BORROWED NARRATIVES

BORROWED NARRATIVES

USING

BIOGRAPHICAL AND

HISTORICAL

GRIEF NARRATIVES

WITH THE

BEREAVING

HAROLD IVAN SMITH

Routledge
Taylor & Francis Group
New York   London

Routledge
Taylor & Francis Group
711 Third Avenue
New York, NY 10017

Routledge
Taylor & Francis Group
27 Church Road
Hove, East Sussex BN3 2FA

© 2012 by Taylor & Francis Group, LLC
Routledge is an imprint of Taylor & Francis Group, an Informa business

Printed in the United States of America on acid-free paper
Version Date: 20111003

International Standard Book Number: 978-0-415-89394-7 (Hardback)

Library of Congress Cataloging-in-Publication Data

Smith, Harold Ivan, 1947-0
    Borrowed narratives : using biographical and historical grief narratives with the bereaving / Harold Ivan Smith.
        p. cm.
    Includes bibliographical references and index.
    ISBN 978-0-415-89394-7 (hbk. : alk. paper)
    1. Grief. 2. Bereavement. 3. Narrative therapy. 4. Autobiography--Therapeutic use. 5. Bibliotherapy. I. Title.

BF575.G7S584 2012
155.9'370922--dc23   2011037587

Visit the Taylor & Francis Web site at
http://www.taylorandfrancis.com

and the Routledge Web site at
http://www.routledgementalhealth.com

For a long time, he was a name on the cover of good books.
Then I heard him speak. After that, when I read his
books I heard his voice and saw his mannerisms. I
thought, "Someday, I would like to meet him."
Years later, while giving a presentation, I looked up and there he was.
At the end he generously affirmed my ideas.
And one day he called to say that he liked an article
I had written. And to keep writing.
And one day he called to ask why I was working on a holiday.
"Get out of the office and have some fun."
He became my mentor and friend.
He has stretched my soul and
helped me see the world with larger eyes.
I dedicate *Borrowed Narratives*
to Earl Grollman

Those who work with the grieving need colleagues.
At first she was a name on the ADEC Board of Directors.
Then she co-chaired ADEC Kansas City with me.
Over time, she became a gracious affirming friend
who taught me a wider definition of colleague.
She patiently critiqued chapters of this book.
Her life enriched me, her death impoverishes me.
Her memory is a blessing to me.
I also dedicate this book to Catherine Johnson.

Contents

Preface

Borrowing Stories—First-Person Singular

By the time you've run your mind through it a hundred times, relentlessly worked every tic of your terror, it's lost its power over you … [Soon it's] a story on a page, or, more precisely, everybody's story on a page.

John Gardner (as cited in Strauss, 2010, p. 5)

This book began a long time ago. During my childhood, my siblings and I spent many Saturday afternoons listening to the stories spun by our grandfathers, Walter Lee and Ivan Lee, whose farms did not have television or radio, indoor bathrooms or furnaces, air conditioning, electricity, or running water. Both grandfathers believed that children were "to be seen, *not heard!*"

The afternoons passed predictably with stories exchanged and punctuated by the ticking clocks and creaking rocking chairs. During winter, came the added sound of the crack-and-pops of potbelly stoves and, in the summer, pauses to wipe the brow and moan, "Whew, we got a hot one today!"

It has been a long time since I sat in a rocking chair on a Saturday afternoon in Indiana listening to a story slowly unfold. Walter Lee

Eckert used a corncob pipe to slow the story; Ivan Lee Smith stalled with a cigar. Those deliberate pauses heightened our anticipation and provoked an impatient, "And *then* what happened?"

Some stories took the better part of an afternoon to "get there." Some stories had stories within them that had to be explored, like small tributaries of great rivers. Both grandfathers often started a story, "Now, I knew of a fellow one time …" or "That fellow who used to live up by the Paulson place …"

I wonder now why particular stories stuck; why stories, or story fragments, remain on the tip of my memory. One story focused on the placement of a stop sign, in that part of rural Indiana something of a luxury. Finally, to test the accuracy of the story, we all piled into trucks and drove to the isolated bend in the road for confirmation of details.

More than once when someone challenged the story, the story-teller snapped, "Who's telling this story? *Me* or you?" An admonition, "Then tell it *right*!" followed, then a rebuttal, "I am telling it the way it *happened*!" Like a tennis match, uncles sought to get in "the last word." "No, you are telling it the way you *wanted* it to happen." Sometimes, it became more heated and my parents concluded it was time to go look at the horses or grab a fishing pole and head to the pond.

As a child, I believed that God called me to be a "preacher." Out of all the children in my church, my school, and my neighborhood, God had called *me*! No one challenged my declaration. After all, God had called the boy Samuel in ancient Israel so why not Harold Ivan. Fundamentalist churches had *preachers* who were generally exuberant storytellers, whereas mainline congregations had ministers, some of whom could, on occasion, tell a decent story. My father advised me, "You'd better do good in history in school because preachers have to know history." I did well in history not just memorizing dates but trying to understand the whys of those dates and the competing inter-pretations assigned to dates, events, and shaping personalities.

I received a significant inheritance from my grandfathers: story-ing skills and an appreciation for storytelling. I am a steward not just to my grandfathers' storytelling: not a mere recitation of facts, but a story that grabs a listener's attention. I wonder how my grandfathers would tell the stories I tell or what they would think of my story skills. Would my stories prompt a "Now, boy, that's a good story!" I hope so.

Sometimes I tell stories to myself, particularly on long drives, to keep them from going stale. To see if, in *this* telling, something fresh might "leap out" from the story. Stories get a bit threadbare over time.

The second major influence was an afternoon in the early 1980s spent in a former monastery in Dubrovnik, then Yugoslavia. Historically, this community of holy men specialized in writing *martyrlogum*—the short accounts of the saints and the faithful. Long after a monk died, stories he had preserved from previous generations were passed on to a new generation.

In graduate school I learned a fascinating hymn, "For all the saints, who from their labors rest ..." As I migrated into a more liturgical tribe within Christianity, I learned the traditions of All Saints' Day and All Souls' Day—days on the church calendar to honor those who had died "in the faith." Visiting Mennonite and Amish communities in Pennsylvania, I discovered the long tradition of honoring the stories of the martyrs in the Anabaptist traditions. Centuries after their deaths, their lives are celebrated and individuals extract meaning from the narratives to face their challenges.

In Christian tradition there is the understanding that the faithful, though dead, still speak. Christians listen to the narratives of Abraham and Sarah, Jonah and Jeremiah, Isaac and Rebecca, Deborah and Esther, Ruth and Naomi. These biblical figures became "alive" in my childhood through the creativity of Sister Ina, Sister Alberta, Sister Frances, and Sister Hazel, Sunday School teachers. Thus, if you have spied on me playing in the backyard, often I was pretending to be a biblical character doing some mighty act. Recreating the story of David slaying the giant Goliath with only a slingshot was my favorite.

Over the years, the radio broadcasts of Paul Harvey fascinated me. He ended a portion of the program with a chunk of a story that left listeners hanging. After the break for one last sponsor, he returned with "And *now* for *the rest* of the story." Then he snapped, "This is Paul Harvey ... good day!" I dissected his stories. What made a particular story make me listen to the end of his broadcasts?

I became fascinated with "the rest of the story" for a long line of grievers:

- The 6-year-old Texan who lost her mother just before Christmas, 1917.
- The young military officer who stood in the cold Colorado wind as his 3-year-old son was buried in 1921.
- The African American child whose best friend was killed in the bombing of the 16th Avenue Baptist Church in Birmingham in 1963.
- The young boy in the oil fields of Texas whose sister died far away in New York City in 1954.
- The father who stood in his pajamas at a casket in the East Room of the White House softly stroking his 16-year-old son's hair in 1924.
- The angry widow who mailed a treasured piece of art to the "other woman" who had been with her husband when he died in 1945.
- The courageous widow who peacefully led 2 million grievers in a funeral procession through the streets of Manila in 1987.
- The shy child whose abusive mother, younger brother, and alcoholic father died before her 10th birthday in 1894.
- The English landscape artist who longed for a darker shade of black paint to capture his grief following his best friend's death in 1841.
- The "manly" man emotionally paralyzed by the deaths of his wife and mother on the same day—Valentine's Day, 1884.

The "rest of the story" is that these grievers walked through the dark pain of grief, at times believing hope was a mirage, yet dared to believe that tomorrow would, in time, appear on the horizon.

I borrow stories from their seasons of grief in my work with the bereaving.

Now I want to offer you a way to find, hone, and use "borrowed" stories.

Acknowledgments

Initially, a manuscript is an author's ideas captured in words—or pixtels—on a succession of pages or screens. In editing and proofreading the author reads what is *supposed* to be there. Any author is blessed to have readers generously willing to loan their "eyes" to track words, sentences, and paragraphs; to follow ideas that sometimes wander all over the landscape and patiently offer specific guidance to tighten, to better convey the author's thinking and intentions. Because I suffer from "length-itis" I need colleagues and friends' sharpened pencils to deflate the manuscript and corral loose ideas. Fortunately, these readers graciously said, "*Maybe* you can use that story somewhere else but *not here.*"

I owe a great deal to colleagues who read and reread drafts.

Richard Gilbert, Rhonda Monke, Catherine Johnson, Stella Corporal-Ruiz, John Larsen, Gregory DeBourgh, Betty Carmack, Brenda Atkinson, Beulah Apple, Dennis Apple, and Joy Johnson. In great gratitude I thank them here.

Special thanks to Doug Fruheling who is librarian par excellence, as are the archivists at the Franklin D. Roosevelt Presidential Library in Hyde Park, New York.

Borrowed Narratives was conceived after a dinner conversation with Ben Wolfe who suggested, "Tell those stories."

Finally, *Borrowed Narratives* would have been impossible without the writings of Robert Neimeyer, which offered a solid theoretical framework that has been like a skeleton and a lighthouse.

And special thanks to my cheerleaders at "The Classic Cookie": Leslie Stoddard, Marina McSorley, Cady McSorley, and Shawn Gore. To the Linda Hall Science Library in Kansas City, which offered an incredible "quiet" environment to write, think, and edit.

PART I

Borrowing as a Process

1

WHY BORROW NARRATIVES?

God has stricken me almost beyond what I can bear.

**Woodrow Wilson after the death of the first lady, August 6, 1914
(as cited in Schulte Nordholt, 1991, p. 137)**

Years ago, so the story goes, a judge asked a bank robber, "Why do you rob banks?"

"Your Honor, that's where the money is!"

If asked, "Why borrow narratives?" I answer, "Because that is where the *gold* is!" Borrowed narratives are resources that can make a difference in an individual's grief experience and, perhaps, alter the ultimate integration.

Oring (2008) urges the use of this approach: "There is experimental research that shows that information conveyed in a narrative is better remembered, more persuasive, and engenders greater belief than statistical information communicated on the same topic" (p. 145).

A Baby Named Patrick

The American public was excited because for the first time in nearly a century a first family was expecting. Moreover, the photogenic Kennedy children—Caroline and John—fascinated the American public. Patrick Bouvier Kennedy was born on August 7, 1963, and died 2 days later from complications of hyaline membrane disease. That fact is unlikely to comfort parents whose assumptive worlds have collapsed following the death of an infant. In those moments, John Fitzgerald Kennedy was not simply the president of the United States but a pain-wracked father adrift in a sea of grief. In Boston's Massachusetts General Hospital in the middle of that hot August night, the president powerlessly watched his son take a last breath. Kennedy turned to aides, "He really put up a fight, didn't he?" Moments later, the president of the United States was on the floor sobbing.

Secret Service agents were uncertain how to respond. They had never trained for the drama unfolding before them. Some agents, who had young children, looked away, fighting to control their own emotions.

That brief story, however, is part of a larger historical grief narrative of a family who has experienced more than their "fair share" of grief, a family some would argue are under a "curse of death." Jackie Kennedy experienced two significant losses in the last half of 1963: in August, Patrick and 3 months later John. Immediately after Patrick's death, Jackie, who had been unable to hold the baby, wept, "Oh, Jack, oh, Jack. There's only one thing I could not bear now—if I ever lost you" (Andersen, 1996, p. 353). Naturally, he assured her that nothing was going to happen to him. Jackie went to Dallas with him as something of a "proof" that she was "over" her grief for the baby and would be available for the tough reelection campaign in 1964. Campaign aides thought Americans needed to see another example of a Kennedy overcoming a wound that life had dealt. Large crowds in Texas turned out to see Jackie and to scream her name. In fact, John Kennedy's last words to her might have been a scolding, "If you have your dark glasses on, you might as well have stayed at home" (Perret, 2001, p. 398).

This borrowed narrative is one of many that I use when lecturing about grief or working with grievers. This story could make a difference in a therapeutic moment for your client. This narrative could invite a grieving client to conclude: "So I am not the only one who has experienced this loss!"

The Power of a Story

Stories are everywhere. Some historical stories rest close to the surface; others are deeply imbedded like coal deposits deep below Appalachian Mountains and streams.

Few remember points one, two, and three of my presentations to clinicians. Many, however, remember a story—or a fragment of a story—about a "slow moving limousine with three people riding in the back seat" that I often tell at the end of a seminar.

It is not simply the story of Caroline Kennedy riding rather than walking with her mother and uncles in her father's funeral procession. The glue in the story is a 6-year-old grieving child trustingly thrusting her hand out the window of the presidential limousine and Special Agent Robert Foster taking her hand and holding it all the way to St. Matthew's Cathedral. I have closed many presentations with these words: "Be on the lookout for slow-moving limousines. They are everywhere! You cannot 'fix' the griever but maybe, just maybe, you can hold their hand on a portion of their grief journey."

Use of the Story by Clinicians

How will clinicians use a story to support a point, to drive home a conclusion, or to inspire a griever? How will clinicians retell a slice of the story to invite a story from the griever's repertoire of experience? How will clinicians use a story to support a conviction, perhaps doubted by a griever, that a tomorrow is on the horizon even in the thickest fog? That the death or burial does not have to be the last line of the narrative?

Borrowing an historical or biographical narrative fragment gives the client an opportunity to make a link to the story. In some cases grievers find permission in the story to honor their story.

The clinician must extract from the story—not unlike the sculptor Michelangelo chipping away the marble to reveal David. The clinician chips away the nonessential elements or details that might puzzle or distract from the story structure. Some stories become too heavy with detail; the griever feels bombarded.

The goal for clinicians is "minding" the story and being good custodians of the story. It is critical to make the story sound as fresh this time as the first time you told it. It will be the first time for some—if not all of your audience or for a particular client—to hear it. It may be the only time a griever will hear the story, or it may be the first time to hear that story linked to her particular grief experience.

The point is simple: If you borrow a narrative, tell it well.

Influence of Narratives

Humans are inveterate collectors and creators of fables, tales, myths, stories, and narratives. Momigliano (1993) contends that Plato and his peers "experimented in biography" as a way of teaching philosophical truth. They focused on the "potentialities rather than the realities of individual" philosopher's lives. Thus, Socrates was dead yet "a guide to territories as yet unexplored" (p. 46). Borrowed narratives may, if told well, act as magnets to a griever's untold story. The borrowed story may lead the griever to say, "Me too!"

Many readers, no doubt, as children, attempting to delay sleep, plead, "Tell me another story. Just one more story. Please?" I have never forgotten the great tales of Paul Bunyan told by Mrs. Alice Cannon as a way to start our postlunch naps in the fourth grade.

Storytelling is one way humans make meaning of and find sense in the loss experiences of their lives. Unfortunately, some stories never get "caught" by a griever; other stories ramble along the dark corridors of memory.

George Washington, the first U.S. president, remains a megahero in American political narrative. Would the colonies have emerged from George III's grasp without our George? Would Americans have ever heard of George Washington if Daniel Parke Custis had not died in 1758, leaving Martha the wealthiest widow in the colonies? Or if young George had not been a bachelor. Or *if* Martha's plantation had been in Georgia or the Carolinas? Or if another suitor had captured Martha's heart, how might American history be different? Or if the heir to his father's estate not died (Lengle, 2011)?

Washington was thrust into intense grief when Patsy, his beloved 16-year-old stepdaughter, died after a seizure at the dining room table at his home, Mount Vernon, in 1773. Washington experienced intense grief when his headstrong stepson Jacky died at age 21 in 1779. How many adults rearing grandchildren today are aware that George and Martha Washington, well along in years, raised two of Jacky's children?

How many daughters or sons of widowed mothers know that George was estranged from Mary, his mother? Would we ever have heard of George, the second son, if his eldest stepbrother Lawrence—the heir to their father's estate—had not died in 1752? Or if George's mother had agreed to George's wish to join the British Navy? George Washington might have fought for the British (Lengle, 2011)!

Many individuals find their grief—and postloss relationships with family members—complicated by the settlement of estates, large and small, especially in dysfunctioning families. What borrowable data might be found in the narratives of Minnie Taylor's death in 1917? The money Minnie left for Claudia, her 6-year-old, over time, funded an education at the University of Texas and, eventually, her marriage to an ambitious but poor Congressional aide, Lyndon Baines Johnson. To gain full access to her mother's bequest, Claudia had to sue her father. Moreover, Claudia's relationships with a succession of stepmothers were less than storybook. The money Claudia inherited after her mother's death funded Lyndon's first campaign for Congress and the purchase of a radio station, KTBC, and the expansion of the family's communication business. These holdings, coupled with money from her father's estate, financed her husband's Senate campaign in 1948. He won by 87 votes (out of 900,000 cast), earning LBJ the nickname, "Landslide Lyndon" (Goodwin, 1991, pp. 86, 101). If that string of events had not occurred, how altered might the personal and grief narratives be for millions whose lives were shaped by the death of a loved one in or their experience in Vietnam?

The Unseen Narratives

Historians do not always comment on or link historical events and personalities with the grief their subjects have experienced; in some cases, biographers offer a brief glimpse into a grief episode or stash a brief mention in an endnote. In a death-denying culture, the author focuses on keeping the narrative upbeat and celebratory. Skidmore (2004), in his superb *After the White House,* examines the years Theodore Roosevelt lived after his presidency. Skidmore comments on the rejection Roosevelt felt when Woodrow Wilson denied his request to raise troops to fight in World War I—in essence, a second wind for the Rough Riders. Wilson and Roosevelt were both cognizant of the presidential election of 1920 on the horizon and that they were the presumed candidates, a rematch of 1912.

Roosevelt urged his sons to enlist; all four did. Teddy found great delight in following their combat exploits.

> T.R.'s romantic attachment to war, however, was shattered when his youngest, Quentin, the son Teddy considered "the weakest," a pilot, was shot down over France in July, 1918. Friends reported overhearing Teddy sorrowfully muttering to himself behind closed doors, "poor Quinikens" [his nickname for Quentin]. (Skidmore, 2004, p. 102)

Skidmore argues that Roosevelt would have been elected to a third term in 1920, "but it was not to be." T.R. died on January 6, 1919, of an embolism days after experiencing that first Christmas without Quentin.

In the telling of the larger stories, small substories get overlooked. That Sunday morning in 1917, before Quentin sailed for France, he attended an early morning service at Christ Church Episcopal in Oyster Bay, New York. Some feared that it might be his last service; that he, like so many other American young men, would not come home. When the Roosevelts received the cable that Quentin was dead—early the next morning, a Sunday, they arrived at Christ Church for the Eucharist service—a service Theodore seldom attended. The rector and some in the congregation were surprised to see the Colonel and Mrs. Roosevelt present; many grieving families would have preferred privacy. A heartbreaking moment erupted for the congregation when the Colonel and Edith knelt at the same altar rail where Quentin had knelt. The rector later recalled, "There were no dry eyes, and the words could scarcely be spoken, but their force was there: 'Preserve thy body and soul into everlasting life.' This time also was the last communion, but we did not know it" (Reisner, 1922, p. 335). That was the last time Theodore Roosevelt received the Eucharist.

Historians and biographers, generally, do not explore the possibility that Theodore Roosevelt died of "a broken heart." Many stick to "the facts." To some, this would be conjecture; to others psychohistory. For many historians and biographers, emotions are not part of the lexicon of their academic field. "An embolism" will do nicely. Ghaemi (2011), however, counters, "the historian, at least the one who seeks to write narrative history, is always engaging in psychological history" (p. 270).

By exploring this narrative as a thanatologist, however, I discovered that Quentin, a pilot, was shot down over France on July 18, 1918, and died immediately (although his father would not know that he died immediately); his father lived less than 6 months. Admittedly, Roosevelt had health issues. He nearly died and pondered suicide while exploring the Rio Bravo in Brazil in 1914; in fact, many thought he had not experienced good health since that expedition (Millard, 2005). Did grief for Quentin contribute to his death? Had Roosevelt, as a father, acted vicariously in urging his youngest son to join the army?

One detail is important in understanding Roosevelt's stress. Given the limited communication in that era, Theodore Roosevelt had to wait 10 days—10 anxious days and long sleepless nights—for official notification of death and the conditions of the death. He worried that if the Germans knew the body was the son of Roosevelt—given his prewar bombastic verbal attacks on the kaiser—Quentin's body would be desecrated. (In fact, photos of Quentin's body were widely distributed among and prized by German troops.) The report that the Germans had buried Quentin with full military honors offered slight comfort to Roosevelt and Edith. Roosevelt wrote Premier Clemenceau:

> It is a very sad thing to see the young die when the old who are doing nothing, as I am doing nothing, are left alive. Therefore it is very bitter to me that I was not allowed to face the danger with my sons. But whatever may be their fate, I was glad and proud that my sons have done their part in this mighty war against despotism and barbarism. (T. Roosevelt, 1954, p. 1355)

What in this slice of the Roosevelt grief narrative might be, or could become over time, comforting to mothers and fathers grieving for the death of a daughter or son in Iraq or Afghanistan?

One detail heightens my interest in Roosevelt as a model of grief. After his mother and first wife, Alice, died 12 hours apart, on Valentine's Day 1884, Roosevelt scrawled in his journal, "The light has gone out in my life!" He drew a large X on that day's page. No doubt he believed that, for days later he added, "For better or worse, my life has been lived" (E. Morris, 1979, p. 244). *The New York World* on February 15, 1884, predicted, "it is doubtful whether he will be able to return to his labors" (p. 242) in the New York State Assembly.

Could that 25-year-old widower have imagined a future or a *bright* future? Seventeen years later, following the assassination of William McKinley, Roosevelt, then vice president, became president—a future he never could have imagined that traumatic Valentine's night in 1884. In his "bully" persona he had pontificated, "There is nothing more foolish and cowardly than to be beaten down by sorrow which nothing we do will change" (T. Roosevelt, 1954, p. 1356). Did his own words slip back into his consciousness those midnights as, after Edith had gone to bed, he grieved for Quentin? Although he had predicted that his wife Edith would "carry the wound to her grave" (Brands, 1997, p. 803), he did! By Edith's death in 1948, Edith had lost three sons in wars (Wead, 2003).

What might a grief counselor extract from the Roosevelt narrative, especially to share with a griever trying to quarantine or tame grief? Using this story gives the clinician the opportunity to explore the client's what-ifs or the client's "My life is not worth living without ..." This narrative offers an opportunity to seed a future—especially if the client places the Roosevelt story in memory's escrow.

Kelly (1955) raised questions about why individuals grieve in a particular manner (in Roosevelt's case, in private, after family members had gone to bed). He also wondered "in what direction" grief "is likely to carry them" (as cited in Neimeyer, 2009, p. 11). Grievers, Neimeyer contends, "live in uncertain futures" which are like "living on the frontier, confronting challenges and innovating solutions" while moving forward.

What if Theodore Roosevelt could have harnessed that grief? What if Roosevelt, honoring his son's death, had lived to lobby for Woodrow Wilson's fledgling League of Nations? What if he had prevailed on hostile Republican senators, friends like Henry Cabot Lodge, to ratify the treaty ending World War I? What if Roosevelt had been elected in 1920 rather than Warren G. Harding, whose administration would be scandal-ridden? Cowley (2001) values what-if questions because "they can show that small accidents or split-second decisions are as likely to have major repercussions as large ones" (p. xiv). Asking "what if"—a process labeled *counterfactual* in academic language—can be a "tool to enhance the understanding of history" (p. xiii) and one's personal history. Many grievers experiencing traumatic loss juggle what-if questions: What if I had said my son could not go out that night with his friends? What if we had delayed our drive by 5 minutes? What if he had missed that plane commandeered by terrorists in 2001?

Neimeyer (2009) contends that "constructivists typically emphasize the role of personal meanings in shaping people's responses to events" (p. 20), particularly their losses. How did Edith Roosevelt grieve double losses within 6 months? How did she grieve the suicide death of her alcoholic son Kermit in 1943 in Alaska or Theodore III in battle in France in 1944? Did Theodore III being awarded the posthumous Medal of Honor lessen her grief?

Reinventing One's World

As a child I was fascinated by the weekly episodes of the television series *Wagon Train*, starring Ward Bond. I imagined myself traveling with those westward-bound pioneers overcoming outrageous obstacles. In Kansas City, the hospital where I am on the teaching faculty is blocks from an area called Westport—where pioneers bought supplies and wagon trains formed and then set out for California or Oregon. Just blocks from my home, outfitters kept thousands of oxen to sell to those ambitious Americans. As pioneers followed their dreams, at times, in order to lighten their wagons, they had to jettison items that were, or had been, of value. Moreover, some buried spouses, children, siblings, and friends along the trail; nevertheless, the wagon train kept moving forward.

Sometimes, a griever's "wagon" is overloaded. How can clinicians help lighten it? How can clinicians, in Neimeyer's words, help grievers "jettison previous patterns and face the discomforts of reinventing ourselves and our worlds" (2009, p. 12)? How can clinicians "defang" some toxic stories grievers hold on to?

Kauffman (2002) contends that grief forces individuals to reassess assumptive worlds that are woven tightly into their stories. How can a griever imagine their equivalent of "California"? I suggest by borrowing narrative fragments and stories from historical and biographical grievers and sifting through those stories for nuggets of encouragement, future, or hope, just as the forty-niners panned for gold along streams in California. The clinician may spend long hours sifting a narrative for the nugget that has the potential to make a difference.

Trajectories of Adaptation

This book focuses on using narratives that demonstrate positive trajectories of adaptation following loss. Alford (2009) argues that life is not so much the survival of the fittest but rather the survival of the "*most adaptable*" (p. 39) or those able to find or make meaning in their losses. Some historical figures from whom I borrow narratives were remarkably adaptable following loss; some lived a long number of years after a death or deaths. Some, like Eleanor Roosevelt, would discover their best days after a husband's death. Eleanor Roosevelt, the widow of the thirty-third president, wrote early in widowhood, "You must do the thing you think you cannot do" (E. Roosevelt, 1960, p. 30). Initially, she thought she could not make a significant contribution without Franklin. She confided to a granddaughter that no one would remember her in a decade. Later, she reflected back on transitioning from first lady to private citizen:

> Every time you meet a situation, though you may think at the time it is an impossibility and you go through the tortures of the damned, once you have met it and lived through it you find that forever after you are freer than you ever were before. If you can live through that you can live through anything. You gain strength, courage, and confidence by every experience in which you really stop to look fear in the face. (E. Roosevelt, 1960, p. 29)

How might you, as a clinician, use that string of words from Mrs. Roosevelt's grief experience to support or encourage a client? How might you as a grief educator use that quote in a class or a presentation or in writing?

Using Quotations to Jump-Start Narratives

In the Grief Gatherings I lead at St. Luke's Hospital, in Kansas City, Missouri, I distribute quotations—like Eleanor Roosevelt's—to grievers. I call these "refrigerator quotes" and ask grievers to put the quotation on a refrigerator door so they and members of the family, or friends, will see it. Some participants photocopy the quotes and pass them on. Others carry the quotes in a purse, notebook, or wallet for further reflection. The more they read and ponder a refrigerator quote, the more meaning it offers.

Mrs. Roosevelt, one of the most widely admired women and widely quoted American activists, has been dead for half a century. Why is her life still valued by Americans? C. Black (2003) identified Franklin D. Roosevelt as "the most important person in the twentieth century" and America's "most accomplished leader" since Abraham Lincoln (p. 1122). Gottlieb, Gottlieb, Bowers, and Bowers (1998) included Anna Eleanor Roosevelt as one of the 1,000 people who shaped the millennium (p. 43). What might a griever, particularly a widow, learn from Mrs. Roosevelt's experience as a widow that might be a resource for meaning making and sense making? Mrs. Roosevelt moved out of the White House convinced her time on the political stage had ended. In late April 1945, when a reporter asked about her future, Mrs. Roosevelt responded curtly, "The story is over." (Lash, 1984, p. 123). She, nevertheless, pondered questions commonly faced by widows 60 years later: "Who am I now?" and "Who might I yet become?" and "What is to become of me without her or him" (Attig, 2001, p. 40)?

If clinicians borrow narratives, how might they be encouraged and equipped to find relevant narratives to borrow?

Admittedly, some biographies have been "cleansed" or "sanitized" to preserve the "hero" associated with the personality. Theodore Roosevelt, paradoxically in his own campaign autobiography never mentioned Alice, his first wife, who died in 1884, 2 days after giving birth to a daughter also named Alice—the Alice who became the most rambunctious of all the first children to live in the White House (Wead, 2003). Which of Theodore Roosevelt's quotes—he, too, is widely quoted nearly a century after his death—might become meaningful if the reader knew more of the grief behind the quote? For example, "For good or ill, my life has been lived out" (E. Morris, 1979, p. 244). That is a dark conclusion—or premature assumption—for a 25-year old. However, as I sat in the funeral for a 23-year-old combat soldier killed in Iraq, the widow's words to the congregation near the end of the service sounded vaguely like Roosevelt's. As Roosevelt could not have imagined a future, neither could this widow.

The Narratives of Eleanor Roosevelt

Eleanor Roosevelt is widely known for her activism and her writing extracted into quotations that appear in compilations of quotes, articles, presentations, t-shirts, greeting cards, posters, or on knick-knack magnets and coffee mugs. Few persons who find meaning in her admonition, "You must do the thing you think you cannot do," know the context in which it was formed. As Eleanor, a widow, age 61, "old" by longevity standards in that era, packed family possessions, she was driven by a woundedness and anger. Just hours after Franklin's death, at his retreat in Warm Springs, Georgia, Eleanor learned that Lucy Mercer Rutherfurd, the woman with whom he had had a public affair in Washington during World War I, had been with him for 3 days. To save his marriage, keep access to his mother's money, and preserve his political future, in 1918 FDR promised to "give up" Lucy. Twenty-seven years later after the agreement was reached, as she rode the funeral train back to Washington and later to Hyde Park, unfinished psychological grief erupted within Eleanor. Immediately after Franklin's death and the succession of Vice President Harry Truman, Bess Truman became First Lady. As she packed around the clock, Eleanor had to confront a question as did thousands of war widows: Who am I *now*?

Eleanor Roosevelt joined a small sorority of former first ladies— Grace Coolidge, Edith Wilson, and Frances Cleveland Preston— who lived their lives out of the public eye. Gradually, she shifted in her identity from being Mrs. Franklin D. Roosevelt, the name used in much of her writing up to that point, to *Eleanor* Roosevelt. A griever might find words from a letter she wrote to her close friend Ellen Woodward, in response to a condolence card, weeks after she had had time to reflect on her situation: "I intend fully to keep my interests and make myself heard on important issues" (May 19, 1945).

A thanatologist might share Eleanor's grief experience and rephrase Eleanor's words to ask a client: "What is *the* thing—as a widow/griever/midlife orphan—you think you *cannot* do?" A clinician might follow-up with "How do you *intend* to pursue your interests?" Or "What interest(s) or causes can you now more fully invest in?" The client response could lead to further therapeutic dialogue and growth.

The noted historian Arthur Schlesinger (1979) concluded, "In a certain sense she was freed by FDR's death." On board a ship to Europe for the first meeting of the United Nations, Eleanor admitted to reporters, "For the first time in my life I can say just what I want. For your information it is wonderful to feel free" (Lash, 1984, p. 126).

Grief as a Consequence of Other Losses

As a serious student of the life of Eleanor Roosevelt, I conclude that doing the thing "you think you cannot do" had been *pre*forged in her consciousness as a result of the string of pivotal antecedent losses in her life: the death of her beloved alcoholic father when she was 10; discovering Franklin's infidelity with her former social secretary Lucy Mercer in 1918; giving up her teaching post at Tadhunter School in New York City to become the most reluctant first lady; and being deeply depressed during her first months in the White House. Eleanor considered divorcing Franklin before they left Albany in 1932, and again after he won a third term in 1940 (Faber, 1980). What goes unnoticed by many historians is that in 1932 Eleanor had to return to the city, Washington, where Franklin had openly flaunted his relationship with Lucy Mercer.

Early on Inauguration Day, March 4, 1933, Eleanor and her friend, Leona Hickok, rode in a taxi to Rock Creek Cemetery to spend time sitting at the statue of Clover Adams—a woman who had suicided after learning that her husband, Henry Adams, a prominent Washington political figure and a Roosevelt neighbor, was having an affair with a prominent neighbor (Dupre, 2007). Eleanor returned to that grave—a sacred space to her—many times during her husband's presidency. Does your client have such a place?

Eleanor, in 1918 after the affair, in 1921 after Franklin developed polio, in 1933 after Franklin was elected president, and after his death in 1945, had to reinvent herself. Eleanor had to create a new Eleanor Roosevelt. Early losses nudged her to evolve from intimate companion to political partner with Franklin; indeed, on some issues, Eleanor had been the scout that tested public attitudes before Franklin committed himself. Eleanor had to face her fear that in Washington she would be compared unfavorably to her Aunt Edith (Mrs. Theodore Roosevelt), considered an outstanding first lady but who, as an aunt, had been emotionally distant to her orphaned niece.

Robert Neimeyer, in the closing plenary session of the 2010 annual meeting of the Association for Death Education and Counseling, highlighted differences between "the *event* story" and "the *back* story." "The king died" is an event story. "The king died *following* the death of his beloved queen" is the back story. Every griever has both an event story and back story—or stories—that deserve thorough vigorous clinical exploration and reflection.

One has to wonder how the Roosevelt marriage would have been different—perhaps better—had Franklin's father not died in 1900 while Franklin was a student at Harvard. James Roosevelt would have "reigned in" Sara and thus given Franklin and Eleanor opportunity to develop a more meaningful marriage without Sara's continuous interference. Eleanor—in alliance with Franklin's political strategist Louis Howe—created an alternative future for Franklin, a future his mother opposed. Admittedly, that future necessitated secrecy about the extent of his paralysis.

Beasley (2010) notes that Eleanor had long resented the emotional and financial control Sara exercised over all of their lives. To avoid being sucked back into Sara's fiefdom, and to avoid the emotional suffocation she would have experienced living "under Sara's thumb at Hyde Park" (p. 32), Eleanor actively promoted Franklin's political future by working in New York Democratic Party offices.

How many surviving spouses and family members have learned things that have challenged their understanding of the deceased? Honor Moore (2008) later discovered her father—an Episcopal bishop and activist—had a long-term homosexual lover. Peter Selwyn (1998) discovered that his father's death had not been an accident but rather a suicide—a fact not scripted in the family narrative. Sally Ryder Brady (2011) discovered that throughout her 46-year marriage, her husband had been gay.

How many grievers have to navigate the discovery of the presence of an intimate other or secrets? How many grievers might find insights into Eleanor's experience of a husband's deception that continued, literally, to Franklin's dying breath?

Seeking Relevance in Historical Narratives

In essence, the clinician pursues an historical or biographical narrative just as a scientist studies a slide under a microscope or an economist explores numbers: "What have we here?" What, in this narrative of an episode of grief or chain of losses might be meaningful to those currently experiencing grief or to those who will use their reading and reflection as something of an escrow deposit for future grief? By letting the narrative tumble over in their minds, readers may make applications that the clinician had not considered. The process of borrowing narratives can be a two-way learning experience.

In *Borrowed Narratives,* I contend that the examination of grief narratives—or grief episodes—in the lives of the historically and biographically significant has value for a griever engaged in meaning making. It may be like examining film scraps on the cutting room floor that directors have edited out of a final cut of the movie. Are there clues, examples, or models that prompt: "Take note of *this* in your grief?"

In cooking, sometimes "minor" herbs, spices, or other ingredients are used, in small portions, to create, or enhance, a particular flavor. Some ambitious chefs may begin a recipe uncertain as to how the ingredient will influence the end product. So it is with the lives of grievers. Small slices of the back story may become a significant therapeutic gift that diffuses feelings of alienation, hopelessness, and loneliness that many grievers feel.

Cultural Influences on Narrative

In cultures that seek to make fast work of grief, or in which grievers seek one way tickets to "Over-it-land," too many are left on their own to seek meaning in and make sense of their losses. Few are encouraged to thoroughly get *into* grief. There is, in some quarters, a growing impatience for a category in a future edition of the *Diagnostic and Statistical Manual of Mental Disorders* (*DSM*) to brand "slow grievers" as problematic, prolonged, or complicated, and to add "disorder" to the description like a caboose on the end of a train. By imposing a label clinicians imply that a griever *ought* to be doing a better job "getting over" their grief or "moving on." One can only wonder how certain historical grievers would be branded.

Value of History and Memoir in Grief Work

Biography, history, and memoir offer resources to see through the life and to peer into the experienced grief, particularly in a time period before mental health care professionals or support groups were available, and in a time period when grief etiquette maintained rigid standards for acceptable behavior, such as wearing black clothing or armbands or declining social invitations for a year. Many are unaware of the extensive thanatological literature that existed in earlier historic periods when grief was such a part of daily lives—when disputes between nations were more commonly settled through warfare than diplomacy; when illness, plague, and childbirth resulted in multiple marriages; and short life spans were the norm. Many are underaware of the influence that grief has had on the arts, music, drama, and literature, particularly poetry.

Clinicians often look for resources to aid receiving and clarifying the grief narratives of and caring for their clients, or in offering hospitality to the grief narratives, particularly those that are different from their own experience. Given the cultural diversity within American and Canadian societies, particularly in urban environments, diverse grief practices must be understood and enfranchised. Recently, en route home to Kansas City, after exploring grief and funeral practices in Hanoi, I had accepted an invitation to deliver lectures for Horan & McConaty Funeral Home in Denver. As John Horan drove me to where the lectures would be given, we discussed my impressions of Vietnam. I discovered that in neighborhoods near the funeral home in Aurora, Colorado, live a large community of Hmong resettled in the United States. Horan & McConaty has become their funeral home.

Could directed reading in historical and biographical narratives strengthen the "bandwidth" of compassionate response? Yes. Could such materials be used to enhance therapeutic relationships? Yes.

Borrowed Narratives and Future Making

"What do I do *now*?" is a predicament for grievers in a culture urging, "Move *on*!" Advice packaged in platitudes, such as "She's in 'a better place,'" encourage individuals to bypass the depths of grief. Rarely are the bereaving urged to get *into* their grief.

In investing in thorough grief, how many can imagine what Gilbert (2006a) terms "a next" or a future? Might historical examples of individuals who creatively engaged their grief to discover a next be important to a client?

Webb (1999) advocates using "people potential" in counseling. Clinicians and grievers tap into the grief narratives of individuals known or admired. In Webb's construct, a clinician would ask a griever to identify an historical griever. Then the clinician asks, "So, what advice might this griever give you?" Given our culture's commitment to heroes, personalities, and celebrities, narratives from their grief experiences offer a resource to explore. Borrowing from some grievers who have written extensively about their grief is like extracting sap from a Vermont maple tree.

As we will explore later in this book, clinicians and grievers can *mine* historical narratives or memoirs for anecdotal insight on grief. "*Fictive* heroes" might become, after reflection, a supportive resource from which grievers draw insight and hope. The clinician, acting as "thanobiographer," could ask an individual who admires Coretta Scott King:

"How do you think Coretta would react in your situation?"
"What might Coretta counsel you in regard to your children?"
"What might Coretta say to you that you would find helpful and hopeful in exploring a future?"

The Example of Leland and Jane Stanford

Stanford University in Palo Alto, California, is among the nation's elite research universities. Few, however, pay close attention to the university's legal name appearing on degrees and publications: The Leland Stanford *Junior* University. Leland and Jane Stanford's only son, Leland, Jr., age 15, died during the family's visit to Italy in 1884.

The Stanfords decided to create a university "to educate the children of California." After her husband's death and early in the life of the institution, Jane fought to keep the university open during the prolonged settlement of her husband's estate and several economic recessions.

In Stanford's first graduating class, one member was 8 when his father died and 10 when his mother died. This boy was separated from his two siblings to be raised by an uncle whose son had died. This Stanford graduate would make a difference in the world. Who would have heard of Herbert Hoover—the great humanitarian who fed Europe after World War I and served as the 31st president—if the Stanfords had not imagined "a next" and created a university as a living memorial to their son (Stanford University, n.d.)?

Admittedly, few grievers have the Stanfords' financial resources. Grievers do have resources and time to invest in deliberately and intentionally remembering a loved one. The story of the Stanfords' active remembrance could lead someone to conclude, "I *can* do something."

Lois Banner, historian and biographer, contends that "biographers are detectives and interpreters attempting to illuminate the past and to interweave its threads in new and compelling patterns" (2009, p. 582). Jeffreys (2011), as grieved parent and clinician, would urge to create a new social orientation.

Clinicians, grief educators, bereavement coordinators, and grief group facilitators, through reading and reflective engagement with *Borrowed Narratives*—and exposure to the methodology of thanatological biographical exploration—will find processes they can use in their own research and adaptation of borrowed narratives.

Unexplored lives offer raw resources that can make a difference in encounters with contemporary grievers committed to both sense making and future making. The clinician does not have to expose the client to the entire grief roster of Eleanor Roosevelt—more than 21 major deaths of family and friends.

Admittedly, grievers, or audiences, may respond, "I did not know *that* about Herbert Hoover, or Arthur Ashe, or Eleanor Roosevelt." But once they know, what can they do with that knowledge?

If the grief of historical and biographical personalities counts—and it does—after sharing borrowed narratives a clinician confidently can say to a griever: "*Your* grief counts, too! In time, someone will borrow from your narrative."

Conclusion

John Donne, the Anglican priest and author well acquainted with death, penned lasting words, "No man is an island, entire of itself." No one's grief should make her feel like a marooned exile on an island. Perspectives can be widened and hope can be rekindled through the use of borrowed narratives. What would Theodore Roosevelt, Jane Stanford, or Martha Washington think if they knew that years, decades, or centuries after their loss experience, that their decisions and words are of value to grievers?

The narratives are there.

The grievers are there.

What is needed are skills to find, probe, and borrow those narratives.

A Story for the Road

Searching for narratives offers little surprises to the curious and persistent. Some surprises come at the end of long days that have not been as productive as we hoped. Researching the retirement years of Grover Cleveland in Princeton, New Jersey, where he had a warm relationship with students, I asked a reference librarian in the Princeton (N.J.) Public Library for assistance. I explained that I was looking for stories about Grover Cleveland's years there. The librarian responded, "Oh, you really should talk to …" and named a librarian who had extensively studied Cleveland's postpresidential life in Princeton and the life of his widow, Francis Cleveland Preston, the first presidential widow to remarry. The second librarian turned something of a needle in the haystack into productive insights into Cleveland's postpresidency and a stack of photocopies. The persistent researcher enjoys the hunt for resources that she can use to keep readers reading and grievers thinking. Sometimes, one needs to inject some humor into a spring after continuing-education experience. Or, a small detail could be the magnet that draws a griever's attention. Several individuals urged me to notice the graves adjoining Cleveland's in Princeton's burial ground. Maybe it was important to them, or perhaps it comforted their families, to be buried near a U.S. president. Real estate agents live by the mantra: "Location, location, location." Maybe permanent location is worth giving more attention to. After spending time at President Cleveland's plain grave marker, I slowly toured the neighborhood of his fellow dead. At one grave, I burst out laughing. One of Cleveland's neighbor's markers reads: "I told you I was sick!" The irony? Grover Cleveland, in 1893, spent a lot of time, as did members of his staff, insisting that he was not sick. In fact, he had a cancerous tumor removed from his mouth and the surgery took place on a yacht to divert nosey reporters (Algeo, 2011). Over a cold beer, Cleveland would have chuckled about his neighbor Grace's inscription.

2
MINING NARRATIVES

Our lives are a connection of stories—truths about who we are, what we believe, where we come from, how we struggle and how we are strong.

Brene Brown (*Up to Date*, KCUR-FM, August 5, 2010)

Where do clinicians find borrowable narratives that can be resources for clients? How can biographies be *mined* for psychological significance? The clinician begins by selecting a historical or biographical personality to explore.

Principles for Mining Narratives

A borrowed narrative is more than a string of interesting dates and facts that support the conclusion, "This individual experienced a lot of grief." The thanatologist probes to discover how the individual experienced and interpreted the death(s). Foundational facts—who, what, where, when—function like pylons. Suppose you select Calvin Coolidge, U.S. president, 1923–1929. On July 7, 1924, his 16-year-old son, Calvin Jr., died of blood poisoning after getting a blister on his toe while playing tennis on the White House courts. Coolidge, a New England Calvinist, struggled with why God would allow his son to die (not an uncommon question for some grievers today). "It seemed to me that the world had need of the work ... that probably he could do. I don't know why such a process was exacted for occupying the White House." Coolidge, in retirement, would comment, "All the power and the glory of the presidency went with him" (1929, pp. 190–191). To understand Coolidge's grief, one has to explore what Worden (2009) calls "historical antecedents" (p. 63), earlier deaths that shape future bereavement.

Calvin Coolidge was 6 years old when his beloved grandfather died; 12 when Victoria, his mother died; 18 when Abigail, his only sibling, died. Three major losses before reaching adulthood left an imprint on his soul, which fueled the depression he fought throughout his life. He wrote of his mother's death, "Life was never to seem the same again." Coolidge, as president, developed a friendship with Edmund Starling, a Secret Service agent with whom he reminisced about growing up in Vermont. One evening Coolidge spoke about his mother. "I wish I could speak with her. I wish that often" (Sobel, 1998, p. 24). Although he carried a picture of his mother "wherever he went," and that picture was in his pocket when he died, "Silent Cal," as he was nicknamed, "never spoke of these matters in public" (p. 24). To some degree, loss shaped his presidency.

A griever does not appear in a clinician's office with a blank slate, but, like Coolidge, brings an accumulation of losses.

Researching the Target Personality

The clinician begins gathering information through preliminary reading in a biographical dictionary or biographical encyclopedia, resources offering a brief overview of the individual's life. The multivolume *The Dictionary of American Biography* or *The American National Biography* offers essays on thousands of noteworthy Americans. Parallel resources are found in *The Oxford Companion to Canadian History* (2004). Many nations have collected similar biographies of its prominent citizens.

An essay on Abraham Lincoln in *American National Biography* focuses primarily on his presidency and his rise to national prominence. In McPherson's (1999) *ANB* essay, I noted that Nancy Hanks Lincoln, Abraham's mother, died in 1818; Abraham was 9. On January 20, 1828, Sally, Abraham's only sibling, died in childbirth; Abraham was 18. Lincoln's grief was heightened because he believed the intoxicated physician her in-laws hired caused her death (Burlingame, 2008; R. L. Miller, 2006). Learning of the deaths (the baby died, too), Lincoln "sat down on a log and hid his face in his hands while the tears rolled down through his long bony fingers" and repeatedly moaned, "What have I to live for?" (Burlingame, 2008, p. 45). Sally's death rebooted memories of his mother's death.

McPherson (2009) reminds that Thomas Lincoln, a grieving but pragmatic father, "needed" a wife to survive in the wilderness because families functioned as economic production units. So, Thomas left Abraham and Sally in a cabin with one wall open to the elements and returned to Kentucky for 9 months to court and marry the recently widowed Sarah Bush (Burlingame, 2008).

McPherson (1999) points to the strong bonding that developed between Abraham and Sarah. Sarah Bush Lincoln, by encouraging his interest in reading, psychologically "rescued" Abraham. That can be true for many children who have thrived under a stepparent's influence and care. Sarah Bush Lincoln survived Abraham. What must her grief for her stepson and president have been like? While researching Lincoln, I explored the Lincoln quote: "All that I am, and hope to be, I owe to my angel mother" (Platt, 1989, p. 233). Which mother: Nancy or Sarah? Lincoln scholars disagree.

In McPherson (1999), I learned that Abraham and Thomas had an adversarial relationship. The illiterate father hired out the brainy boy to other farmers and claimed the money Abe earned until his son was 21; the practice, common in that day, stoked Abraham's resentment. Not surprisingly, Lincoln, in 1851, declined to visit his dying father a day's travel away in Southern Illinois. Lincoln (1851) informed his stepbrother, John D. Johnson, that were he to visit "it is doubtful whether it would not be more painful than pleasant."

Cox (2010) argues that grief is about decisions made or not made. Why had Lincoln's sons never met their paternal grandfather? Why did Lincoln not travel 80 miles to attend his father's funeral in 1851? Why did Lincoln never purchase a tombstone for his father?

Creating a Grid

These early deaths that Lincoln experienced are chronicled, although bare bones, in this preliminary reading. I have enough information to construct a rough grid. I want to know how Lincoln *felt* about these deaths. Having dates facilitates further exploration. During preliminary research, a clinician might decide to explore a particular loss experience to analyze its contribution to the accumulated grief of this individual.

A preliminary grid for Abraham Lincoln looks like this:

Thomas, Betsy (de facto grandparents)	Nancy (mother)	Sarah (sister)	Edward (son)	Thomas (father)	Willie (son)	Abraham
1818	1818	1828	1850	1851	1862	1865
Age 9	Age 9	Age 18	Age 41	Age 42	Age 53	Age 57

It is important to calculate the subject's age at the time of key deaths, although exact death dates are not always available. Did a parent, spouse, or child die on the subject's birthday, a major holiday, or during a particular event? For example, Andrew Johnson's son, Robert, after his father's service as president, suicided soon after his father returned to Greenville, Tennessee. Despite the stigma of being impeached, the grieving Johnson threw himself into a campaign for the U.S. Senate but lost (Gordon-Reed, 2011). Theodore Roosevelt's mother and wife died 12 hours apart on February 14, 1884. How did Roosevelt acknowledge those losses on future Valentine's Days? That might be worth exploring because holidays impact grievers.

Identify the Author(s) of Biographical Essays

Record the name(s) of the author(s) of the essay and be certain of the spelling. You might Google the name(s) to find more information about the author(s). Lepore (2010) cautions that increasingly in the cyberworld anyone can call himself a historian. Generally, in essays on Lincoln in biographical reference works, the essay's author was selected because she or he is recognized as an authority on Lincoln or on some aspect of Lincoln's life.

Some biographical works list the name of the author at the end of the essay. Others identify the author by initials; a list of initials identifying authors generally can be found near the table of contents.

Search for this author's other publications on Lincoln: journal articles, biographies, or chapters in edited works. On the Internet you may be able to find interviews or download lectures, articles or reviews in academic and professional journals.

Pay Attention to Cited References

At the end of the essay you will find sources the author consulted in writing. By examining these sources, you may find more details on a particular death. You may find a citation for a peer or friend of the subject that may prove valuable in your research, for example, Joshua Speed or Elmer Ellsworth, friends of Lincoln.

In a 5,000-word essay in *The Dictionary of American Biography,* the author could not fully explore the death of Lincoln's mother or sister; elsewhere, this author may have written 2, 10, or 20 pages, and offer insights on the impact of the death in later periods in the subject's life. A particular death may have been unimportant to the author. The thanatologist, however, wants to widen the magnification of the historical antecedent.

Historically, deaths of parents and subsequent remarriages were more common given the lack of accessible health care and lack of antibiotics, especially in rural communities. Given the number of women who died in childbirth, males often married younger women and had more children. Those decisions had consequences for children from the previous marriage.

Generally, historians do not aggressively explore the psychological soil of the subject; any information of this nature may be relegated to an endnote. Keller (2006) contends that the emergence of female— and feminist—historians and biographers is widening the lenses of history and biography.

Having made a preliminary assessment of a subject's potential, you can expand the boundaries of your project.

Read Autobiographies and Biographies

Read or skim autobiographies by your subject of interest or biographies about them, particularly by peers, friends, or family members. You may feel empathy for the individual for a particular grief she experienced. If you run into a "dry hole" on Lincoln's grief following the death of his sister, explore another loss he experienced.

Be Clear on the Distinction Between Authorized and Unauthorized Biography

An unauthorized biography is written without the cooperation or permission of the subject or, if deceased, the subject's estate or survivors. A thanatologist should read any unauthorized biography cautiously, especially given a "get 'em!" or "bring-them-down-to-size" debunking mentality about stars, celebrities, athletes, religious leaders, and political figures. Americans love heroines but like to see them, occasionally, humbled. So, read or skim the unauthorized and compare with other sources.

Kelley's (2010) unauthorized biography of Oprah Winfrey may interest thanatologists because she explores the death of Vincent Miquelle Lee, the son born to 15-year-old Oprah. Vernon Winfrey, Oprah's father, told Kelley, "We tried to keep the fact of the baby quiet, even within the family. There was no funeral, no death notice" (p. 40). How a death is interpreted may be as significant as the death. Winfrey told his daughter, "This is your second chance. ... God has chosen to take this baby and so I think God is giving you a second chance, and if I were you, I would take it" (p. 40).

Browse Other Biographies

The author of a biography may be untrained in the writing of or interpretation of history or biography, which Hamilton (2008) contends is a fine art. Theodore Roosevelt, for example, made no mention of Alice Lee, his first wife, in his "official" autobiography (T. Roosevelt, 1913). That absence is conspicuous because Roosevelt was a well-respected published author.

Adopt this maxim: Read. Read widely. Read wisely.

Examine the Article Before and After the Article of Your Interest in a Journal or Chapter in an Edited Book

Dr. Gregory DeBourgh (2008), of the University of San Francisco, a specialist in the use of technology in nursing curriculum, offered a methodological suggestion that has paid rich dividends. Suppose you read an article on Lincoln in *The Journal of American History*, pages 123 to 151. DeBourgh insists that a wise researcher checks the article or chapter preceding and following the article or chapter of primary interest. It is possible that a particular issue of a journal has a specific theme. That additional article could be considered a *lagniappe*, which in New Orleans is "the little extra" the chef places on a plate. Synchronicity, or coincidence, often rewards an inquiring researcher.

Explore Suggestions for Further Reading

Authors often recommend additional reading, which perhaps may interpret the subject differently. A particular death might be addressed more fully in a recommended reading. You will not know unless you check it out.

Pay Attention to Publication Dates

Note the time lag between the publication date and when you examine the material. Is there a source more current? During this interval, a significant biographical or historical book or article may have been published offering new insights based on recent research. Lincoln's bicentennial in 2009 fueled a watershed of new books by recognized Lincoln authorities: Burlingame (2008), Clinton (2009a), Epstein (2009), Foner (2008), and White (2009), as well as less-known and emerging scholars.

Rely on the most recent biographical works. Hopefully the author(s) took advantage of new discoveries or interpretation in the continually expanding Lincoln literature. Richard Miller demonstrates this in his multivolume history of Lincoln. Miller spent countless hours reading microfilms of newspapers from Lincoln's day for fresh insights into the daily life of the 16th president.

Exploring Lincoln, a clinician early on would consult Michael Burlingame's definitive 2,000-page, two-volume biography, *Abraham Lincoln: A Life* (2008), the Cadillac of Lincoln resources. The closing paragraph offers a great model for drafting the conclusion of your article, book or presentation:

... *despite* [emphasis added] a childhood of emotional malnutrition and grinding poverty, *despite* a lack of formal education, *despite* a series of career failures, *despite* a miserable marriage, *despite* a tendency to depression, *despite* a painful midlife crisis, *despite* the early death of his mother and his sibling as well as of his sweetheart and two of his four children, he became a model of psychological maturity, moral clarity, and unimpeachable integrity. (Vol. 2, p. 834)

I asked Burlingame how he came to write this paragraph. As one who lectures on grief, I find this string of *despites* a fascinating literary device to catch the griever's attention. Other historical personalities, like Eleanor Roosevelt, have experienced a chain of *despites*, as have some grievers you counsel. Burlingame added one sentence that is critical: "His presence and his leadership inspired his contemporaries, *his life story can do the same for generations to come* [emphasis added]" (Vol. 2, p. 834).

The grief-related biographical narratives you find could be equally inspiring "for generations to come" or for a particular client or a grief-group participant. John Claypool, a grieving father, after reflecting on his losses, concludes: "If we are still breathing, it is too early to tell the ultimate impact of any event in our lives" (2005, p. 40). Lincoln demonstrates, in my judgment, Claypool's conclusion. I can share Claypool's quote with a griever and link it to a reinforcing borrowed narrative from Lincoln.

No one could have predicted future greatness for that depressed prairie lawyer following the death of his romantic interest Ann Rutledge in 1835, or that prosperous railroad lawyer grappling with spiritual questions after the death of his son Edward Baker Lincoln in 1850 (Carwardine, 2008). Similarly, no one may predict a meaningful future for your client. As a clinician your words may have impact if supported by some detail from Lincoln's grief narratives or from another borrowed narrative. That is, if you know the narrative slice and if you match and communicate that narrative segment effectively.

Explore Specialized Biographical Resources

Specialized encyclopedias or dictionaries are valuable. To explore the grief of George Frideric Handel, composer of *The Messiah* and other classic musical works, a clinician would wisely begin with *The New Grove Dictionary of Music and Musicians,* which is "*the* [emphasis added] standard multi-volume reference book [on music] for the English-speaking world" (Sadie, 2001, p. xiii). Standard reference works in various fields may be found in public libraries (although not necessarily the latest edition) or in a local university library, with increasing numbers online. In Volume 10 of the 2001 edition of *Grove*, I read Paul and Spencer's essay on Handel. I learned that after Handel lost his eyesight—a devastating loss for composers or keyboard performers—he improvised at the organ during concerts. At one concert, a child led him to the organ console—a detail that greatly moved the audience. Admittedly, that detail seems trivial. What may seem initially trivial could become far become more valuable when working with a client experiencing loss of eyesight.

I pondered a passage that might be skipped by individuals with other interests. On April 11, 1759, Handel added a codicil to his will directing that his estate go to the Society for the Support of Decay'd Musicians. So what? Handel died 3 days later! Reading history and biography through a thanatological filter, that decision and those dates—and the brief interval between them—begs the question: Why did Handel add a codicil? Did he know he was dying? Who were the initial recipients of his estate? How did they react after discovering their exclusion from the will? Perhaps like some excluded individuals or institutions feel today. What more in Handel's life might a griever choose to mine?

J. M. W. Turner's *Peace—Burial at Sea*, painted in 1842 after the death of his close friend Sir David Wilkie, was savaged by London critics who dismissed it as too dark. Turner snapped, "I only wish I had had colour to make them blacker" (Gaunt, 1971, p. 15). Wanting to know more about this detail, I read Andrew Wilton's (2001) biographical essay on Turner in *The Dictionary of Art*. Wilkie's death in 1841, when the painter was 54, disturbed Turner and "contributed to his sense of isolation" (p. 466). From thanatological literature, I know that psychological isolation complicates grief (Bonanno, 2009; Stylianos & Vachon, 1993).

Turner died in 1851 and was buried in Saint Paul's Cathedral in London. His "family" was, by that point in his life, fellow landscape artists rather than biological kin—a reality I label "the family of investment." Turner intended that his significant estate finance an asylum for indigent landscape painters. That intention, however, was thwarted by Turner's family who successfully overturned the will. Families still challenge wills and, sometimes, the stated wishes of the deceased are ignored or overturned.

Use Online Sources Cautiously

In a cyber era and given the time pressures clinicians face, some may launch research by going to an online source like Wikipedia. Admittedly, a Web site may offer key dates, relationships, or losses in a subject's life. Sometimes it is unclear who wrote the essay, their skills, or their biases. Were details thoroughly fact-checked? An online source can be a place to gain key words, ideas, or dates to further focus your research. But, let the clinician beware!

One maxim to remember when researching: Thoroughly double fact-check dates and spellings in *all* sources. Even professional historians or individuals writing about family make errors. John S. D. Eisenhower was Dwight and Mamie Eisenhower's second son—but many thought *only* son. In a personal reminiscence of his father's career, John addressed the lingering impact of the death of Doud Dwight Eisenhower at 3½ years old in 1921, before John was born. General Eisenhower called that death "the greatest tragedy of their lives" (J. S. D. Eisenhower, 2003, p. 7). John Eisenhower comments, "The bereaved parents longed to leave" Fort Meade, Maryland, "so full of memories of their loss" for a fresh start elsewhere. A thanatologist notes that Doud "had contracted scarlet fever just before the end of the year and had died *the day after Christmas* [emphasis added]" (p. 7).

Two issues stand out in a brother's narrative who, no doubt, inherited his parents' fears that something would happen to him. Eisenhower used "Ickie" rather than the traditional spelling of Doud Dwight's nickname—Ikky, a play off Ike. Second, Doud Dwight Eisenhower died the day after New Year's, 1921. Initially that seems a minor detail. The death date, however, has critical importance because Eisenhower, in his grief, mistakenly applied for full military dependent funding while Ikky was staying with an aunt in Iowa for 3 months in 1920. That decision triggered an investigation that almost led to his court martial for fraud. D'Este (2002) fumes:

> The fact that Eisenhower had recently suffered the untimely death of his son evoked no sympathy with the unforgiving keepers of army regulations. The amount was duly repaid, and the family finances took a severe hit. To protect her from further travail, it is doubtful that Eisenhower shared his latest troubles with Mamie, at least until he had to cough up $250.67, which could hardly have been glossed over. Eisenhower never again referred to the matter or how close his career had come to derailment. (p. 162)

The point: Check dates and spellings carefully.

Consult Major Biographies

Researching Abraham Lincoln can be overwhelming. The 16th president has long fascinated biographers and historians. James Cornelius, curator of the Lincoln Collection at the Abraham Lincoln Presidential Library, estimates "roughly 17,000 distinct titles" about Abraham Lincoln (2010, p. 7) have been published and more, no doubt, are in press as you read this.

Which biography is a good place to "put in" as a canoeist would put in on a river or lake? Can one trust this biography, especially given the increase in author-published books that are not subjected to peer review? Some books are written by authors with an ax to grind. Some self-defined "historians" write books to "fill" a niche on a political issue.

Amazon.com or BarnesandNoble.com offers a generous selection of biographies on "major" figures. Amazon.com provides a way to sample books before buying or looking for them in local libraries or bookstores. Seeking bibliographic resources on Helen Steiner Rice, who wrote poetry as therapy following the suicide of her husband, I struck out using Amazon.com and interlibrary loan. So I turned to Abe.com, a network of used books stores across the United States, and purchased *Helen Steiner Rice: Ambassador of Sunshine,* an out-of-print biography on Rice that proved valuable. Trivia question: What was Helen Steiner Rice's occupation? Pollitt and Wiltse (1994) report that she was a professional lampshade designer. Scanning brief reviews—or readers' comments—may persuade you to explore, or ignore, a particular biography.

You might interview or consult with a professor of American history at a local university seeking what Gregory DeBourgh calls "a good steer" or being directed to relevant resources—guidance that may save you time, money, or embarrassment if you rely on a writer that is untrustworthy. That professor might also become a good sounding board for questions as you read, be willing to loan you her editorial eye to critique your conclusions, or review your manuscript. Given colleague networking in academia, a professor may recommend, "Here is someone who might be able to help you" or "You might want to run your idea by ..."

Browse in Libraries and Bookstores

Browse biographies and histories in libraries, bookstores, book sections of antique stores, bazaars, and even yard sales. I enjoy what Julie Bosman (2010) describes as "the book-buying tradition of strolling aisles, perusing covers and being able to hold books" in my hand and examine indexes and tables of contents.

Check specialty libraries or bookstores devoted to history, religion, science, whatever. Kansas City's Linda Hall Library of Science's collection on Albert Einstein offered resources, in several languages, to research the scientist's grief—resources unavailable in a general library.

Browse online for a bookstore that specializes in your subject of interest. The Prairie Archives, in Springfield, Illinois, is a literary candy shop for Lincoln enthusiasts and researchers. The owners—as many owners of independent bookstores—recommended great reads that have proved helpful to me. Laurence Kirshbaum describes the particular delight of "going into stores and seeing a book" you "didn't know existed and buying it" and finding it valuable (as cited in Bosman, 2010). Admittedly, I have not always purchased a book but made a note to explore it later.

Use Interlibrary Loan

Interlibrary loan is a marvelous resource, especially for clinicians living in small towns or rural areas. A local library can often borrow a book from another library across town, state, or country, although there may be restrictions on the use of the book. Even if you are not a student, alumni, or faculty at a particular university, academic libraries may allow reading privileges.

Identify a Subject's Contemporaries

In researching Eleanor Roosevelt's grief, I read biographies by her contemporaries such as Hickok (1962) and Parks (1961), and by individuals active on the world stage at the same time or committed to similar causes. I read Metaxes's (2010) *Bonhoeffer: Priest, Martyr, Prophet, Spy* about German pastor Dietrich Bonhoeffer who was hung by the Nazis in 1945. Although this biography offers no direct link to Eleanor Roosevelt, it helped me understand widespread anti-Semitism in the 1930s and 1940s that Eleanor fought vigorously.

I read Levy's (2010) biography of Henry Morgenthau, Jr., who served as FDR's Secretary of the Treasury from 1934 to 1945. Mrs. Elinor Morgenthau was so close a friend to Mrs. Roosevelt that Mrs. Roosevelt delayed the public announcement of FDR's death until Secretary Morgenthau notified his wife, who was hospitalized following a heart attack. The Morgenthau biography is a gold mine for understanding American blindness to the early Nazi atrocities against European Jews and Congressional opposition to increased Jewish immigration.

Using an Index to Expedite Research on Grief

The index can narrow the focus of your research. In a Lincoln biography, search for an entry such as "Lincoln, Abraham, life of." The entry "Lincoln's men" in the index in Epstein (2009) has a large category "Lincoln, Abraham" with subentries "assassination of" and "assassination plots against." I found curious one subentry, "private grief." By skimming the pages listed, I found comments of William Stoddard, a presidential aide, on Lincoln's grief one month after the death of Lincoln's son, Willie.

> The President has recovered much of his old equanimity and cheerfulness; and certainly no one who saw his constant and eager application to his arduous duties, would imagine for a moment that the man carried so large a load of *private grief* [emphasis added]. (Epstein, 2009, p. 113)

In those days, Lincoln's office—and those of top aides—was down the hall from the family quarters. Stoddard commented on the office environment weeks after Willie's death:

> Eight-year-old Tad was again up and about, but ... he sorely missed his older brother Willie. Tad also missed his mother, who rarely emerged from her bedroom, so the child was seen at all hours of the day and night playing in his father's office. When Tad fell asleep on the floor or on a couch, Lincoln would carry him off to bed, and return to the maps and war strategy. (Epstein, 2009, p. 113)

As I read that paragraph, I thought somewhere young siblings are experiencing a mother who is not there or a father overwhelmed by work.

In an index, read subentries such as "death of son" or "death of mother" or the deaths of other family members. Admittedly, the citation in the text may be brief, but still contributes to the formation of the grief grid. Check the index for other family listings: "Lincoln, Thomas" (Lincoln's father) or "Lincoln, Robert" (Lincoln's oldest son). Many indices note the relationship to the subject of the biography by parenthesis or dash: mother, grandfather, and so forth. This will be helpful when common family names run through generations. Roosevelt indices, for example, have multiple Theodores, Annas, Eleanors, Alices, and Franklins. A subject's in-laws will be more difficult to find; you may have to skim the entire index.

Admittedly, indices may contain errors. If there is no specific entry related to key deaths in the subject's life, search the hard way: skimming pages, which, although laborious, may prove profitable.

Pay Attention to Dates

Elmer Ellsworth died on May 24, 1861. That is a fact of a powerful story. How did Colonel Ellsworth die? Expand the significance of a narrative by fleshing out more details, a process Doris Kearns Goodwin terms "widening the lens" (1991, p. xvii). From his bedroom window in the White House, Lincoln saw a Confederate flag flying in Alexandra, Virginia, across the Potomac River. Ellsworth, knowing the flag distressed the president, organized a raiding party to confiscate it. After ripping down the flag, as he descended the stairway in the Marshall Hotel, the innkeeper shot him dead.

This narrative chronicles a personal sacrifice by a friend. This story might be valued by a griever whose friend(s) died in Iraq or Afghanistan—particularly if a friend had exchanged places with the survivor in a Humvee and the griever struggles with survivor guilt.

The Lincolns were deeply moved as they viewed their friend's corpse at the Washington Naval Yard. Lincoln paced in front of the corpse, wringing his hands and groaning, "My boy! My boy! Was it necessary this sacrifice should be made?" (Carpenter, 1887). Then Lincoln ordered the body moved to the East Room in the White House. Hundreds of people experienced viewing an embalmed body for the first time. Favorable impressions fueled the public's acceptance of embalming so that soldiers' bodies could be returned from distant battlefields to their families (Ward, 2007, pp. 39–42).

Ellsworth's story may be meaningful to a friend whose grief is underrecognized and dismissed with phrases, "It's not like she was *family*" or "He was *just* a friend!" Why did Abraham and Mary Lincoln sit on the front row at Ellsworth's funeral and were observed weeping? Why was Mrs. Lincoln present? In those days, women were thought too weak to attend funerals. Mary did not attend the funeral for her son Willie in 1862 or for her husband in 1965.

Explore Footnotes, Endnotes, and Asterisks

If you read only the text, you may miss details in the footnotes or endnotes. Increasingly, to shorten a chapter or to eliminate material that interferes with the flow of the reading, editors place the material in endnotes, a practice Burlingame (2008) suggests keeps endnotes "lean" (p. 839), rather than overwhelming.

Strauss's (2010) memoir, written 18 years after a pivotal experience, recounts an accident that resulted in an adolescent's death. Grief constricted his life and sabotaged his future, particularly during 5 years of litigation. Strauss opens the memoir, "It was still tough to think about this girl who died" (2010, p. 193). In the footnote, he reports, "See the way a forgiving brain runs that sentence. ... *The girl who died*" (p. 193). For many years the accusing phrase in Strauss' mind was: "The girl *I killed*."

Endnotes are like "places to visit" highlighted in tourist brochures. Hamilton (2008) urges, "Read carefully the bibliographies, footnotes, and endnotes of existing biographical works on your subject, and make a list of all the names mentioned—especially in the other author's acknowledgements" (p. 69).

Befriend Reference Librarians

Reference librarians have generously aided my research. Doug Fuehling at Ryan Library at Point Loma Nazarene University likes challenging questions and knows how to navigate reference works and Web sites for answers. He has made valuable suggestions to my research for this book.

While researching historical figures who migrated to Texas after personal losses, I went to the main Dallas Public Library to read its extensive Texas history collection. As I explained my project to a reference librarian, she interrupted, "Well, of course, you are including Maribeau Lamar!"

"Oh yes," I responded without acknowledging that I had never heard of Maribeau Lamar.

"Then," she smiled, "you have come to the *right* place." She escorted me to a table and promised to return. Twenty minutes later she pushed a cart loaded with resources to my table. I soon found gold. Lamar, a newspaper editor in Columbus, Georgia, nursed his bride who had tuberculosis. After she died in 1835, Lamar, like many early settlers, sought a fresh start in Texas. He played a critical role in the fight for independence, and in 1836, was elected vice president of the new nation of Texas. When he ran for president, since both of his opponents suicided (*both* opponents suicided!?), he was elected almost unanimously to succeed the legendary Sam Houston. After Lamar's only daughter died in 1843, he battled depression but died a visionary who founded what became the University of Texas in Austin (Henson, 1999). His contributions to Texas were honored by the naming of Lamar University in Beaumont, Texas. In time, I might have stumbled onto Maribeau Lamar's narrative. With a librarian's assistance, the process was expedited.

Be Cautious in Citing Secondary Sources

If you rely on secondary sources, you rely on the accuracy of an author, or authors, their editor and fact-checker. Invest time in seeking primary sources. I could have accepted Burlingame's (2008) quotation from *The Los Angeles Times* on the death of Lincoln's friend, Ellsworth, but what if there was other interesting information in that particular newspaper article that Burlingame had not used?

I asked Fuehling, my librarian friend, to do a search for the article and send a photocopy. In reading that article, I discovered Ellsworth had written his parents on May 22, 1861, the night before his death, "I am perfectly content to accept whatever my fortune may be." Grievers have long found comfort in recalling a last conversation.

Occasionally, I skim *The Wall Street Journal.* One day I read an article about a new 1,112 page anthology of Ray Bradbury stories. Buried in that article, I found that Tom Nolan had asked the famed author the source of his stories. Bradbury answered, "All my stories are me" and offered an example:

> When I was 8 years old, I was at the beach in Waukegan and a little girl was building a sandcastle with me. She went in the water and she never came out. She drowned. It was my first experience with death. It upset me terribly. … Years later, I remembered that, and I wrote about it; it was called "The Lake." It was published in *Weird Tales.* And all around the world, people wrote to me about that story; and my career was started. I was 26 years old. (Nolan, 2010)

I did not rely on the reviewer's accuracy with the quote. I pursued the story—and the facts—in Weller's (2005) *The Bradbury Chronicles*. By doing so, I learned that a string of deaths (beloved grandfather, uncle, baby sister) shaped Bradbury's childhood and would, in time, be incorporated in his fiction.

A "take away" in an article or book may not be initially evident. Later, the researcher may experience a, "Wait a minute, I remember ..."

Details Make Dates Significant

In the late days of summer 1941, Franklin Roosevelt and staff anxiously prepared a national radio address in response to the Germans sinking the *USS Greer*, an incident Roosevelt considered an act of war. Many Americans feared the sinking would drag the United States into the war in Europe, although during the campaign of 1940, Roosevelt had repeatedly assured Americans, "Your boys are not going to be sent into any foreign wars" (Lash, 1971, p. 630).

On September 6, 1941, Eleanor Roosevelt arrived home in Hyde Park, and alarmed by her mother-in-law's physical condition, telephoned Franklin. The president resisted her entreaty to "come home immediately" because of the preparations for the address. Eleanor insisted that he come to Hyde Park. Immediately! Because Mrs. Roosevelt insisted, Franklin had the opportunity to spend the last 24 hours of his mother's life with her.

Sara Roosevelt, the president's mother, died on September 7, 1941. Franklin, her only son, grieved so deeply that Eleanor had to arrange for her mother-in-law's funeral and burial, an emotionally demanding task since Eleanor "had no affection for her mother-in-law" (C. Black, 2003, p. 660).

Days later, as FDR and his aides sorted through boxes of childhood memorabilia his mother had saved, the president found baby clothes and locks of his hair. Beginning to cry, he asked his aides to leave. While FDR did not show grief in public, that day he grieved privately. That example may encourage one of your clients to find, or create, *mekom hanekhama*—a safe place of comfort (Brener, 1993, p. 31).

In the days following, tension with Nazi Germany eased to the relief of many Americans. Historians and biographers have left unprobed the reality that Franklin Roosevelt was in deep mourning when the Japanese attacked Pearl Harbor on December 7, 1941.

Conclusion

Borrowed narratives offer stories of grievers who have faced, survived, and sometimes thrived in circumstances similar to or not unlike what clients are experiencing. Grievers need stories or story fragments for reflection. Paradoxically, the emotional wilderness of one griever becomes, through a clinician's awareness, an oasis for another.

"Borrowed narratives" are resources clinicians use to help grievers find courage to confront questions that may not have words to formulate—or to ponder the unwelcomed questions that dart into their consciousness. Eleanor Roosevelt, as a widow, wrote in 1950, in the introduction to her autobiography:

> Autobiographies are, after all, useful only as the lives you read about and analyze may suggest to you something that you find useful in your own journey through life. … There is nothing particularly interesting about one's own story unless people can say as they read it, "Why, this is like what I have been through. Perhaps, after all, there is a way to work it out." (1992, pp. xviii–xix)

A Story for the Road

The first Union officer to die in the Civil War was Colonel Elmer Ellsworth, Lincoln's former law student who accompanied the Lincolns to Washington. Burlingame (2008) identifies Ellsworth as one of Lincoln's "favorite surrogate sons" (Vol. 2, p. 177). After arriving in the capital, Ellsworth immediately organized a brigade of Union troops. Their colorful uniforms and precision marching gained a lot of attention as well as the addictive fascination of Willie and Tad Lincoln who soon had matching uniforms and wood rifles. Moreover, Colonel Ellsworth lived for a while in the White House. On May 24, 1861, when Lincoln was notified of Ellsworth's "murder"—that was the phrase Lincoln used—he burst into tears in front of visitors in his office and said, "Excuse me, but I cannot talk." Moments later, he resumed the conversation, "I will make no apology, gentlemen, for my weakness; but I knew poor Ellsworth well, and held him in high regard" (Burlingame, 2008, Vol. 2, p. 177). Lincoln explained that the initial shock of the death was so overwhelming "that it quite unmanned me" (Burlingame, 2008, Vol. 2, p. 177). In a society that disenfranchises male grief (Doka & Martin, 2010), a narrative slice from Lincoln's grief may be valued by a male of any age. If Abraham Lincoln grieved publically for his friends, today's grievers may find permission to grieve for their friends from this historical narrative.

3

CONSTRUCTING A GRIEF GRID

In the telling of our tales we seek help in finding answers, or at least, permission to share the burning questions.

Robert Neimeyer (1998, p. 54)

Barely a day goes by when I do not think of her. There would be so much to tell her.

J. K. Rowling (Iggulden, 2006)

As a child growing up between hog farms in Kentucky, I enjoyed watching *The Naked City,* a television drama about detectives in New York City. Every week's show opened with the deep-voiced announcer saying: "There are eight million stories in the naked city." Thirty minutes later, during the credits, the same announcer reminded, "There are eight million stories in the naked city; this has been one of them" (Wythoff, 2010). Similarly, I believe millions of grief narratives are waiting to be explored and borrowed.

The Grid

To match a borrowed narrative with a particular client, an individual's *grief grid* needs to be constructed. A grid is influenced by the experience with other losses, perhaps over generations.

Clinicians are familiar with the concepts of mapping, clustering, or webbing. If using that structure to graft losses, each loss would appear independent. A grief grid, however, makes losses interdependent. The *New Oxford American Dictionary* (2010) defines *grid* as "a framework of spaced bars that are parallel to or cross each other" (p. 764). Cities maintain grids of streets, sewers, and water lines; utilities maintain distribution grids to distribute electricity or natural gas to clients. In recent times, a *computer grid* has emerged. A number of computers are "linked together" through internet connections, "so that their *combined power* [emphasis added] may be harnessed to work on difficult problems" (p. 764). A grid also has meaning in geography and nautical navigation and spying. Thus, scientists have constructed an imaginary grid of parallels and medians over the surface of the earth so that a ship, plane, or object can be located at a specific point and become a target (Coubeil & Archambault, 2010).

A grief grid is a process a clinician can use to audit a client's loss repertoire and enhance the therapeutic interaction. The grid forces the question: How does this loss intersect with other losses?

In gridding grievers, clinicians want to know about the deaths of friends, family members, colleagues, and pets. To say, "Oh, she was only a friend" or "It was just a dog!" verbally disenfranchises important losses. A death in an individual's friendship network or their "family of investment," may distress more than a death in the biological family.

A Death Is Never Completely Past Tense

Admittedly, clinicians use the word *bereaved* for clients. I prefer *bereaving* because *-ed* implies past tense and is something of a statement about cooperation with the cultural impatience for grievers to obtain "closure." Strauss (2010) describes the impact over an 18-year period after the death of a girl he struck while driving a car. That death became a "ghost" in his life after the girl's mother said to him: "Whatever you do in your life, you have to do it twice as well now. … Because you are living for two people" (p. 62). Moreover, Strauss contends that in marriage what had been *my* secret became *our* secret and impacted the marital relationship.

Gridding Losses

Grids must incorporate the losses a client self-disenfranchises: "I was so young when that happened" or "I don't remember much about that death." Jeffreys (2011) insists that some grievers gain "a better grasp of the reality of their loss after they put it in some kind of historical perspective" (p. 60). Initially, some grievers will perfunctorily list deaths. Jeffreys suggests an exercise to engage memories: "Writing the history of a relationship … can help individuals express feelings they are unable to verbalize" (p. 270). The clinician can jump-start the conversation by asking, "Tell me five significant things about the individual or about your relationship." You can follow up on a disclosure such as, "My uncle was a sports nut" with "Tell me one story that demonstrates that." The client may offer a narrative slice: "I will always remember the last time he took me to a Yankees game …"

The following questions, adapted from Jeffreys (2011), facilitate gridding:

> What other losses have come to mind since you sustained this latest loss?
> Do you have "unfinished business" from previous losses that may be impacting this loss?
> How did you and your spouse/partner/family/friends respond to each of these losses?

For some individuals the clinician will need to allow time in the session for constructing a thorough grid. Reviewing the grief grid in future sessions provides opportunities to expand the original inclusions and, over time, becomes a fuller assessment. Other questions that a clinician might find valuable in constructing a grid:

> What is the earliest death that you can recall?
> Which significant death in your family do you know the least about? Why do you know little about this loss?
> Were you included or excluded from attending rituals? Was it your choice or was the choice made for you?
> What do you remember about conversations related to this death? Did your family talk about death?
> How do your religious beliefs and traditions influence the way you respond to death and grief? (Jeffreys, 2011, p. 99)

Ask the client to date the initial grid so that the client is saying, "These are the losses that I remember and acknowledge on [insert] date."

The Comprehensive Grid

The comprehensive grid captures *significant* losses—or the consequences of losses—experienced by the client. Losses before the client's birth can impact a family narrative. Ron Reagan (2011) notes
that although his paternal grandfather died "before I was born," that
death tinted the environment in which his family narratives developed. H. I. Smith (2006a) labels this reality "the long shadowed grief"
particularly common after stigmatized deaths. One has to make room
in the grid for all the dead and for a realistic appraisal. "Speak no ill
of the dead" may be a barrier to some clients.

Borrowing a Grid

To guide the client's graphing of their accumulated losses, a clinician may share a historical or biographical figure's grief grid. Or the
clinician might ask a particular griever, as homework, to do some
research and draft a grief grid for a historical or biographical person
they admire, such as Abraham Lincoln.

A Grief Grid for the 16th President

Abraham Lincoln, U.S. president, 1861–1865, was no stranger to
grief. By age 26, he had experienced the deaths of three significant
women: mother, sister, and Ann Rutledge. If I explore his romantic relationship with Ann Rutledge, I have to acknowledge the relationship is the subject of much speculation by historians and amateur
history buffs. Some agree with William Herndon, Lincoln's law part-
ner-biographer, that Ann was the woman Abraham loved; Mary was
the woman he married (Clinton, 2009b).

Ann's death on August 25, 1835, devastated Lincoln. Burlingame
(2008) reports that Lincoln was left "so profoundly grief-stricken that
many friends worried that he might lose his mind" (p. 100) or take
his life. Elizabeth Abell, who witnessed his grief, commented, "I have
never seen a man mourn for a companion more than he did for her"
(p. 100). Burlingame contends, "Ann's death unconsciously reminded

him of those old wounds … causing him to re-experience 'the bitter agony' he had endured" (p. 101) when his mother and sister died.

By researching Lincoln's grief behavior following Ann's death, counselors gain insight helping in assessing his grief for friends Elmer Ellingsworth and Edward Baker who died in 1861, and for his son Willie, who died in 1862. The Ann Rutledge component may be helpful when working with grievers whose fiancée, partner, or significant other died. If the relationship has not been publically acknowledged, as may be the case for closeted gays and lesbians, the survivor also grieves for a future that had been richly imagined and desired (H. I. Smith & Johnson, 2008).

Deliberately Exploring *Under*recognized Losses

Every grief leaves a residue that I explain with this analogy: Suppose you have been drinking milk from a glass and that glass is empty. If still thirsty, you do not pour cola into that glass because the milk left a thin residue inside. Previous losses also leave residues.

The significance assigned to a previous death may be underacknowledged. A married or partnered client may not be forthcoming about the death of an individual with whom he or she had had an affair. The narratively clouded death can become toxic. Families with secrets initiate children into the family-framed expected responses for future losses. When an individual is expunged from family narratives and conversations, that communicates: If you die, you will be expunged! Clients report a parent never again mentioning a deceased sibling; indeed, grandchildren may be unaware of this aunt or uncle. When I visit my paternal grandparents' graves, I notice the adjoining small marker, "Joseph Dean Smith, infant." I never heard my uncle mentioned in family gatherings. I wondered why my father never cried until I was offered this explanation: Your father cried so much when his brother died that he damaged his tear ducts. That made sense when I was a child. Now, long after the deaths of my father and his siblings, there is no way to probe that most unlikely explanation.

"Defrosting" a Family Narrative

As a child, I helped my mother periodically defrost the refrigerator by chipping away ice that had accumulated around the refrigerator coils. Some clients need to "defrost" a grief to make a place for a deceased individual who has been frozen in "the absent" or relegated to the margins of family narratives. The clinician may have to nudge the defrosting process by probing, "Tell me more about this loss." Unfortunately, a narrative may have been so edited that the griever possesses few details. Some families adhere to a "Don't ask, don't tell, don't probe" perspective on anything that challenges the scripted family narrative.

In preparing to write a book celebrating his father's centennial, Ron Reagan (2011) researched his father's life before being elected governor of California and president. Reagan examined what Neimeyer (2010) calls "the back story" of Jack Reagan, his paternal grandfather. He discovered Jack had lost both parents by age 6. (Thus, Reagan's father, as a child, had no living paternal grandparents.) Moreover, his grandfather's sisters had died: Catherine in 1901 and Anna in 1903 and his only brother, an alcoholic, died in 1920. Ron Reagan recalls,

> Not one bit of this was broached during my father's discussions of Jack as I was growing up. None of us—my mother included—even knew that Jack had a brother and sisters. ... We certainly weren't apprised of their tragic early ends. Was my father aware of them? (2011, p. 100)

Ron Reagan wondered if his grandparents—Jack and Nelle—kept such details from his father or if these details were "simply omitted from my Dad's story" (2011, p. 100)? These unacknowledged deaths were still part of Ronald Wilson Reagan's grief grid and, therefore, part of Ronald Prescott Reagan's *inherited* grief grid.

A clinician may sense strong reluctance to pursuing a missing link. Jeffreys (2011) suggests confronting the reluctance: "Let's take a few minutes to look at how your reluctance is serving you. What do you think would happen if you probed" this death (p. 305)?

Tapping Into a Celebrity Grief Grid

Adolescents and young adults are generally more knowledgeable of and interested in celebrities than historic figures and humanitarians. If you ask a child or adolescent to name their heroes, expect sports figures and pop-culture icons. In a culture addicted to celebrities, children grow up wanting to be famous. For some, fascination with "the latest" of a celebrity offers an escape from their own reality. Ponton (2002) identifies three common elements: courage, resiliency, and development. Never, he says, count a celebrity out; some periodically reinvent themselves. Because celebrities are not immune from life's realities, some grievers find exploring the grief of a celebrity valuable in constructing their grid.

A Griever Named J. K.

J. K. Rowling experienced a meteoric rise to fame through her *Harry Potter* novels. Rowling, in an interview with the London *Telegraph*, said, "I was writing Harry Potter at the moment my mother died ... I had never told her about [him]." Rowling concedes that her mother's death "left her 'a wreck'" and "was the inspiration for Harry's orphan status" (Iggulden, 2006).

Admittedly, at Christmas 1990, Rowling had been surprised by how frail and exhausted her mother was. Nevertheless, on Christmas Eve, she kissed her mother and went off to spend the rest of the holidays with a boyfriend. Early on the morning of New Year's Eve, her father phoned with the news that her mother had died. Steffens (2002) reports that J. K. "blamed herself for not noticing" how ill her mother was and for preferring to spend time with her boyfriend. Rowling phrased two sentences that may resonate with a client of yours: "I wasn't there. That stirs up such guilt" (p. 35). Steffens (2002) offers an insight you might use in encouraging a griever to grid, journal, or memoir. "To escape from her sadness, Rowling turned to her writing. The world of Harry Potter did not turn out to be a refuge from her pain *but a place to experience it in a different way* [emphasis added]" (p. 35). Simply, therapeutic conversation is a safe place to experience pain in a different way.

An adolescent or young adult might find borrowable material in Rowling's personal grief grid. Rowling's family moved to Wales "almost exactly" at the time her favorite grandmother, Kathleen, died. "No doubt the first bereavement of my life influenced my feelings about the new school, which I didn't like at all" (J. K. Rowling Official Site). When the publisher, to attract boy readers, insisted on publishing her novel with initials rather than her first and middle names, Rowling, having no middle name, chose K. to honor her grandmother. Soon after her grandmother died, her mother was diagnosed with multiple sclerosis. Rowling reveals the emotional rollercoaster of those days:

> It was a terrible time. My father, Di [her sister] and I were devastated, she was only forty-five years old and we had never imagined—probably because we could not bear to contemplate the idea—that she could die so young. I remember feeling as though there was a paving slab pressing down on my chest, a literal pain in my heart. (J. K. Rowling Official Site, accessed April 4, 2011)

Many clinicians will find Rowling's next line of interest. "Nine months later, desperate to get away for a while," the grieving daughter went to Portugal and found a job teaching English. Although she planned to finish the manuscript and return to England, she met and married a Portuguese man and had a baby. The "short and catastrophic" marriage of "thirteen months and a day," left her "quite shell-shocked." Rowling returned to Edinburgh at Christmas 1993 with a baby and a manuscript. Rowling regrets not having shared the book concept with her mother. She told Oprah:

> But the odd thing is that's just life, isn't it? The books wouldn't be what they are if she hadn't died. I mean her death is on virtually every page of the *Harry Potter* books, you know. At least half of Harry's journey is a journey to deal with death in its many forms, what it does to the living, what it means to die, what survives death—it's there in every single volume of the books.
>
> So, if she hadn't died I don't think it's too strong to say there wouldn't be *Harry Potter*. There wouldn't—you know? The books are what they are because she died. Because I loved her and she died. (Winfrey, 2010)

The Grief Grid of Mary Lincoln

The grief grid of Mary Lincoln, U.S. First Lady, 1861–1865, is complicated. Mary Todd was born on December 13, 1818, into a socially and politically prominent Kentucky family.

1830	Mother dies; father remarries. (Mary is age 12.) Father and new wife have 9 more children.
1839	Mary moves to Illinois to get away from her stepmother. (Mary is age 21.)
1842	Mary courts and marries Abraham Lincoln after a stormy engagement. (Mary is 24.)
1849	Elizabeth Palmer, Mary's supportive maternal grandmother, dies. (Mary is 30.)
1849	Robert Todd, Mary's father, dies; siblings from first marriage sue over settlement of his estate. (Mary is 31.)
1850	Eddie Baker Lincoln, son, age 4, dies in epidemic. (Mary is 32.)
1860	Abraham Lincoln elected president. (Mary is age 42.)
1861	The Civil War erupts. (Mary is age 43.)
1861	Death of Colonel Elmer Ellsworth, close family friend.
1861	Death of General Edward Baker, family friend for whom the Lincolns named their deceased son.
1862	Death of William Thomas Lincoln, son, age 12. (Mary is 43.)
1863	Death of General Benjamin Helm, brother-in-law, husband of favorite sister. Helm fought for the Confederacy. (Mary is 44.)
1865	Abraham Lincoln is assassinated. (Mary is 46.)
1871	Tad Lincoln, son, age 19, dies. (Mary is 52.)
1875	Robert, son, confines Mary to Batavia Asylum. (Mary is 56.)
1882	Mary Lincoln dies on the 33rd anniversary of her father's death. (Mary is 63.)

On the surface, this is a string of dates and facts. Certain details, however, heighten the consequences. Consider the impact of the death of Confederate General Benjamin Helm, married to Emilie, Mary's favorite stepsister. Both Lincolns had great affection for the Helms; Abraham had offered him a Union command at the start of the war. Clinton (2009a) observes, "Mary hid her grief … [to] protect her husband" (p. 206) from his critics (she was already accused of being a Southern sympathizer). Both Lincolns lost cousins, friends, and acquaintances in the bloody conflict. Not surprisingly, Abraham Lincoln carefully read casualty reports and penned numerous condolence letters.

My conclusion that the Lincolns were grief saturated would be clearer if I created overlapping grids for the president and for the First Lady. When counseling couples who are grieving for a child, plotting an overlapping grid is essential since a spouse or partner may have disenfranchised the other's grief.

Drafting a Preliminary Grid

Step 1

Ask a grieving client to diagram her or his death grid and bring it to a session. After reviewing it, ask questions that invite conversation such as: Who supported your grief? Who challenged or dismissed your grief? How is the individual remembered in your family? How would you capture this death in a word or phrase?

Admittedly, the early grid is skeletal. Through conversation and reflection, more details will be integrated into the grid. Gridding rewards those who, in Strauss' experience, "look hard through the window of memory" (2010, p. 176).

Step 2

Ask the griever to describe the death in a word or phrase. If she answers, "devastating" or "probably for the best" follow up with: "How was your father's death 'probably for the best'?" A griever might answer, "Dad's greatest fear was ending up in a nursing home like his mother!" Other insights might follow that observation.

Step 3

Ask the griever to describe the death in a sentence. One griever wrote, "I have always wished that I could have known my grandmother who died before I was born." A widower wrote, "I wish my wife could have lived three more months for our fifty-fifth wedding anniversary."

Step 4

Ask the griever to write a paragraph describing the loss. You might share a sample paragraph from a historic griever without initially identifying that griever: "No one talked about it much; the 1950s were a time when a death or any other tragedy was viewed as just that: personal. I didn't know that of course. I was only seven." Or "I guess I learned at an early age never to take life for granted. But rather than making me fearful, the close reach of death made me determined to enjoy whatever life might bring, to live each day to the fullest." Both paragraphs were written by George W. Bush years after Robin, his 4-year-old sister, died of leukemia in October 1953 (G. W. Bush, 1999, p. 15).

"Re-Viewing" the Grid

Periodically ask the client to initiate conversations about the deaths in the grid. Now what words or phrases come to mind? A clinician may focus on a particular loss to ask, "Is there anything that you are pretending not to know about this loss?" If the client hesitates, repeat the question emphasizing a different word: "Is there anything you are pretending not to know about this loss?" You might borrow this question from Brady (2011), "What do you know that you didn't know you knew until now" (p. 6)?

A griever from a grief-denying, grief-suppressing family, marriage, or relationship might want to construct a grief grid for each parent or stepparent. What losses did they bring into the relationship? Laura Bush, for example, brought surviving a devastating automobile accident—she was the driver—that resulted in a young man's death. Although George Bush knew, their adolescent daughters were unaware until they learned from a member of the then-governor's security detail (the guard assumed that the girls knew) (L. Bush, 2010).

Gridding in the Dysfunction*ing* Family

In dysfunctioning families, there may be a logjam of unknown losses or unacknowledged losses. (I use *dysfunctioning* rather than *dysfunctional* because strong families may dysfunction as a result of a specific death; second, *dysfunctional* has lost much of its value by overuse.) Some stumbled on a "ghost" in the grief closet of the family: perhaps a previous marriage that ended in death or divorce, or "other" children from other relationships. Some have questioned paternity. In some dysfunctioning families, extended family members have, over the years, lost contact, particularly following the situations, perhaps settling the estate, that challenged the fragile equilibrium of the family.

"As the Story Goes"

Some families "bleach" the death narrative; thus, the deceased is a faint, or fainter, ghost banished to the margin of the family narrative. In other families, details, long unacknowledged, become muddied.

Ron Reagan discovered this reality as he explored an incident foundational in the narrative of Ronald Wilson Reagan, first published in his 1965 biography, *Where's the Rest of Me? The Ronald Reagan Story* and "refurbished" in his 1990 autobiography, *Ronald Reagan: An American Life*. As the story goes, late one night in Dixon, Illinois, an 11-year-old came home.

> My mother was gone on one of her sewing jobs, and I expected the house to be empty. As I walked up the stairs, I nearly stumbled over a lump near the front door; it was Jack lying in the snow, his arms outstretched, flat on his back.
>
> I leaned over to see what was wrong and smelled whiskey. He had found his way home from a speakeasy and had just passed out right there. For a moment or two, I looked down at him and thought about continuing on into the house and going to bed, as if he weren't there. But I couldn't do it. When I tried to wake him he just snored—loud enough, I suspected, for the whole neighborhood to hear him. *So I grabbed a piece of his overcoat, pulled it, and dragged him into the house, then put him to bed and never mentioned the incident to my mother* [emphasis added]. (1965, p. 33)

That was not the first time, according to Eliot (2008), that young Reagan saw his father, in an alcoholic stupor. Passed out on the front porch, however, where a neighbor might see, demanded action. So, young Reagan dragged his father into the house, up the steps, and into bed. This, the younger Reagan insists, was a "hinge story" describing his father's awakening "to adult responsibility" (2011, p. 96). Ronald Reagan (1965) recalled, "I felt myself fill with grief for my father at the same time I was feeling sorry for myself" (p. 7). He continues, "Seeing his arms spread out as if he were crucified—as indeed he was—his hair soaked with melting snow, snoring as he breathed, I could feel no resentment against him" (pp. 7–8).

Ronald Reagan, Ron insists, "did what heroes" or many storytellers do: "He manned up, took charge, muscled his pop to bed, and spared his mother's feelings" (Ron Reagan, 2011, p. 97).

An old adage advises, "Best let sleeping dogs lie." This guidance is adapted by families hesitant to closely examine a threadbare family story. Even just threatening to tell the story can make some family members anxious. The silence, however, leads some to conclude, "Must be more to that story."

You might have a client who has experienced familial rationing of details who needs an example. In 2009, wanting to know more about his father's childhood, Ron Reagan (2011) traveled to Dixon and walked through his father's childhood home. The experience shattered his father's narrative:

> Only it didn't happen that way—it *couldn't* have happened that way. My father, just turned 11, was small for his age; he'd have stood maybe five feet tall and weighed barely 90 pounds. Jack, nearing 40, probably tipped the scales at 180. Dutch wasn't big enough or strong enough to drag Jack anywhere, not over the threshold and into the front hall, *and certainly not up the narrow, angled stairway to his parent's bedroom* [emphasis added]. (p. 97)

It takes courage to challenge an entrenched family myth. Many children of alcoholics, reading Reagan's biography, recognize parallel incidents in their own lives. They too have seen parents passed out or violent.

Ron Reagan proposes an alternative account: Dutch (Ronald Reagan's childhood nickname) nudged or shook his father who awakened long enough to get to his feet and stumble into the house and up the stairs to bed. Reagan concludes, "Jack's role during this incident *has effectively been edited out of my father's internal script* [emphasis added]" (2011, p. 98).

Jack Reagan has been marginalized throughout the family narrative: "Nobody likes Jack—not in my family, anyway," Ron Reagan admits. "When I pursue the subject of Jack with my mom, her tone turns slightly chilly and reserved" (2011, p. 98). Nancy Reagan dismissed her dead father-in-law "as a drunkard and ne'er-do-well, someone who caused her husband pain" (p. 98). Jack, however, died in 1941—long before Nancy married Reagan in 1952. So where did her opinion come from? Ron insists that Nelle Reagan, his grandmother, or his father's brother, Moon, would never have "bad-mouthed" Jack.

> The only way my mother—and, by extension, the rest of us—could have gotten a negative impression of Jack was through his other son, Ronald. Not that Dad intentionally set about destroying his father's reputation. Quite the contrary: He never failed to acknowledge Jack's good qualities, if he seldom lingered on them. It was more his repeated expressions of pity for Jack—never anger. (2011, p. 98)

A counselor might recommend a client read *My Father at 100* and follow up with these questions:

> What might your family members have edited out of scripts of a particular death?
> Have you challenged some of the dominant explanatory narratives in your family?
> Where could you begin to explore the cracks in the story?

The client may need to be graciously cautious. Narrative truth, as Selwyn (1998) discovered, for some family members "remains a fresh wound, even after years of denial, as raw and searing as the day it happened" (p. 108). On the other hand, family members may remember and give prominence to things that never happened to deflect attention from things that did happen. Lopata (1981) calls this process, "the sanctification of the dead."

When Families Camouflage Narrative

Families may not conceal a death fully, but edit or withhold full disclosure. The Roosevelt family could not, in their social circles, and in consideration of Theodore's political ambition, acknowledge that Elliott, his brother, died of consequences of alcoholism, that he had been living in a scandalous relationship, or that his death might have been suicide. Hence, Elliott's death was reported in *The New York*

Times under the headline "Elliott Roosevelt dies of heart disease" ("The Obituary Record," August 16, 1894).

When Family Members Resist Gridding

There may be little enthusiasm, but rather resistance, within the family—or by knowledgeable family members—to ask questions about a death. For some the admonition "Speak no ill of the dead" is nonnegotiable; for others, "Honor father and mother" is enough to dissuade questioning. Thus, the clinician may have to persuade the client to see the process as "an investment" or compare gridding to full disclosure in a medical history; the more thorough the disclosure, the better a physician can care for the patient.

What Stands Out for Grid Makers

Siblings sometimes maintain dissonant grids. While agreeing that Dad died on November 25, 2007, they interpret the death differently. One might say, "My father died of lung cancer" without elaborating. Another says, "My father would never give up smoking—even though he knew it would have given him more years with his grandchildren. I cannot tell you how many times I pleaded with him: 'Dad, give up the cigarettes.'" This may require diplomacy if family members smoke. Gridding is like dodging landmines. G. K. Chesterton cautions, "There is so much good and evil in breaking secrets" (Brady, 2011, p. 89). On the other hand, there is an Alcoholics Anonymous (AA) adage, "A family is only as healthy as its secrets."

Pursuing Gaps in a Grid

Gaps in the grid are common, especially in early drafts. I have long relied on Kochmann (1997) as a guide to facts and dates on the presidents. If I ask individuals, "How many children did President Reagan have?" the common answer is four (or three since Maureen died in 2001). Wead (2003) in *All the President's Children* names four children: Maureen, Michael (adopted), Patricia, and Ronald Prescott. If I check Reagan's autobiography, I find support for four. "The same year

I made the Knute Rockne movie, I married Jane Wyman, another contract player at Warners. Our marriage produced two wonderful children, Maureen and Michael, but it didn't work out, and in 1948 we were divorced" (1990, p. 93).

Reagan, a master storyteller, summed up 7 years of marriage in 37 words. Reagan, while filming *That Hagan Girl*, became physically exhausted after being asked repeatedly to dive into a tank filled with icy water, until the director got the shot he wanted. Late that night "an exhausted, frozen" Reagan, experiencing stabbing chest pains, was admitted to Cedars of Lebanon Hospital and diagnosed with viral pneumonia. Jane Wyman, his pregnant wife from whom he was separated, rushed to his bedside and found him "near death" (Eliot, 2008, p. 202). After 6 touch-and-go days, his fever broke. As Reagan was being prepared to be discharged, Jane went into labor in another hospital. (The pregnancy had been kept secret so that Jane could continue working on the movie she was making.) Christine Reagan, born on June 16, 1947, lived 9 hours and was cremated. Reagan finished his movie although looking "as if he had aged five years during his week-long stay in the hospital" (Eliot, 2008, p. 202). One of the few places where Christine's death is noted is in Matuz (2004). This gap underscores the importance of double-checking facts and raises questions: Why did Reagan not include Christine's death in either autobiography? Why did the publisher not add, at least, a footnote in the re-release of the autobiography for Reagan's centennial in 2011?

Some might counter that Christine's death is a minor biographical detail. Moreover, in that day, many families experienced neonatal losses. Sometimes a troubling memory is so painful that individuals create detours. Thus, underacknowledged narrative strands in the extended family grief narrative of your client may be blocking the integration of the losses.

Conclusion

The grief grid assists griever and clinician in constructing a realistic overview of the death repertoire of the client. Admittedly, constructing the grid may go slowly and raise many potentially troublesome questions. Welwood (2002) offers an insight on intimacy in marriages that merits consideration: "Most couples throughout history have managed to live together their whole lives without engaging in personal conversations about what was going on within and between them" (p. 282). That acknowledged, with gentle prodding by a clinician, a joint willingness might develop to explore the silences.

A Story for the Road

Immediately after the death of General Benjamin Helm at the Battle of Chattanooga, brother-in-law Abraham Lincoln issued an order allowing Mary's stepmother to cross enemy lines to escort the widowed Emilie Helm and her children from Tennessee back to Kentucky. Emilie desperately needed money for her family's survival. So, under presidential order, she traveled to Washington to seek a waiver to sell cotton she owned. Lincoln, concerned about his wife's mental condition following Willie's death, hoped his sister-in-law would stay and be a companion to Mary; Mrs. Helm declined. In the fall of 1864, given worse economic plight, Emilie pleaded for Lincoln's permission to transport 600 bales of cotton to an eastern port to be sold. Lincoln consented only if she pledged loyalty to the Union (Helm, 2007). Swearing allegiance to the Union, Mrs. Helm fumed, would dishonor the memory of her deceased husband. Tensions accelerated after the death of Levi Todd, Mary and Emilie's alcoholic brother, who was buried in a pauper's grave. Emilie lashed out at the Lincolns: "Your bullets have made us what we are," that is, destitute widows and orphans (Clinton, 2009a, p. 224). The Todd sisters never reconciled. That was true for many families in the Civil War era and today.

4

CHAINING BORROWED NARRATIVES

If I talk long enough, you will say, "Oh that is my history too."

Maya Angelou (2011)

The Golden Gate Bridge has long fascinated me, not just the two majestic towers stretching into the sky but more important, the thick cables from which hangs the roadbed linking San Rafael and San Francisco. I always notice the cables, aware that inside each cable are tightly woven strands of individual wires that create incredible load-bearing strength.

So, too, with stories. There are narrative threads within stories—sometimes tightly interwoven into stories that provide great strength for grievers.

Stories Sharing a Common Thread

What do C. S. Lewis, Eleanor Roosevelt, Jane Fonda, John Dillinger, Herbert Hoover, Ken Burns, Lady Bird Johnson, Thomas Merton, B. B. King, Malcolm X, Abraham Lincoln, Arthur Ashe, and Andrew Jackson have in common? As children these individuals experienced the death of one or both parents. Consequently, all experienced and survived emotionally challenged, and in some cases emotionally impoverished, rescripted childhoods and adolescences. Nevertheless, all of them, except Dillinger, as adults made a positive lasting contribution to American society. An awareness of strands within their narratives could lead some grievers to conclude: "If they survived their losses, I can survive *mine*!"

Chaining

Chaining is a process of identifying a common thread in a griever's story that links to narratives of others who have experienced a similar loss. A borrowed story of being a child-griever can become inspirational raw material for a contemporary griever's reflection, interpretation, and decision making. If, that is, the griever becomes aware of particulars in the narrative. For example, what about a child or adolescent griever who mothballs grief in order to care for a parent? Might that child find encouragement in the narrative of Arthur Ashe, who, after his mother Mattie, 27, died when he was 6, told his father, "Stop crying, Daddy. I will take care of you." Almost 40 years later he sought the care of a psychologist. Ashe reflects,

> I have understood that this quality of emotional distance in me … may very well have something to do with the early loss of my mother. I have never thought of myself as having been cheated by her death, but I am terribly, insistently, aware of an emptiness in my soul that only she could have filled. (Ashe & Rampersad, 1993, p. 50)

Ashe's unacknowledged grief had a significant price. How will the child or adolescent learn of the narrative if clinicians do not offer it?

A few grievers have challenged me for using Jane Fonda's narrative of her mother's death. Some individuals retain resentment toward Fonda for her activist positions during the Vietnam War 40 years ago. I often respond, "What do you know about Jane Fonda's childhood?" (The common answer is "Nothing" or "Her father was Henry Fonda.") One, however, cannot understand Jane Fonda without pondering the impact of her mother's suicide—and her father and grandmother's collusion in covering up the cause of death—when Jane was 12.

Jane knew that Frances Fonda had died in a "hospital," but not a *mental* hospital. Henry Fonda, divorced from Jane's mother, told Jane and Peter, her brother, that their mother had died after a heart attack. In fact, Frances had slit her throat with a knife she picked up during her last supervised visit to the home. That day, Jane had refused to see her mother despite repeated requests from the governess. After her death, Frances was immediately cremated and ritualed in a brief funeral service with only Henry Fonda and Jane's grandmother present. The children had no reason to question the accuracy of their father's account.

Sometime later, friends insisted that Jane go to the library to read a particular magazine article about her father. While reading that article, she learned how her mother died. Jane sought confirmation from her governess, but never discussed the issue with her father. She thinks he died thinking that she still believed her mother had died after a heart attack (Fonda, 2005). Jane Fonda offers a warning:

> When I was in my forties and the tears for Mother did finally come— unexpectedly and for no reason—they were unstoppable. They came from so deep within me that I feared I wouldn't survive them, that my heart would crack open, and like Humpty-Dumpty, I'd never be able to put it back together again. (p. 18)

Discovering Gaps in the Explanatory Narrative

Many adults have discovered that the narrative of a parent's death was false or less than accurate. In counseling, the griever may seek to bridge that gap. After Jane Fonda secured her mother's medical records, she discovered that her mother had been repeatedly molested as a child by a family friend and that reality had triggered her lifelong battle with depression.

Linking the Strands

The clinician needs more than one borrowed story in any category such as death of parent, sibling, friend, or in any complication of grief, such as being unable to attend the funeral. If a clinician has only one borrowed narrative in her pool of narratives, the benefit to the client is limited. I find a strand in Fonda's story that links to the narratives of two other children who learned that a parent's or grandparent's death had not been accidental.

Margaret Truman, age 20, during her father's campaign for the vice presidency in 1944, was puzzled by a conversation with her Aunt Natalie Wallace about the effect Truman's vice presidential nomination might have on the family (Truman, 1986, p. 234). Margaret was stunned when her aunt suggested, "I suppose it will all come out now, about the way your grandfather died. The reporters will dig it up. I'm sure it's going to upset your mother and grandmother terribly" (p. 234).

Margaret responded, "I thought he died of a heart attack or something like that."

"He shot himself." Three crisp words changed Margaret's life; suddenly, pieces of the puzzle of the family narrative fit. "I could not have been more astonished if she had told me that she had seen Frank Willock Wallace ascend into heaven" (Truman, 1986, p. 234).

As Jane Fonda sought confirmation from her governess, Margaret sought confirmation from Vietta Garr, the longtime Truman family cook. After Margaret disclosed what she had heard, Garr nodded and explained that Mr. Wallace had a growth on the back of his neck and feared it was cancerous. Later that day, when her mother returned home, Margaret did not raise the issue but waited until Senator Truman came home to ask what he knew. Margaret recalled:

> I have never seen him so angry and upset. He seized my arm in a grip that he must have learned when he was wrestling calves and hogs around the farmyard. "Don't you *ever* mention that to your mother," he said.
> He rocketed out of the house and down through the backyard to Aunt Natalie's house. I have no idea what he said to her, but it is not pleasant to think about, even now. (Truman, 1986, p. 234)

Later, while writing a memoir about her mother's life, the lenses opened wider and Margaret concluded that her aunt had an agenda in disclosing the secret. "She was obviously striking back for twenty-eight oppressive years" of Marge, Margaret's domineering grandmother, "breathing down her neck" (Truman, 1986, p. 234). The silence, however, remained intact as one more individual had been captured by the web of silence. Six years after her mother's death in 1982, Margaret reflected:

> I wish I could tell you that years later I asked Mother if her anxiety about her father's death was a hidden reason for her opposition to Dad's nomination. But to the end of her life, I never felt free to violate the absolute prohibition Dad issued on that summer night in 1944. More

than once, in these later years, I had hoped Bess would talk to me about her father, but she never did. (Truman, 1986, p. 235)

Bess and Margaret rarely joined Truman on the 1944 campaign trail but remained at home in Independence, Missouri (Sell, 2010). Truman enlisted Margaret, "You must help me keep all the family in line. Most of 'em on both sides are prima donnas and we must keep our eye on the ball" (p. 237), that is, protecting the cause of Mr. Wallace's death. Margaret reflected:

> In this letter Dad was strengthening the bond of silence he had forged with me on the night of my encounter with Aunt Natalie. He was also sending Mother a message. He was certain that I would show her the letter or she would ask to read it after I opened it. He was trying to say that he understood her anxiety and he cared deeply about it. (Truman, 1986, p. 237)

Laura Bush and "The Secret"

Did Laura Bush experience anxieties during her husband's campaigns for governor in Texas and for the presidency in 2000 and 2004? Her involvement as a high school senior in an automobile accident in which a classmate died was not seriously explored by the media or pundits, although Oprah asked about it in an interview with Mrs. Bush. So carefully had the secret been kept that two of George's cousins were stunned to learn of the incident (L. Bush, 2010).

Every Family Has Secrets

Unfortunately, some grievers become "custodians of the secrets." Another link in an adult child's later discovery of suicide as the cause of death and the price of secrecy comes in Peter Selwyn's (1998) memoir, *Surviving the Fall*. Selwyn, an only child "without a father," knew only what his mother chose to tell him: his "clumsy" father died after accidentally falling from a window in an office building. That was the family script for occasions when the curious young boy, and later adolescent, asked questions. Because Selwyn noticed discomfort when he asked about his father, over time he began to suspect that there was more to the story. Then he discovered a key detail in the family's sanitized narrative—that his father was clumsy—was false. His father jumped from the window to his death. The scripting, however, was more damaging to him than the suicide.

Based on these narratives, I urge surviving parents and family members, especially after a suicide, to "Always tell the child the truth—age-appropriate truth." Smith (2006a) observes, "Suicide alters the stories we tell others about ourselves, and the stories we tell ourselves" (p. 4). In the Internet age, the child will likely uncover the truth and dissect the most intricate web of falsehoods. Even well-intentioned collusions to protect the child or protect the family may, in time, become more toxic than the facts. Neimeyer (2000), a suicide survivor, acknowledges, "Early, provisional meanings of the death tend to be revised as the reality of living with loss raises new questions and undermines old answers" (p. 550).

Theodore Roosevelt's Son's Suicide

According to the "official" account, Kermit Roosevelt, Theodore's son, died after contracting amoebic dysentery in the Middle East. In reality, in June 1943, when Kermit, an alcoholic Army officer stationed in Alaska, realized that he, unlike his brothers, was being kept from combat, he ended his life with a Colt .45 automatic pistol. Edith Roosevelt, his mother, was told that he had died after a heart attack. It was not until 1980—23 years after Edith's death—that the details of Kermit's death became public (Wead, 2003, p. 353).

Exploring Common Denominators in Chained Narratives

What common denominators in loss narratives might be valuable for widowers grieving for a spouse or, these days, for elder adults, several spouses? What did James Van Buren, John Tyler, Andrew Jackson, Chester Arthur, Thomas Jefferson, and Woodrow Wilson have in common? All were widower-presidents although Tyler and Wilson remarried while in office. What common denominators in the grief of these presidents might be meaningful to widowers today?

The marriage of Andrew and Rachel Jackson became a controversy in the presidential election of 1828. The Jacksons married in 1791, thinking Rachel's divorce in Kentucky was final. The divorce, however, was not finalized until September 1793. The Jacksons married again in January 1794, but critics labeled Rachel a bigamist and, therefore, unfit for the White House. (Jackson fought more than one duel over such slurs.)

In 1828, after Jackson defeated John Quincy Adams, Rachel traveled to Nashville to select gowns for Washington. As she shopped, she overheard vicious gossip about herself and returned immediately to The Hermitage where she suffered a severe heart attack on December 17, 1828. Mrs. Jackson, 61, was buried on Christmas Eve in one of the gowns she had purchased to wear in Washington (Schneider & Schneider, 2001, pp. 359–360).

Jackson confessed to his friend John Coffee, "My mind is so disturbed … that I can scarcely write, in short my dear friend my heart is nearly broke" (Meacham, 2008, p. 6). During his 8 years in the White House, Jackson looked at his wife's picture every night before going to bed. After returning to his Tennessee plantation, he visited her grave daily. Many, these days, find visiting the grave "too frequently" troubling. I suggest to the widowed: Andrew Jackson went to his wife's grave every day. No one dared suggest that he "needed help" or "ought to see someone." If someone implies that you are visiting the grave too frequently, offer them a little historical insight from Andrew Jackson.

Chester Arthur as Widower

Chester Arthur was devastated by the death of his wife, Ellen, on January 12, 1880. What future did he have without her? He had no way of knowing that in a few months, Republicans would draft him as a compromise candidate for the vice presidency. Returning to New York City after the convention as the vice presidential candidate, once safely behind closed doors in his home, "he could not stop himself from breaking down in tears as he remembered his wife who wasn't there to share his good fortune" (Karbell, 2004, p. 43). His sister Regina recalled that a large crowd gathered outside his home and "essentially forced him to celebrate publicly, which he did politely but unenthusiastically" (p. 43). Arthur suffered psychological anguish because, after reflecting on his marriage, he lamented how much he had neglected Ellen during his rise to political influence, although Ellen never protested his absences from their home.

James Garfield was shot on July 2, 1881, after only 4 months in office, but languished 80 days before dying on September 19, 1881. During that long interval, the government was paralyzed. Rumors floated that the ambitious Arthur had been behind the assassination. Immediately after Garfield's death, reporters arrived at Arthur's home asking, "How is he taking the news?" The new president, a servant told them, was "sobbing like a baby" (Karbell, 2004).

Every day during his time as president, Arthur placed fresh flowers beside his wife's picture (as would Mrs. Grace Coolidge by the picture of her deceased son). In his wife's honor, he donated a stained glass window for installation in St. John's Episcopal Church, across Lafayette Square from the White House. Every night the president found comfort in looking out across the lawn to that window.

Chains of Parental Grievers

It is well known that Abraham and Mary Lincoln's son, Willie, 12, died in the White House in February 1862, from typhoid fever. Many are less aware that Calvin and Grace Coolidge mourned for their son, Calvin, Jr., age 16, who died in July 1924 from blood poisoning after he suffered a blister on his toe while playing tennis on White House courts. Some young adults are unaware that Jackie and John Kennedy grieved the death of their 2-day-old son, Patrick Bouvier, in August 1963. How did these First Families "manage" their grief in the public eye, particularly the Kennedys given the media fascination with them? What common denominators in their narratives might be borrowed and found meaningful by individuals grieving the death of a child?

The Loss of Privacy

News photographers used telescopic photo lens to shoot through open windows of Massachusetts General Hospital where baby Patrick, born 5 weeks premature, fought for life. One picture appeared on the

August 16, 1963, cover of *Life* accompanied by the headline "Hospital Vigil over the Kennedy Baby." Inside the issue, three-fourths of one oversize page featured a photo capturing the president in a crowded elevator at the hospital captioned "a worried father visits his stricken son" (p. 26B). By the time that issue of *Life* appeared on newsstands, Patrick had died. The last line of the story noted "neither the devoted care [of physicians] nor the nation's prayers could save the President's son" (p. 26B).

Privacy to Grieve

Many parents never appreciate their freedom to grieve without invasive media. My colleague, Richard Gilbert, calls this fixation "celebrity" grief. Chochinov (2005) labels this "vicarious grief." Gilbert, a chaplain, remembers sneaking a family out the hospital's back door, past the garbage dumpsters, to avoid photographers (personal communication, April 22, 2011). The grief of others is deemed newsworthy following a kidnapping, a school shooting, or an automobile accident, especially on a "slow news day." The privacy of many who have lost children or other family members in Iraq or Afghanistan has been disturbed by picketers at funerals.

Missing the Funeral Rituals

Missing a funeral ritual can be a significant secondary grief. Jackie Kennedy, still hospitalized at Otis Air Force Base, could not attend the funeral for baby Patrick, nor could Rose Kennedy, the grandmother, who was in Paris. With some directed reading—given the extensive Kennedy literature—a grieving parent could discover a palate of emotions President and Mrs. Kennedy experienced.

At the John F. Kennedy Presidential Library in Boston, I read through files containing approximately 1,000 condolence telegrams, letters, and cables that the Kennedys received from the famous and the unknown. I was taken by the number of condolences that included a phrase "having lost a child ourselves."

Barbara Bush, who was living in Long Beach, California, could not attend her mother's funeral in September 1949 because she was pregnant, and cross-country air travel in those days was exhausting. Marvin Pierce, her father, insisted that she not come to Connecticut lest the baby be harmed. Mrs. Bush recalls, "What a miserable time that was" as "I sat in California" (B. Bush, 1994, p. 36). George H. W. Bush arranged for friends to come to their home to be with Barbara through those days.

A second "chain" is the experience of famed opera soprano, Beverly Sills, whose father, Morris Silverman, died in 1948. When Beverly got a chance to do concerts on a cruise ship to Buenos Aires, her parents urged her to accept. Sills recalls:

> My father died five days before I returned to New York. He was only fifty-three years old. My parents and my father's doctor had all decided it was wiser for me to go to South America than to stay at home and see Papa waste away. For a long time, I felt an enormous sense of guilt of having left my father's side when he was so sick.
>
> I frequently tell myself that I'm very much like my father, and that if I were gravely ill, I'd also send away a child of mine. (Sills & Linderman, 1987, pp. 44–45)

Dwight Eisenhower was involved in planning the invasion of Normandy and could not return to Kansas in March 1942 when his father died. Yet, Eisenhower conceded that he could not just "go ahead with business as usual." So, "I closed the door to my office and sat thinking about the life we had had together" (D. Eisenhower, 1967, p. 304). Later that day he wrote:

> I have felt terribly. I should like so much to be with my mother these few days. But we're at war. And war is not soft—it has no time to indulge even the deepest and most sacred emotions. I loved my dad …
> Quitting work now—7:30 PM. I haven't the heart to go on tonight. (p. 305)

The Value of Chained Borrowed Narratives

Awareness gained from a chain of borrowed narratives might be helpful to a client whose grief is intensified because he could not attend a funeral or memorial service. Moreover, chained borrowed narratives offer a variety of responses to a loss. Eisenhower was not emotionally close to his father yet he grieved when David Eisenhower died. Suppose a griever is self-indicting insisting, "There must have been something more I could have done!" The clinician might initiate a therapeutic conversation:

> President John Kennedy's son, Patrick Bouvier, died on August 9, 1963, two days after birth, due to complications of being born five weeks premature and given that day's limited resources for caring for preemies. The son of a president with that day's best medical care still died. How did the president grieve? What advice might John Kennedy offer you about your baby's death?

In fact, John Kennedy actively mourned for Patrick. At the end of the Mass for Infants and after family members left the chapel, the president held Patrick's tiny casket in his arms. He did not put the casket down until Cardinal Cushing insisted (S. B. Smith, 2004). JFK rearranged his schedule to spend much of the following 90 days with Jackie and the children, out of the public eye, on Squaw Island. Some believe that the child's death intensified the marital bond between the couple (Douglas, 2008; S. B. Smith, 2004). Kennedy aide Arthur Schlesinger, Jr., later observed, "Their marriage never seemed more solid than in the later months of 1963" (Pitts, 2007, p. 236). Such narrative segments may help dispel the myth that a high number of couples divorce after the death of a baby or child (Murphy, Johnson, & Weber, 2002).

Given that many fathers have not bonded with the baby, their grief for a perinatal loss may be underrecognized, with condolences primarily directed to the mother. John Kennedy's actions may enfranchise a grieving father. President Kennedy was sleeping in the hospital when he was awakened at 2 A.M. and told Patrick was having difficulty. Knowing the child would die, the doctors took Patrick out of the oxygen chamber for the president to hold. At 4:04 A.M., August 9, with his father holding his fingers, Patrick took his last breath.

Kennedy did not want his aides or hospital staff to see him crying, so he returned to the room, closed the door, sat on the bed, and wept. While in the unit, he had noticed a severely burned child near Patrick. He asked for the name of the mother and wrote a note to encourage her. At the funeral service, with only 13 people present, the president wept "copious tears." When he returned to the White House, he telephoned Enud Sztanko. The "very depressed" president, talked a long time on the phone, "specifically asking why God would let a child die" (S. B. Smith, 2004, pp. 396–397).

If the president can ask the God question, that story might give a griever permission to ask their questions. Douglas (2008) suggests that Patrick's death drove Kennedy to immerse himself in preparation for talks for a Test Ban Treaty so that a nuclear explosion would not kill children.

The link between the historical personality and your grieving client might not only be the relationship (wife, son, husband) but an emotional regret or self-indictment like Chester Arthur.

A Particular Young Couple

If you had even noticed the young couple in Sloan-Kettering Cancer Center as their 4-year-old daughter died in 1953, what would have suggested that someday they would live in the White House and the child's oldest brother would someday be president? George and Barbara Bush, at that time, were just a young couple from Texas hoping for a miracle and wanting the best medical care for Robin, their critically ill daughter.

The clinician might point out to grieving parents that by doing thorough grief work, they, too, might have an unimaginable future; dodging the grief work, however, hamstrings their future as a couple and as individuals. The counselor might disclose that the Eisenhowers did not talk about their 3-year-old son's death, because "it was too painful." "Each retreated into a private world of sorrow and suffered in silence, their only common bond their beloved son's death" (D'Este, 2002, p. 156). Sharing this tidbit could present an opening to ask the client: "Do you want to repeat the Eisenhowers' experience of marital silence?"

A Grieving Eleanor

In 1909, a young Eleanor Roosevelt, grief-stricken following the death of her 9-month-old son, the first Franklin Delano Roosevelt, Jr., lamented in her diary, "my heart aches for Eleanor" (Cook, 1992,

183), meaning herself. The baby "might have lived," she concluded, if she had nursed him longer (p. 187), an unlikely assumption since the baby had congestive heart failure. A depressed Eleanor wrote her friend Isabella Ferguson:

> Sometimes I think I cannot bear the heartache which one little life has left behind but then I realize that we have much to be grateful for still, and that it was meant for us to understand and sympathize more deeply with all of life's sorrows. (Cook, 1992, p. 525)

The baby's death, however, strained the relationship between Eleanor and Franklin.

> I was young and morbid and reproached myself very bitterly for having done so little to care for this baby. ... in some way I must be to blame. I even felt that I had not cared enough about him, and I made myself and all those round me most unhappy that winter. I was even a little bitter against my poor young husband who occasionally tried to make me see how idiotically I was behaving. (E. Roosevelt, 1937, p. 165)

After Eleanor's death, her close friend Father William Levy described her intense "devotion to the memory of her third baby" (Levy, 1999, p.145). Eleanor Roosevelt never forgot burying the infant. "To this day," she later wrote, "I can stand by his tiny stone in the churchyard and see the little group of people gathered around his tiny coffin, and remember how cruel it seemed to leave him out there in the cold" (Cook, 1992, p. 183).

Among the First Ladies between 1917 and 1969, only one, Lou Hoover, was not a grieving mother. Few grievers knew of the guilt that Eleanor Roosevelt and Mamie Eisenhower carried for a child's death.

Mamie Eisenhower's grief was complex. Having grown up in wealth, living in officer's quarters at Fort Meade, Maryland, she had pressured Major Eisenhower to hire a maid. Ike, who had grown up in poverty, rejected the idea but finally gave in. Doud Dwight "Ikky" Eisenhower, their 3-year-old son, was exposed to scarlet fever by that maid. Thus, Mamie blamed herself for the baby's death on January 2, 1921. If she had not insisted on hiring that maid, Ikky would not have died (D'Este, 2002, pp. 155–157).

Mrs. Roosevelt in 1909 and Mrs. Eisenhower in 1921, were but two among tens of thousands of mothers who "lost" babies and young children; few sought professional care. Simply, grief for babies was aggressively disenfranchised with the guidance: Have another baby. Both Eleanor and Mamie became pregnant immediately. Mrs. Eisenhower, according to her granddaughter, Susan Eisenhower, never dealt with her feelings about Ikky's death until days before she died in 1979 (1996, pp. 66–69).

Linking to the Human Family

C. S. Lewis, well-acquainted with grief before the death of his wife, Joy, alluded to the subtle temptation to think oneself the world's greatest griever. "We want to prove to ourselves that we are lovers on the grand scale, tragic heroes; not just ordinary privates in the huge army of the bereaved, slogging along and making the best of a bad job" (Lewis, 1961, p. 63). Perhaps you have had a group participant who believed her grief trumped the grief of other group members.

Chaining borrowed narratives reminds grievers that loss is a human reality, and that grievers populate a large fraternity. No one, no family, no historical figure is long immune to grief. Martin Luther King, Jr. reminded grievers in his sermon at the funeral for four of the young girls killed in the bombing of the Sixteenth Avenue Baptist Church in September 1963:

> There is an amazing democracy about death. It is not an aristocracy for some of the people, but a democracy for all the people. Kings and beggars die; rich men and poor men die; old people die and young people die. Death comes to the innocent and death comes to the guilty. Death is the irreducible common denominator of all men. (As cited in McKinstry, 2011, p. 84)

Implications for Clinicians

Admittedly, early in therapy, it may be difficult for the griever to find a link with a borrowed narrative. They may suggest, "I'm different because ..." Lewis (1961) acknowledged, "I find it hard to take in what anyone says. Or perhaps, hard to want to take it in" (p. 1).

Pointing the griever to the narratives of others who have walked this path—this particular path—may heighten the curiosity of some to read further and, perhaps, to identify other personalities to add to the chain. Long after the termination of therapy or participation in a group, the griever may continue to expand the links to include other grievers. In some distant point they might, as a de facto grief educator, share some narrative slices with other grievers.

Actively Honoring the Deceased

Presidents Jackson and Arthur intentionally maintained a relationship with their dead through specific acts, a reality that is part of the idea of "continuing bonds" (Klass & Walter, 2001; Silverman & Klass, 1996). Jackson and Arthur created a new "inner representation" of the deceased that allowed them to face a world and enormous political responsibilities intensified by the absence of a spouse as White House hostess. Both presidents knew that their wives would have enhanced their years in office (eight for Jackson, four for Arthur) and their postpresidential years.

The clinician might link these historical narratives with observations from Thomas Attig (2000): "Grieving is a journey that teaches us how to love in a new way now that our loved one is no longer with us" (p. xviii) and "Consciously remembering those who have died is the key that opens our hearts, that allows us to love them in new ways" (p. 27).

The clinician could inquire: If Presidents Jackson and Arthur "consciously remembered" their wives, how are you "consciously" remembering your loved one(s)? Or, what are some ways you could consciously remember your deceased?

A Story for the Road

Many grievers struggle with the fragileness of life. Others indict themselves: "If I had not been late that day ..." Sometimes, we survive "close calls" that would have forever changed our lives. Cowley (2001) talks about moments that change the history of a family, a nation, a world.

Jackie and John Kennedy came very close to not becoming the First Family. After Thanksgiving they relaxed in Florida after the close campaign, and John focused on transition planning and selecting a cabinet. On Sunday morning, December 11, 1960, a would-be suicide bomber parked outside the Kennedy compound in Palm Beach, Florida, and sat waiting in a car parked near the front door. When John came out the door to leave for Mass, Richard Pavlick intended to flip a switch connected to seven sticks of dynamite. The senator (technically, because the Electoral College had not met, Kennedy was not yet president-elect) would have been killed and the nation would have faced, perhaps, a constitutional crisis. Richard Pavlick, however, aborted his plan when Mrs. Kennedy, holding baby John, came to the door to say goodbye to her husband. Pavlick drove off. He was arrested four days later. If Jackie had slept in that morning, history would have been significantly altered.

5

DIVERSIFYING BORROWED NARRATIVES

The funeral was a disaster. All of us men turned to jelly, we became a bunch of cry-babies totally useless for the practicalities of the moment. Fortunately, the women were there to organize everything.

Gabriel Garcia Marquez (as cited in Martin, 2009, p. 436)

The criticism still stings! After teaching a continuing education seminar, I reviewed the evaluations and one leaped off the page: "ALL OF YOUR EXAMPLES IN THE POWER POINT WERE OF CAUCASIANS!" I took another look at my PowerPoint presentation. Now, the criticism resounded like cymbals. How could I have been so insensitive?

Clinicians see and interpret grief through particular cultural, religious, gender, and class lenses. The client could insist, in the words of that December song, "Do you see what I see?" Any protest—"but it was not intentional"—would sound hollow.

Cultural Insensitivity Happens

Cultural insensitivity happens too frequently in clinical and academic settings. That day my insensitivity negated what I wanted to communicate. Now as I prepare PowerPoint presentations I ask: What will grievers see or hear that will help them be more receptive to a borrowed narrative? I may have the best story in the world but must consider if I overlooked a "stumbling block?" Is there anything in the way I borrow and use a narrative that minimizes the impact on grievers?

Diane Eck (2001), of the Harvard Spiritual Diversity Project, insists that the United States is the most spirituality and ethnically diverse culture in history. Her definitive text, *A New Religious America: How a "Christian Country" Has Become the World's Most Religiously Diverse Nation* challenged my perspective. Death and dying have, for many grievers, a clear link to spirituality, religion, and meaning making. Barack Obama demonstrates this reality:

> There's no one definition of what an American family looks like. In my own family, I have a father who was from Kenya, I have a mother who was from Kansas, in the Midwest of the United States; my sister is half-Indonesian; she's married to a Chinese person from Canada. So when you see family gatherings in the Obama household, it looks like the United Nations. (Kornblut, 2009)

Such diversity has accelerated since Lyndon Johnson signed the Immigration and Nationality Reform Act of 1965, eliminating most racial quotas in American immigration law.

The World Is in My Zip Code

In 2010, en route home from Hanoi to Kansas City, I stopped in Denver to do presentations for Horan & McConaty Funeral Home. As John Horan and I talked about my experience in Vietnam, he informed me that a large community of Hmong people lived in neighborhoods near his funeral home; in fact, Horan & McConaty is *their* funeral home. More recently, in lecturing to Civil Air Patrol chaplains, one was Hmong. In teaching a class in grief at a small university in Kansas weeks later, one student was Hmong. Who in the 1960s could have anticipated a sizeable Hmong community living and grieving in Denver or Green Bay and elsewhere (Verbeten, 2011)? Or the media's fascination in 2011 with Hmong funeral rituals in Fresno for General Vang Pao, a Hmong legend, that drew 6,000 grievers (including my student)? The 7 days of rituals included high-pitched chants, feasting on 10 freshly slaughtered cows daily, and burning a giant pile of paper money to buy his soul into the spirit world (Arax, 2011). General Vang Pao had been the conduit between the Hmong tribe and the Central Intelligence Agency during the Vietnam War.

Immigrants bring funeral and grief rituals and traditions with them. In fact, the narratives of many immigrants are punctuated with grief: grief for their nation or the nation they once knew, grief for family members and friends left behind, grief for family members who died in civil wars or who died in violation of human rights. With increasing Americanization in second- and third-generation family members, narratives and traditions disappear, are scaled back, because of the loss of fluency and nuance in language and the devaluating of first-culture narratives and traditions.

What Sensitive Clinicians Need

The United States Department of Health and Human Services defines cultural competence as "a set of congruent behaviors, attitudes, and policies … that enables effective work in cross-cultural situations" (as cited in Rose, 2011, p. 12). Clinicians need resources to receive and, at times, clarify the grief narratives of their clients in order to offer hospitality to those grief narratives, particularly narratives different from the clinician's experience and tradition. Given the expanding cultural diversity in American suburban settings because of affordable housing, and increasingly in rural communities, diverse grief practices must be understood and enfranchised. Clinicians must work to locate resources that will support their clients, realizing that exposure to client realities will, according to Jackson and Samuels (2011) "expand rather than constrict the lens" (p. 235) clinicians use to "receive" narratives. These authors argue that clinicians need more than competence but must be "culturally attuned," which "emphasizes that the knowledge and skill required in practice are intimately linked to the cultural standpoints of others" (p. 237). One excellent resource for use as a launching point is Matlins's (2000) *The Perfect Stranger's Guide to Funerals and Grieving Practices.*

Two-Way Enhancement

Diversity offers opportunities to tap into the vibrant pool of potentially borrowable grief narratives. How can clinicians become culturally wise? First, I believe, by acknowledging our lack of familiarity with a particular background. Second, through reading and reflecting on borrowed narratives from ethnic groups and *testimonio,* first-person accounts from the marginalized. I have found the following grief narratives meaningful in expanding my understanding.

Booker T. Washington

An awareness of the life and work of Booker T. Washington is pivotal in understanding African American history. Washington provided phenomenal leadership in an era of outrageous, aggressive Jim Crow racism. Having a meal with Theodore Roosevelt and his family in the White House in October 1901 nearly touched off rioting across the South. Senator Benjamin Tillman of South Carolina declared, "The action of the president in entertaining that nigger, will necessitate our killing a thousand niggers in the South before they will learn their place again" (Norell, 2009, p. 246). Tillman's words represent the brutal reality of racism that is hard for many to understand today and is necessary to include here to comprehend the racist environment Booker T. Washington challenged.

Although biographers have examined Washington and Tuskegee Institute, at which he was its first leader, Washington's grief grid is overlooked.

April 5, 1856	Born to Jane Ferguson, a slave, and an unknown father.
	A sister dies in infancy (date unknown).
1884	Fanny, 26, his wife of 2 years, dies; infant Portia survives. In 1885 Washington marries Olivia Dickinson.
1889	Olivia Dickinson dies at Massachusetts General Hospital. His brother-in-law, a teacher in Mississippi, is murdered by the Klan (date unknown).

Twice a widower by age 33, Washington was stunned by Olivia's death because she was his wife, coleader of Tuskegee, and a tireless fund-raiser. Washington, unfortunately, left little anecdotal material on his grief for clinicians to explore. Smock (2009), who found little on grief in his study of Washington's correspondence, explains, "Typical of his actions when faced with adversity throughout his life, he simply threw himself into his work with more determination" (p. 70). Does that sound familiar?

Washington left a legacy but at a significant emotional cost. One unexamined link between Washington and Theodore Roosevelt was that both as widowers had, at least for a period, been single parents before remarrying.

Condoleezza Rice

Condoleezza Rice has been a significant player on the world's political stage. The Stanford political scientist signed on as a senior "tutor" on foreign affairs for Governor George W. Bush, of Texas, as he contemplated running for the White House. After Bush was elected in 2000, he immediately offered Rice the position of national security advisor. Dr. Rice weighed the opportunity in light of a significant obstacle: her elderly father. An only child, her mother died in 1985, Rice moved her father to Palo Alto so he would be closer to her. In a sense, Angelina Rice's death "turned daughter into parent" (Bumiller, 2007, p. 89) as his health declined. How, Rice pondered, could she accept the president-elect's invitation if it required "abandoning" an aged, ill father?

George Bush offered her the option of flying home to California once a month (Rice, 2010). Rice weighed the decision. What father— especially a minority father who had long been his daughter's cheerleader and who had, over the years, sacrificed to provide educational opportunities for her—would not want to see his child in such a responsible position? Yet, Condoleezza could not ignore the what-if factor: What if, after accepting the offer, she happened to be halfway across the nation, or world, when her father's health took a dramatic turn and she could not be there for him? The question became moot in late December 2000, when Dr. John Rice died. Seemingly, Condoleezza was now free to accept the position; yet she wondered if her father had "given up" to avoid being an obstacle to this opportunity.

Given the economic realities of today's world, some 48.9 million Americans (66% of which are female) are caregivers for individuals over age 50; many adult children wrestle with reversed role decisions. Indeed, the literature indicates that a high percentage of caregivers are working women (National Alliance for Caregiving/American Association for Retired Persons, 2009, p. 4). Most clinicians have or will yet have caregiver-clients who struggle with the weight of responsibilities. Indeed, following the death of one parent and the subsequent increased responsibilities for the surviving parent, the individual may have little time or energy to give to grief work.

January 20, 2001, as Condoleezza Rice sat just steps from George Bush as he took the oath of office, she wished her father had lived to experience that moment and a series of moments, such as the one in 2005 when she became secretary of state. "If only he could have …" ricocheted through Rice's mind. Your clients may also have if-only thoughts or self-indict: "I should have done more."

For Rice, September 11, 2001, had a personal element when she notified President Bush that an airplane had crashed into the World Trade Center; that a second plane had crashed into the other tower. Then she reported a plane had crashed into the Pentagon. Her assessment: The nation was under attack! What rambled through her mind that day was the sound of the bomb going off in Birmingham 38 years earlier. "And it is a sound that I can still hear today" (Rice, 2002).

On Sunday, September 15, 1963, Rice, an elementary student, was in Sunday school in Birmingham, one of the most racially segregated cities in America, when racist terrorists detonated a bomb in the basement of the Sixteenth Street Baptist Church just as Sunday school classes ended. Denise McNair, age 11, Rice's best friend and neighbor, and three other young girls died instantly. Rice, although blocks away at the church her father pastored, felt the blast and the resulting chaos and fear. She told the graduating class at Stanford University in 2002 that the first thing she experienced when notified of the World Trade Towers attack was the sound of the bomb's denotation that Sunday in 1963. That bombing led Rice to conclude that "Birmingham wasn't a very safe place" for a black child (LaGanga, 2000). She later reflected,

> Those memories of the Birmingham bombings have flooded back to me since September 11. And, as I watched the conviction of the last conspirator in the church bombing last month [May 2002] I realized now that it is an experience *that I have overcome but will never forget* [emphasis added]. (Rice, 2002)

Unfortunately, this society pressures traumatized grievers to "get over it" and "move on." By sharing Rice's observation, "an experience that I have overcome but will never forget," you give clients permission to keep their grief. A society that encourages individuals to move on needs stories from alternative voices speaking from deep-grooved experience. The African American spiritual captures the reality felt by those that think "nobody knows the trouble I've seen." Individuals, whether well credentialed and powerful, or "ordinary," who have had their assumptive world shattered by a particular death, have wisdom that is borrowable. The narrative of another African American could contain the raw materials for reducing the stress of your client. Parenthetically, it should be noted that your client has access to mental health care services; those touched by the bombing in Birmingham did not. McKinstry (2011), who was in the church that day—and who lost four friends—recalls,

> Days passed, and then weeks, and we simply walked through our same routines—predictable routines disturbed only briefly that Sunday morning.
>
> No one asked me, "Carolyn, are you okay?"
>
> "Carolyn, do you miss your friends?"
>
> "Carolyn, are you afraid?"
>
> "Carolyn, do you want to talk about what happened at church?"
>
> Nothing was said—not at home and not at school. (p. 90)

Finally, a fellow student told her: "Well, frankly, Carolyn, I think you're making more out of this than you should" (McKinstry, 2011, p. 92). Years later, when the case was reopened and individuals were tried, Carolyn was, stunningly, called by the defense. She describes her trauma, "I felt like a knife had cut deep into the old painful wound, sliced open the healed scar, and caused it to bleed freely once again" (p. 256).

A heightened personal sense of vulnerability may act as a Bunsen burner on the crucible of grief. Condoleezza Rice, Dexter King, and others learned that the world seemed safer when a father or mother—who had lived through so much—was only a phone call away. Many grievers miss the calming sound of the loved one's voice or wonder what the loved one would say about a particular crisis. On September 11, 2001, Condoleezza Rice was the one who telephoned relatives in Birmingham to assure them that she was safe (Felix, 2002).

Can you identify a client who might profit if you borrowed from the grief of Rice or the trauma of McKinstry?

A Griever Named Barack

Barack Obama reflects the diversity in contemporary American society. Cobb (2010) describes him as "a biracial man with family members on four continents—and therefore is the face of the next generation, one that is multiracial and cosmopolitan" (p. 3). Barack Obama, Sr., a Kenyan student, abandoned his wife and son to attend graduate school at Harvard and, slowly, made the absence of a father become a permanent reality.

In November 1982, Obama, then a senior at Columbia, received a late-night telephone call from an aunt in Nairobi informing him that his father had driven off the road, crashed into a tree, and died. Barack noted, "my father remained a myth to me, both more and less than a man" (Remnick, 2010, p. 116). He later reflected that he had felt no pain at the death, "only the vague sense of an opportunity lost" for some level of relationship in the future (as cited in Obama, 2004, p. 128). Obama broke the news to his mother. In 1992, Stanley Dunham, his maternal grandfather, who had been like a father to him, died.

In 1995, as Obama's half-sister, Maya Soetoro-Ng, completed a master's degree in New York City, Ann Dunham, their mother, was given a terminal diagnosis. Soetoro-Ng's goal had been to finish her degree then move back to Hawaii to care for her mother for "those last days." Soetoro-Ng recounts learning how ill her mother was:

> But because I was young, I thought we had more time. I was in a state of denial and thought she might last for years. But when I returned from class one day she called and made it clear she didn't have much time. I told her that I was scared and she said, "Me, too." I got on a flight that day. (Remnick, 2010, p. 287)

Soetoro-Ng had less than a full day with her 52-year-old mother; Barack did not arrive until the day after his mother's death. Days later, in a Japanese garden at the University of Hawaii, the siblings offered short eulogies celebrating their courageous mother. Then the family drove to a cove at Lanai Lookout, near Honolulu, where they scattered their mother's cremated remains into the Pacific.

Obama lived with his grandparents from age 10 to 18, and called Madelyn Dunham, "Toot," shorthand for *tutu*, the Hawaiian word for grandparent. Dunham had a profound influence on her grandson, especially during the years his mother lived in Indonesia. In early October 2008, at a critical transition in Obama's campaign for the presidency, Dunham fell and broke her hip. (She was also battling cancer on her own terms.) At her insistence, the hospital discharged her to go home under Soetoro-Ng's care. Her health deteriorated quickly. Obama learned that his grandmother "might not make it"— four words that have changed the schedules and priorities of many grievers. Despite the tight race with John McCain, Barack, who had long regretted not being with his mother before she died, flew to Honolulu—a 9-hour trip each way, which at that point in a presidential campaign can seem a lifetime—to spend time with his grandmother. Leaving the campaign trail sparked both human-interest stories and pundits' comments. Given the publicity, his grandmother laughed, "With all this hullabaloo, it's going to be embarrassing if I *don't* die" (Andersen, 2009, p. 278). Obama explained his motivation to the press: "One of the things I wanted was to have a chance to sit down and talk with her. She's still alert and she still has all her faculties and I wanted to make sure that I don't miss that opportunity right now" (as cited in Andersen, 2009, p. 278).

Two days later, Barack resumed campaigning. "I'm still not sure she'll make it to Election Day," he confessed on *ABC's Good Morning America*. "We're all praying and hoping that she does" (Andersen, 2009, p. 278). Madelyn Dunham died on the last full day of the campaign. A grieving candidate, captured in the glare of media, responded, "She has gone home. She died peacefully in her sleep with my sister at her side, so there's great joy instead of tears" (Zeleny, 2008).

On December 23, 2008, Obama and his family attended a memorial service for his grandmother at Honolulu's First Unitarian Church and then motored to Lanai Lookout where President-elect Obama and Soetoro-Ng now scattered their grandmother's cremated remains into the Pacific at the same point of shoreline as they scattered their mother's. They were now what Brooks (1999) terms "midlife orphan."

On January 20, 2009, Obama wished his mother and grandparents could have experienced the historic day with him, a feeling shared with many people of color. Their parents and grandparents, especially those who had experienced Jim Crow racism, could never have imagined such a day would come. Michele Norris, an NPR commentator, remembered that her African American father had been discharged from the Navy on January 20, 1946. Given the racism her father experienced during military service and in Birmingham after his discharge, she reflected: "I, too, thought of my father on Inauguration Day, wondering what he would have made of the ascension of a black president of the United States, a black commander in chief. The answer brought tears to my eyes" (Norris, 2010, p. 126).

A Griever Named Wilma Mankiller

Some grief is not limited to a single generation. During Andrew Jackson's administration, under the United States Indian Removal Act of 1830, some 16,000 Cherokees, Choctaws, Creeks, Chickasaws, and Seminoles were forcibly "removed from lands of their ancestors" and relocated to Oklahoma—a travesty called "The Trail of Tears." No one seemingly cared about the lingering trauma inflicted to these Americans forced to abandon tribal burial grounds. More than 4,000 individuals died either in captivity or on the 800-mile trek (McLaughlin, 1993, p. 7).

Almost a century later, bureaucrats in the Department of Indian Affairs pressured for another resettlement. Wilma Mankiller recalled, "I experienced my own Trail of Tears." While no one, this time, held a gun at the heads of First Nation people, economic threats forced acceptance of the decision.

> I learned through this ordeal about the fear and anguish that occur when you give up your home, your community, and everything you have ever known to move far away to a strange place. I cried for days, not unlike the children who had tumbled down the Trail of Tears so many years before. I wept tears until they came from deep within the Cherokee part of me. (Mankiller, 1998, p. 198)

Mankiller's family tried to adapt to life in San Francisco. In 1960, Robert, her brother, working picking apples in Washington state, died after a kerosene heater exploded. In 1971, after Wilma's father died from kidney disease, the family returned his body to Oklahoma for burial on the reservation. Soon, Wilma was diagnosed with kidney disease and became a transplant recipient. In 1976, she returned to Oklahoma to live on the reservation while pursuing a graduate degree at the University of Arkansas at Fayetteville. Despite the long hours commuting, the degree ensured a better future for her. Early one morning, Mankiller was involved in a highway accident; the other driver died. When Mankiller learned that Sherry Morris, her best friend, was the other driver, she was consumed by grief. Not long after, Mankiller was diagnosed with myasthenia gravis, a muscle disease.

Fast-forward a decade. Wilma Mankiller was elected chief deputy of the Cherokee Nation. Two years later, she became principal chief—the first woman to hold the position. In 1991, she ran for reelection and won. She would not allow grief and tragedy to be the last line of her resume (Mankiller & Wallis, 1993).

A Griever Named Rigoberta Menchú

Thirty-three seems a young age to win the Nobel Peace Prize unless you have survived "hell" in the jungles of Guatemala and led indigenous people to resist. Menchú was born in 1959 to a peasant family in the Cliché branch of Mayan culture. Some in the Guatemalan aristocracy and military were determined to reduce, even wipe out, the indigenous tribes who made up 60% of the nation's population (Menchú, 1998, p. 479). At the age of 8, Menchú joined her parents and siblings in the fields picking coffee on plantations or *fincas*.

As a child, Menchú witnessed, over a 15-day period, the starvation death of her 2-year-old brother, Nicholas. Her mother could not stay with the ill child but had to work or lose her job and the money to support the family. Moreover, Menchú's mother did not speak the dialect of the area where they were working to get help. The grief was prolonged when mother and daughter returned to their village and, over the coming days, family members returned from the *fincas* where they had been working and learned of the death. Menchú insists, "From that moment I was angry with life, and afraid of it, because I told myself, 'This is the life I will lead too; having many children and watching them die'" (Menchú, 1984, p. 41). She remembered those days with an enormous hatred "that has stayed with me until today" (p. 41). Later she mourned for a another brother who died as a result of ingesting insecticides that had just been sprayed on the crops he was harvesting. As a Catholic, Menchú applied the church's teachings on social justice as she worked for workers' and women's rights. While an adolescent she, along with members of her family, achieved prominence for that effort. Her activism, however, drew the attention of national leaders and the military. Soon her father was arrested and tortured for being a member of the Committee of the Peasant Union.

In 1979, at age 20, Menchú formally joined the movement. In September 1979, Petrocinco, her 16-year-old brother, was kidnapped by the army. Soon hundreds of the military gathered villagers for a public meeting at which an officer announced that the individuals who had been captured must be punished. The Menchú family came, given Petrocinco's disappearance, to see if he was one of the prisoners. Men, women, and children packed the square as Petrocinco and the others were executed. Although Menchú's mother tried to get to her son, her other children, fearing for her life—and theirs—restrained her. The villagers, who had no way to fight the soldiers, experienced mass traumatization.

Twenty individuals died in that massacre. Despite heavy rains, a mass funeral was arranged and the villagers buried their dead. Silverstone (1999) reports that almost all of the villagers remained at the graves in respect for the dead. Menchú's mother acted bravely and did not cry in public because that might cause villagers to lose their willingness to resist the army. For a week, the family grieved in private. They could honor Petrocinco's memory, the Menchús concluded, by refusing to be intimidated in their fight for justice. For safety, the family separated without telling each other their destinations.

On January 31, 1980, Menchú's father participated in a sit-in at the Spanish Embassy in Guatemala City. Organizers hoped the action would gain the attention of the world press to the suffering of the indigenous peoples. They assumed, unfortunately, that an embassy was a safe place because of diplomatic protocols. Guatemalan security forces, however, firebombed the building; Rigoberta's father and 38 others—including embassy staff—burned to death.

In April 1980, Menchú's mother was arrested while trying to buy food. She was repeatedly raped and savagely tortured by cutting for refusing to disclose the whereabouts of family members (her family members knew she was being tortured but were powerless to rescue her). After she died from multiple injuries, her body was tied to a tree and left to the animals. Menchú struggled not only with the reality of these horrendous inhumane deaths, but because none of her family members' remains have been recovered. Thus, Rigoberta Menchú has never been able to provide a "proper" burial, which "is of the utmost importance in the Mayan tradition" (van Lippe-Biestenfeld, 2005, p. 25).

During an eight-month period, September to April, three of Rigoberta's family members were savagely killed. Menchú went into hiding and eventually fled into Mexico and later to Europe, where she labored tirelessly to call attention to the plight of the poor and to the military's atrocities. In 1982, her autobiography, *Me llamo Rigoberta Menchú*, created a sensation—and outrage against the Guatemalan military—across Europe; her writing was translated into 12 languages.

The Nobel Committee, recognizing Rigoberta Menchú's courage and tenacity in defending the rights of indigenous peoples, awarded her the 1992 Peace Prize. The prize, by attracting attention to the ongoing Mayan holocaust, angered the government. Death threats have kept her from returning to Guatemala.

In Mayan thought, ancestors play an active role. Thus, Menchú prays each morning to her ancestors for strength and invites them to stand with her against injustice. In an interview with Irene van Lippe-Biesterfeld, Menchú noted that 200,000 Guatemalans have been killed and approximately 450,000 are missing. Thus, most indigenous families have lost multiple members. Under Menchú's influence, more than 3,000 mass graves have been identified. She laments, "All those figures are not enough to shame or frighten the world" (Menchú, 2005, p. 14). She groans, "Nobody seems to hear anymore all the millions whom I am talking about" (p. 15).

Menchú has also recognized the "living" corpses who did not die but live traumatized lives. How, she has asked, can there be a God who allows such atrocities to occur? How can a global society ignore these deaths in light of the United Nation's Universal Declaration of Human Rights?

Having lived through what she has, Menchú wonders "where I would be had I not been through so much sadness in my childhood, if my people and my own family had not been butchered? What would I have accomplished in life (Menchú, 2005, p. 234)"? After removing the word *butchered,* many adults, perhaps some of your clients, could express the same thoughts.

A deep spirituality has made Menchú fearless. She offers words that might be meaningful to those whose have had family members killed.

> If I were to encounter the people who tortured my mother—tomorrow, I would give them a chance—first, to show remorse; second, to admit their crime; third, to help me locate the remains of my family and all those others so that we can give them a decent burial and get some distance from the tragic memories that torture us and our children. Fourth, I would give them a chance to ask our forgiveness. (Menchú, 2005, p. 26)

Requests for forgiveness, Menchú replies, "would not fall on deaf ears" (Menchú, 2005, p. 26). Such atrocities—and the systemic sabotage of children's rights to a happy childhood—destroys their futures and locks millions in a permanent sadness, especially in a nation where mental health care is limited. Menchú used the Nobel's $1.2 million cash prize to create a foundation named after her father. In Jewish culture, such an act would be called a *tzadkiah.*

In 1996, Menchú became the UNESCO Ambassador for a Culture of Peace. In 1997, she was present in Norway when the Guatemalan government sat down with rebels to end the 42-year conflict that had fueled an unrelenting grief in the nation's peoples. Menchú offers lessons to clinicians. First, she insists, "We have to keep the grief as a testimony" to the dead (Menchú, 1984, p. 199). In feminist studies, the use of subjective experience has been prized, particularly the voices of the marginalized. There is a need to borrow from traditionally silenced or discounted voices, particularly from the subalterns, individuals who live outside of mainstream society. Their voices count. Consequently, clinicians must become aware of the emergence of *testimonio,* the literary genre that provides narratives from those who have experienced injustice. Their public testimony or "verbal journey" "allows the individual to transform past experience and personal identity, creating a new present and enhancing the future" (Cienfuegos & Monelli, 1983, p. 46). *Testimonio* offers another point of view from the experience of those who witnessed it.

The memoir of Carolyn Maull McKinstry (2011) and many others could be considered examples of *testimonio*. Menchú opens her book, *An Indian Woman in Guatemala:*

> My name is Rigoberta Menchú. I am 23 years old. This is my testimony. I didn't learn it from a book and I didn't learn it alone. I'd like to stress that this is not only my life, it's also the testimony of my people ... my personal experience is the reality for a whole people. (1984, p. 1)

Identifying Narratives Reflecting Diversity

Clinicians need borrowable stories that are universal, with ethnically sensitive, and are appealing. Those briefly mentioned in this chapter are but a small sampling. Countless thousands of *testimonios* are awaiting exploration.

Methods for Exploration

How does a clinician find borrowable ethnic narratives? Narratives by King, Rice, or Washington are readily accessible in libraries. Other narratives, equally poignant with meaning, require detective work. For example, I recently found the memoir of E. Lynn Harris (2003), a gay African American novelist, which captures multiple nonfinite losses in children, the death of his biological father one year after Harris met him, and a succession of deaths of gay African American friends in the AIDS epidemic.

Step 1 Ask ethnic clients to recommend narratives they have found meaningful, or ask who they admire as heroes, humanitarians, or celebrities. A client may not name an individual immediately, but after reflection or talking to family and friends, may offer suggestions that open the mutual exploration.

Step 2   Consult minority librarians, particularly in reference departments. Repeatedly, librarians have directed me to specific reading that I might not have found on my own. While visiting in San Francisco, I read in the Harvey Milk Room of the downtown public library, a depository of gay, lesbian, bisexual, and transgender resources. I used the Irene H. Ruiz Biblioteca de las Americas, part of the Kansas City Public Library system; the Ruiz holdings on Hispanic biographies are more expansive than other branches.

Browse specialized reference resources in local libraries. You may find resources such as:

> Hine, D. C. (Ed.). (1993). *Black Women in America: An Historical Encyclopedia* (2 vols.). Brooklyn, NY: Carlson.
>
> Saari, P. (Ed.). *Prominent Women of the 20th Century*. Detroit, MI: UXL/Gale.
>
> Commire, A. (Ed.). (1999). *Women in World History*. Detroit, MI: Gale.
>
> Malinowski, S. (Ed). (1995). *Notable Native Americans*. Detroit, MI: Gale.
>
> Telgen, D., & Kamp, J. (Eds.). (1993). *Notable Hispanic American Women*. Detroit, MI: Gale.
>
> Smith, J. C. (Ed.). (1992). *Notable Black American Women*. Detroit, MI: Gale.
>
> *The A to Z of Women in World History*. (2002). New York: Facts on File.
>
> *The Encyclopedia of Asian History*. (1989). New York: Scribners.

Step 3   Ask ethnic clergy, who often use biographical narratives in sermons, teaching, and funeral eulogies, for suggestions. In Joseph Lowery's (2011) collection of sermons, I found eulogies he gave for Rosa Parks in 2005 and for Coretta Scott King in 2006, as well as his spirited defense of the political content in his eulogy for Mrs. King. Lowery offered several insights into the creation of eulogy in African American churches: "Always in a Black funeral, we celebrate the life of the dead and challenge the living to take up the mantle and carry it on. That is what a Black funeral is about" (p. 97).

Step 4 Borrow proverbs from ethnic groups. A proverb could be a magnet to draw out a story from an ethnic griever. Check resources such as *The Concise Oxford Dictionary of Proverbs* (Simpson & Speake, 1998), *Little Oxford Dictionary of Proverbs* (Knowles, 2009), or *The Routledge Book of World Proverbs* (Stone, 2006). In Hong Kong I found two proverbs worth keeping: "A day of sorrow is longer than a month of joy" (p. 125) and "He who seeks revenge should remember to dig two graves" (*Chinese Proverbs*, 2010, p. 131).

Step 5 At the Grief Gatherings I lead, I distribute inspirational quotations on grief from Condoleeza Rice, Nelson Mandela, Malcolm X, B. B. King, which I ask participants to place on their refrigerators. Maya Angelou (2002) offers rich insights such as, "Death of a beloved flattens and dulls everything" (p. 194). Some grievers find permission to grieve thoroughly in this quote from Dionne Warwick (2010, p. 234): "I still deal with both of these losses daily," referring to the deaths of her mother and her sister.

Step 6 Ask ethnic grievers to teach you. Ask grievers: What narratives have been helpful to you? Before you use a borrowed narrative with a client, rehearse it by asking a colleague to "receive" it. Ask: What do I need to understand to sensitively communicate this?

Step 7 Borrow narratives from celebrities. While browsing new memoirs in a bookstore, I found Natalie Cole's *Love Brought Me Back: A Journey of Loss and Gain* (2010). As I skimmed pages, one paragraph leaped out:

> The impact of losing my dad at age fifteen was incalculable. Some twenty years later, while in rehab, I was told by a wise counselor that I still hadn't mourned the loss. I'm not sure I ever will. My teenage years will forever be defined by my father's death. (Cole, 2010, p. 99)

I constructed a grid of Cole's string of losses within a 2-year period, a reality captured in her phrase, "Death piled upon death. Too young, too soon, too suddenly" (Cole, 2010, p. 39). Because hepatitis C had damaged Cole's liver and kidneys, she waited, like thousands of individuals, for a transplant. Even in a busy musical career, she reflected on the losses she had experienced:

Marvin	(March 22, 1985) Former husband and "the love of my life," father of her son Rob.
Drue McCrae	(March 1987) Nanny for Rob, Natalie's son.
Sammy Davis, Jr.	(May 16, 1990) "Fictive" uncle and mentor.
Janice, cousin	(1985) Died of a stroke in her 30s; 4 years earlier, Natalie and Janice survived the fire in the Las Vegas Hilton by walking down 24 stories of steps; Janice never recovered from smoke inhalation.
Bay, aunt	Favorite aunt dies in 1994.
Kelly Cole, brother	(October 24, 1975) Kelly, 36, dies of AIDS.
Cooke, sister	(May 2009) Cooke suffers stroke. On May 19, Natalie is notified that a kidney is available for transplant. Cooke dies while Natalie is being prepared for surgery. Natalie learns when she came out of recovery that her surgery had gone well but that Cooke "had passed."

Cole dismissed her surgeon's insistence that her prognosis for the future "was bright." "He didn't understand. How could he? How could I face a future without Cooke? How could I deal with my good fortune while she, in a matter of a few short weeks, had been dealt a fortune of utter devastation" (Cole, 2010, p. 131).

Cole lamented that, at age 59, she had a new life but that, at age 64, her sister's life ended. "On the day after my amazing medical procedure, grief overwhelmed celebration, complex confusion overwhelmed simple gratitude" (Cole, 2010, p. 132). Cole described the summer after the transplant as the most difficult in her life as she wrestled with the questions: "Why *me*? Why was I the one to be here and she was the one who left?" (p. 142). Other deaths demanded her attention that summer: "I was missing my father, missing my brother, missing my Aunt Bay, missing my cousin Janice, missing my soul mate Marvin, missing Rob's nanny, Drue, and mostly missing my precious sister Cooke" (p. 145).

A card from the donor's sister, over time, Cole insists, "helped bring my faith back" (Cole, 2010, p. 149). Natalie realized that she had lived only because tragedy had upended another family. When Cole resumed her musical career in a Hollywood Bowl concert, the donor family was guest of honor. Cole's narrative is like a stream for a canoeist; many places to "put in."

We live in an era of celebrities. Yet, in one entertainer's narrative is a story of two other women: Jessica who died and her sister Patty who authorized the donation. Natalie reflects, "Our dramas may seem separate, but my drama has brought me to an inescapable conclusion: that we are deeply and permanently connected" (Cole, 2010, p. 2).

This compelling narrative is available for borrowing because Cole chose to write a memoir and, second, because Jessica's family allowed their "drama" to be included in Cole's narrative.

Why Diversity Is Important in Clinical Settings

McDevitt-Murphy, Neimeyer, Burke, and Williams (2009) assert that "the demography of death is not democratic" (p. 3). According to the 2000 Census, African Americans experience homicide at the rate of 22.3 per 100,000, whereas Caucasian homicides are at 2.3 per 100,000. These researchers conclude that understanding "the ways African-Americans experience grief, loss, and trauma is an important public health concern" (p. 3) and a pressing concern for thanatologists. William Dean Howells observed that "Americans want tragedies with happy endings" (as cited in Bram, 2009, p. 250) and want "good" to be extractable from loss.

Clinicians must acknowledge what Rosenblatt and Wallace (2005) identify as a significant barrier to be surmounted. "European Americans who provide" mental health services "may not have sufficient openness to African-American narratives that speak about racism" (p. 233) or awareness of the entrenched reach of racism. Homicides occur so frequently in some families and that means a multigenerational pool "of survivors who struggle to face life following" chains of traumatic loss (McDevitt-Murphy et al., 2009, p. 3) develops; many fear retaliation if they testify in criminal cases.

Warwick (2010) concedes, "I know losing my mommy and my sister will always be a great loss. But in my heart, when I think of them, I know they are both now without pain or stress and are in a better place" (p. 234). She adds, in reference to heaven, "I know those who have faith in God, as all my family does, have been able to greet each other again. So I know my family is all together, keeping a watchful eye on the family members who are still here" (p. 234).

Many grievers live with unanswerable questions that raid their minds like guerrillas in war; others live in an absence of hospitality to their questions, particularly from clergy and from mental health care workers. Christine King Farris (2009) captures her confusion about that Sunday when a gunman killed her mother, Mrs. Martin Luther King, Sr., in this "lingering" question: "How did a day that began with the promise of such joy end up with us all so pained in that room?" She acknowledges, "There will never be an adequate response to that question" (p. 151). Many grievers would nod in affirming that conclusion.

Living, in the absence of answers, or adequate answers, is a challenging barrier to integration of the loss. A clinician, aware of narratives, can be a companion on that journey.

Conclusion

The diversity of the United States offers gifts to clinicians: stories that stretch our hearts, that offer tidbits of encouragement on days we ponder career change. Diversity is not something to fear but to celebrate.

A Story for the Road

While lecturing in Vietnam I became familiar with the diary of Dang Thuy Tram, *Last Night I Dreamed of Peace.* Tram was a 26-year-old North Vietnamese female army combat physician. She pens memoir material that some grievers might recognize as a parallel to their lives, and material that I borrow when lecturing to nurses and health care professionals. She reminds me to suspend the stories I know from the "American" side of the Vietnam war to consider what it was like for the Vietnamese. I was taken by a story of her response to a soldier with a terminal case of stomach cancer in its final stage. In primitive surgical conditions near the front, she responded to his need for medical care.

> I perform a probing operation and discover with great regret that the cancer has metastasized. It is impossible to do anything for the patient,

so I resign myself to suturing the wound and watched death close in upon him. That afternoon, standing at his beside, I feel an ache in my heart as though it is being cut. He forces a smile as he talks to me, but the tears are filling his eyes. "I am not blaming anyone. You and other comrades in the clinic have tried your best to cure me, but the disease is incurable." (2007, p. 62)

Dang Thuy Tram reminds clinicians that sometimes our best is insufficient for the client. Sometimes, we show up and try. And we keep showing up, especially in these troubled economic times, when caseloads are increasing, social service agencies are cutting back, and some people arrive at our doors bearing outrageously complicated grief.

6

BORROWING MEMOIRS

What do I really know of Upton? What do I know of his life? Of our life together? What do I know that I didn't know I knew until now?

Sally Ryder Brady (2011, p. 6)

Increasingly, as Baby Boomers become caregivers and grievers for aging or ill parents and for dying children or friends, many find themselves in narratively rescripted or rescripting circumstances; some find that the presumed family narrative has worn thin. Following a death, an individual may uncover land mines in unknown family narratives, even unsuspected. Surprises in life tend to weigh heavily on those who experience them and those who bear the news. Dying and grieving prod a close look at assumptions about relationships, heretofore unquestioned. Rynearson (2011) suggests that while an individual cannot change the facts, she can change how she narrates those facts. I contend that process may be encouraged by reading the narratives of other grievers. How does a griever integrate what he or she now knows into the batter of narrative?

Borrowing From the Experience of Another Griever

Increasingly, grievers are turning to memoirs for insights and inspiration in recrafting narratives about relationships; in some cases it is like borrowing the starter in making bread. In reading and reflecting upon another griever's experience, grievers have opportunities to examine and extract from the testimony of a particular witness who has experienced, perhaps, a similar loss. Long before some individuals can talk about what they are experiencing, or have experienced, many read for clues from others. The courage of other grievers in disclosing particular details may empower the reader to be honest.

What Qualifies as a Memoir?

Webster's New Oxford American Dictionary (2010) defines *memoir* as "an autobiography or a written account of one's memory of certain events or people" (p. 1091). The memoir explores feelings more than facts and focuses on details, or lessons, in the author's life that would attract readers. Socrates observed at his trial in Athens in 399 BC, "The unexamined life is not worth living" (Strathern, 1997, p. 65). Memoir, then, is a written examination of a portion of a life, not unlike placing a specimen under a microscope. Minzesheimer (2008) indentifies memoirs as "an older form of personal confession." Simply put, memoirists acknowledge, "This is what I experienced during a particular chapter of my life."

Many adults are writing—some are publishing—crisis and loss-related memoirs on death, divorce, job loss, bankruptcy, catastrophic illness, drug addiction, or depression. The memoirist confesses, "I was not immune from this loss but here is how I survived!"

Increasingly, memoirs are being written by individuals who are not famous but have experienced something that interests others. Increasingly, memoirs capture a stream of multiple hardships, losses, or suffering. Fame may help sell memoirs but does not guarantee lasting relevance or sales. In a society well acquainted with Fodors and Rick Steves's guides to foreign travel, a particular memoir is something of a guidebook when surviving a particular loss. A memoir read today can be an escrow account upon which the reader draws upon some day.

Why are memoirs needed in the video era? Harkins (2008) suggests that a memoir needs both words and serious reflection. The memoirist has spent time thinking through the experience, sometimes years later. Although "a photo can freeze the moment. . . the written word can slow down for layers of meaning and stop chunks of time in their tracks for later rumination" (p. 6).

Memoirs are a way that many writers and readers confront the questions: Did my experience count? Did I face up to this challenge of loss and grief honorably? What lessons did I learn? What wisdom can I share with others?

The Boundary Between Memoir and Autobiography

Clinicians and grievers may need clarification on the precise differences between memoir and autobiography. Harkins (2008) makes this distinction: "A biography or autobiography chronicles the events, accomplishments, and trials of a *person's entire life* [emphasis added] that can be verified by exterior proofs." A memoir focuses on "a time period, a phenomenon, or an issue critical to a person's interior formation" (pp. 6–7). Harkins adds,

> When we choose to construct our memories and ideas in the form of a memoir, we must put together the past in a way that makes sense for our readers, folks unknown to us. Here we must take care to put our insights into a context that creates a sense of reality without overwhelming [the reader] with extraneous material. (p. 7)

The ongoing question, "How did she get through *this?*" keeps the reader turning pages. At some point the reader asks, "Could I handle this as well as the author did?" Martin and Flacco (2009) further clarify that *memoir* indicates "that a book contains a deeper self-revelatory component than a mere recital of deeds and accomplishments" (p. 265).

The memoir-writer must pay attention to the adage, "the truth, the whole truth, and nothing but the truth," as James Frye (2003) subsequently learned when Oprah Winfrey challenged his memoir *A Million Little Pieces*, which she had promoted through her book club. Grievers reject a memoir that comes off as offering too polished an accounting or one that does not ring true. A memoir must be factual even if it makes the author less than noble or heroic. In some memoirs, I have been amazed by the vulnerability of caregivers acknowledging their foibles.

Characteristics of Memoir

Burch (1999) identifies these characteristics of a memoir:

- *Explores* an event or series of related events that remain lodged in memory

- *Describes* the events and then shows, either directly or indirectly, why the event is significant or, in short, why the author continues to remember particular incidents
- *Focuses* on a time period rather than a long span of years
- *Centers* on a problem or focuses on a conflict and its resolution, and on the understanding of why and how the resolution impacted one's life

Borrowing from contemporary cyberexperience, when individuals browse a Web site for a restaurant or bookstore, they may keep narrowing the search for the location of a particular bookstore, in essence narrowing the map to provide specifics on its location. Likewise, some details dismissed as extraneous by some grieving readers are valued by others.

Taylor (2005) insists that boomers "hunger" for memoirs because they are "trying to figure out the plot and theme of our own story and are eager for hints" (p. 5) from those who have been there, done that, got the t-shirt. A memoir can be an oasis of hope for a griever.

Authenticity is critical. One can lecture or write about losing a son without having experienced that loss. Gordon Smith, U.S. senator from Oregon, however, writes a memoir from the trenches of grief in *Remembering Garrett: One Family's Battle with a Child's Depression*. Smith grabs the reader early: "I can still hear the knock at the door. I can still feel the dread that filled my heart" (2006, p. 1). I found those words to be to a clue that he intended to write from the gut, without sugarcoating.

One night as Smith prepared for bed, his wife called him to come downstairs. Their world forever changed when a police officer said, "Senator and Mrs. Smith, I don't know how to make this easy, but I have the duty to tell you that your son, Garrett Lee Smith, was found dead in his college apartment. It appears to be a suicide" (G. Smith, 2006, p. 2).

That string of words, or some variation, is how thousands of individuals learned that a loved one died by suicide. They, too, experienced the knock on the door or heard someone say, "The police are here to see you." Some expend incredible emotional energy trying to diffuse the words to "move on" or to bypass dealing with the full impact. Smith chose rather to confront the reality by writing a readable memoir, concluding, "Sharon and I remember Garrett each and every day. And we also remember the pledge we made to bring some good out of our son's tragic death" (G. Smith, 2006, p. 188). In 27 words, Smith gives readers permission to remember and to honor their dead; indeed, this string of words may be a life preserver to grievers early in the experience or those who have not yet found freedom to be a rememberer.

I tell grievers, "You have permission to remember your loved one each and every day." Yet, those words have a stronger impression when Gordon Smith says them. Or when Tony Blair, the former prime minister of Great Britain, reveals that after his mother's death, "Life was never the same. ... I miss her each day of my life" (2010, p. 11).

If Tony Blair can remember his mother "each day of my life," so can your client. Thus, memoirists are guides for the grief path as Boomers hunt for insight into good-bying, good-dying, and good-grieving. After reading a memoir, many conclude: So I am not the only person experiencing this! In a sense, the memoirist becomes a borrowed friend for a portion of the journey or what Hispanics call an *accompanero*.

Memoir as Alternative Narrative

Some grievers will not invest in counseling; others cannot obtain ongoing counseling because of limited insurance coverage, financial limitations, or geographic isolation. Some bail when the going gets tough. Thus, a recommended memoir might be what my colleague Gregory DeBourgh, of the University of San Francisco School of Nursing, calls "a good steer" or recommendation that "fits."

For some, a memoir might facilitate exploration of the reader's reaction in a counseling relationship; it might lead the client to explore personal potential memoir material. Some grievers find reading memoirs a type of "*literary* support group" that reduces their sense of isolation. For some readers, a memoir may be the nudge to pursue therapy, particularly if the memoir-writer portrays counseling experience as beneficial and valued.

Use of the Loss-Themed Memoir

Bibliotherapy has long been recognized as a means for grievers to explore the lived experiences of others. Clinicians have recommended literary resources for exploration and reflective response. The actor playing C. S. Lewis, a complicated mourner given the number of losses he experienced, in *Shadowlands* (Attenborough, 1993), the movie account of his life, observes to a student, "We read to know we are not alone." The safety of the printed page may offer a griever an "awakening moment" captured in an "I never thought of it quite that way before." Picardie (2008), a blogger at Oxford, comments on Lewis's words, "I suppose it might be better to say we WRITE to know we are not alone."

A clinician might match memoir reading assignments to spur reflection or encourage a client to pursue writing a memoir. Clients report being told, "After what you've been through, *you* should write a book." Harkins (2008) recognizes that journals, photographs, and long conversations with family and friends are "our servants of memory." After reflection, these become the fabric we use to quilt a memoir. On the other hand, if those memoirs are not used they may fade like photographs left too close to direct sunlight. Memoir writing may first be a way of telling ourselves the truth.

Memoir writing is like quilting only with words. Through reflection and evaluation, grievers sew together narrative fragments of a particular loss. The Hawaiian language offers a word I use in my grief groups, *humuhumu*, which means "fitting the pieces together." Hawaiians also use the phrase "talking story" ("Talking story," n.d.). In Hawaii, I overheard on several occasions, "We need to get together and *talk story*," meaning to catch up with each other. Some grievers need to "talk memoir." Indeed, favorable response to spoken memoir may lead to a written memoir.

Writing a Memoir

A memoir can also be a significant way to memorialize the dead, one of Worden's (2009) four tasks of bereavement: "To find an enduring connection with the deceased in the midst of embarking on a new life" (p. 50). The reader accompanies Garrett Lee from that late night knock at the door to the fulfillment of his pledge to bring good out of the death when President George W. Bush signed the Garrett Lee Smith Memorial Act providing federal funds for suicide prevention for adolescents.

Growing up hearing Southern gospel music, I was familiar with a song written by Charles A. Tindley, whose mother had died when he was 4 and whose wife had died quite young: "We will tell the story of how we've overcome. We will understand it better bye and bye" (Terry, n.d.). We tell our way into understanding; the more complex the loss or the circumstances of the loss, the more telling is necessary. Sometimes, at some point in writing a memoir, grievers experience their equivalent of a eureka moment.

Abigail Thomas, a leading proponent of memoir writing, capsules the process: "Writing memoir is a way to figure out who you used to be and how you go to be who you are" (2008b, p. 2). I share that quotation in support groups when I ask grievers to write a memoir slice. Memoir writing can be a bridge—even a pontoon bridge—between a griever's initial understanding of the death and a more reflective perspective that only time can bring. A. Thomas (2008b) points out that the word *memoir* comes from *memory*, which comes from the same root as *mourn*.

Up to this point, our focus has been on borrowing narratives from historical or well-known figures. In years past, to have a memoir published one had to be famous, well known, notorious, or to have done something significant. Publishers, over the years, discovered that fame or name recognition did not turn the printed page, or pixels, into a bestseller. Now, a growing collection of *borrowable* stories from less familiar or even unknown grievers are being published, particularly by small, independent publishers, and they are being read; sometimes, these memoirs are given as gifts to grievers, "Here, you might be interested in this." (Indeed, friends gave C. S. Lewis multiple copies of *A Grief Observed*, the grief memoir that he had written and published under the pen name N. W. Clerk.)

Today's Memoir Writers

A memoir, such as *Angela's Ashes* by Frank McCourt (1996), may long survive the author and become, in the thinking of Irvin Yalom, the author's "ripple." In his 2008 memoir on elderhood, the psychiatrist observes: "Rippling refers to the fact that each of us creates—often without our conscious intent or knowledge—concentric circles that may affect others for years, even for generations" (p. 83). Admittedly, memoir is in the eye of the beholder, creating the healthy tension between comforting and disturbing.

A. Thomas (2008b) models strategies for writing a memoir in her *Three Dog Life,* chronicling her losses after her husband was struck by a car while walking the dog. Although her husband did not die, he suffered significant brain trauma that challenged their marriage. Thomas had to mourn for what had been, for what was, and for what would never again be. Through writing she responded to the question phrased by Boss (2011), "What does this situation mean to you?" In time, Thomas had to institutionalize her husband but only after she wrestled with the ancient phrase in her wedding vows, "for better or worse ... in sickness and in health." Thus, in Boss's construct, Thomas had to *reconstruct* her identity.

The Clinician's Acquaintance With the Memoir

Clinicians need to sample from the wide palate of memoirs available for professional development, insight and reflection and, secondarily, in order to make recommendations responsibly to clients and colleagues. Keeping up with the rapidly expanding memoir literature is, admittedly, a daunting task. Publishers signed 295 contracts for memoirs in 2007 (Minzesheimer, 2008, p. 1D). Borrowing fishing vernacular, clinicians today have a well-stocked pond in which to fish for borrowable memoir slices.

Where to Begin to Explore the Field

How does a busy clinician find borrowable material?

The Clinician Needs to Become Familiar With the Memoir Genre

A clinician does not have to read an entire memoir but can read selectively, asking: What does this memoirist say about death, loss, or bereaving?

Look for Memoirs in the Professional Writing and Presentation of Colleagues

Some clinicians have found a citation or explanatory footnote in a book or journal article that attracted their interest. Prior to reading Attig (2001), I knew little about C. S. Lewis's personal life other than glimpses in his memoir, *A Grief Observed*. Through Attig's essay, I gained insights into Lewis's grief following his wife Joy's death. His way with words incited my curiosity and the research that resulted in the inclusion of the Lewis chapter in this book. Based upon my reading and reflection, I contend that Lewis' grief for his wife can only be understood in light of the numerous antecedent losses he experienced. If I had not read Attig, I might not have had reason to read Lewis extensively.

Read Book Jackets and Reviews

Publishers offer a capsule view of the memoir on the inside book jacket of a hardback or the back cover of a paperback. In a bookstore or library, skim the table of contents as well as the indices for vignettes and quotations. You might do an Internet search-and-skim, particularly with Amazon.com.

Ask Clients to Name Heroes or Individuals They Admire

Has a client's hero written a memoir? If so, has the client read it? How recently? By reading it now, or rereading it, the grieving client can gain a fresher perspective than when they read untouched by loss. Grievers may read with more focus than nongrievers and some read between the words. An in-session conversation might begin this way:

> John, you told me that you are a football fanatic. You mentioned that
> you had great respect for Tony Dungy, former coach of the Indianapolis
> Colts. I know that you know a great deal about his coaching success. I

am wondering how much you know about his personal life, particularly his grief experience? Are you aware that his 17-year-old son died by suicide just before Christmas in 2005? How did Coach Dungy "handle" his grief?

A clinician may reboot a client's interest in a particular memoir eliciting this response, "Yeah, Dungy did lose a son. I had forgotten about that." A client may not remember enough details initially to make a strong connection. By the next visit, after rereading some of the book, the client may have an enhanced awareness of, if not appreciation, for Dungy's experience as a griever. Slices in a memoir can become grist for the therapeutic mill or for reflection and the client's writing. The clinician might offer the client a sample from Dungy's memoir, *A Quiet Strength*:

> People sometimes ask if I went through a typical grief cycle and what I learned from having gone through it. I learned two primary things from our experience and from talking to countless other parents. First, there is no *typical* grief cycle, and second, it's not something I *went* through. I'm still grieving, as is Lauren [his wife]. I don't know that I'll ever look at this in the past tense, as something I've emerged from. (2007, p. 263)

The clinician and client find a section helpful. For example, in Mark Vonnegut's (son of novelist Kurt Vonnegut) 2010 memoir, *Just Like Someone Without Mental Illness Only More So*, he devoted only two pages to his father's death. Vonnegut, a child psychiatrist says, "So one month short of my sixtieth birthday I became an orphan. I had lost my mother twenty years earlier. I was no longer on deck. There's nothing quite as final as a dead father" (p. 193). He did offer insights into his role as his father's medical proxy and his decision that his aged father "was not shipped to a futile neuro-rehab in New Jersey" (p. 192). This was a turnabout: Years before, during Mark Vonnegut's psychotic break, his father took responsibility and had him hospitalized. Now, Vonnegut "took responsibility for letting him go" (p. 192).

Define Why This Memoir Is Potentially Valuable

Some clinicians may dismiss what I am suggesting as cherry-picking borrowable passages, perhaps taking material out of context. The Dungy (2007) narrative is written by a father well known and well respected in the sports world. Some clients will be more interested in his memoir than a memoir written by an opera singer, nuclear physicist, or a politician.

Second, the memoir slice I borrowed focuses on the death of a son by suicide and a death just before Christmas, an emotionally charged time that haunts many grievers. Indeed, the grief could become more acute in future Decembers. Many attempt to ignore the long December holiday season; others mothball their grief for that round of holidays (H. I. Smith, 2001b).

Third, the suicide occurred on the cusp of navigating the "second" season or the playoffs, a major source of stress for a coach of championship contenders. The question for his employers (the owners of the Colts who initially told him, "Take all the time you need"), and for players, for sports commentators, and for fans was: Will Dungy return to coach the Colts? Will his grief distract from his ability to coach them to a division and league championship and a Super Bowl win?

Dungy returned to the field 10 days after his son's death. He noted in *A Quiet Strength*, "Getting back to work certainly helped me heal" (2007, p. 263). The clinician might ask the client: "How could Dungy go back to work so quickly? What inner, or quiet, strengths did he rely on?" Dungy writes as an evangelical Christian. Portions of his narrative appeal to individuals who share his understanding of religion and his hope in God sustaining him. Some passages, however, would be troublesome to grievers who do not share a similar faith perspective. The death of his son, Dungy concedes, "will never make sense to me, and the pain of losing him will never go away" (2007, p. 260). He continues, "But in the midst of it all, I truly believe that hope is available to *all* of us—for joy in today and peace in the certainty that heaven's glory awaits us" (p. 260). Not all "Christian" grievers believe in "heaven's glory." Some grievers will find Dungy's words evidence of escapism, "spiritual spin," or what Welwood (2002) calls an "emotional bypass."

Some grievers may find Dungy's interpretation of his son's suicide offensive. Some who before a death shared his religious views, may find his words unrealistic, annoying, or simplistic. One father angrily snapped at me, "He has no idea of what grief is! *Yet!*"

Dungy does not dodge the question of why bad things happen.

> Why did Jamie die? I don't know. But I do know that God has the answers, I know He loves me, and I know He has a plan—whether it makes sense to me or not. Rather than asking *why*, I'm asking *what*. What can I learn from this? What can I do for God's glory and to help others. (Dungy, 2007, p. 261)

With an evangelical Christian griever I might suggest this probative question: After reading and reflecting on Dungy's experience as a suicide survivor, if you could ask him one question, what would you ask? After reflecting on the client's question, I might follow up with: How do you think Dungy would answer? Would he be open to insights from your experience?

Based on the griever's responses, I might invite an individual to write a letter to Dungy responding to his narrative from the griever's perspective. That letter—although never mailed—could prove meaningful in future sessions.

Clinicians must pay attention to public figures, celebrities, or athletes who offer commentary on their grief (this seems particularly common after the death of a well-known athlete), or an athlete whose grief is the subject of comment by commentators or columnists. Quite frankly, for x number of grievers, if Coach Dungy said it, it is so. I worried when Dungy returned so soon to calling signals. Would his behavior be interpreted as "now *that* is how you do grief"? Some might find Dungy's model of, at least, his public grief, as the gold standard to achieve. Sometimes a celebrity's initial grief responses get coverage while the "overtime" experience is unknown or not deemed newsworthy.

During sports broadcasts, professional commentators offer "color commentary" to speculate, interpret, or applaud a sport's figure's behavior. In January 2011, *The New York Times* commented on safety Ed Reed leading the Baltimore Ravens to victory over the Kansas City Chiefs despite the apparent recent suicide of his brother just days before. Terrell Suggs, a Ravens' linebacker, told a reporter, "Ed and the Reed family, they're going through a lot right now. We wanted to give him three hours of peace, just go out there and have fun with your football brothers." The headline for the article was unequivocal: "Reed pushes his grief aside and provides stability" (Crouse, 2011, p. 8). Thus, while a public figure may put on a game face in the glare of the media, in private the experience may be different. The fan, however, will not be exposed to that reality.

Reread Portions of the Memoir With the Griever

The bereaving client may, over time, rethink an initial response to or appreciation of a particular memoir. She may want to expand her response since she has more experience and insight from which to filter the memoir. Ask the griever to reread the memoir, or a portion of it, as homework. You might then ask: What did you find in this reading that you did not notice in a previous reading?

The Clinician Must Be Prepared to Permission the Griever's Perception

The clinician might respond with a permission-giving statement: "*Some* grievers have told me they found Dungy's viewpoint unrealistic." By this approach, you give this griever permission to respond negatively or more authentically.

Deputize Friends to Read and Recommend Memoirs

When friends or colleagues read a new memoir—or a memoir getting a lot of media attention—ask them to read for grief and loss issues. The clinician cannot read everything in the expanding memoir genre and must sample widely. I am not a sports fan, but I have friends who are sports enthusiasts and walking repositories of facts, statistics, trivia, and opinion. So, if a friend can recommend a sports figure's biographical or memoir insights, I explore that recommendation so that I have a better awareness before recommending it to a griever. Remember: Read before recommending.

Ask Bookstore Owners and Employees for Recommendations

Once owners or employees know the range of your interests, they may recommend books. I have long considered bookstores a laboratory for new reads and spend a couple hours each week browsing memoirs and biographies for death and loss themes. Since the title of a particular chapter may be a tip off, I examine the table of contents and the index.

The Clinician Can Orchestrate a Parallel Memoir

Ask grieving clients to write a memoir slice on a topic covered by a memoir that matches their loss. Ask the griever to write a brief review of the memoir for homework answering this question: What leaped out at you in this memoir?

Memoir Writing in Grief Groups

In grief groups at Saint Luke's Hospital in Kansas City, Missouri, I ask participants to write a three-page, double-spaced "memoir slice" (H. I. Smith, in press) focusing on one aspect of the deceased's life or their relationship with the deceased. A. Thomas (2008a) recommends the three-page segment as a nonthreatening way to write memoir. In my experience, the memoir segment offers a way to corral thoughts that may have been rambling helter-skelter along the corridors of the mind. Some memoir material has been awaiting an opportunity to get loose, like the cat waiting for someone to open the back door. I suggest selecting one of the following as a jump-start for writing three pages:

Who was your loved one's favorite comedian?
What was your loved one's idea of a healthy breakfast?
What was the best surprise birthday gift you received from your loved one?
What was the deceased's favorite vacation spot?
What was the deceased's favorite movie or actor/actress?
What was the best compliment you ever received from your loved one?

In the next group session, I offer opportunities to read aloud the memoir segment. Some grievers resist the assignment, fearing the writing will, in the words of one participant, "just stir things up." I explain that writing memoir segments is a way to get *into* the grief. I modify Attig's conclusion to suggest memoir writing can be a way to "welcome them back into our lives" (Attig, 2001, p. 27). Attig adds, "grieving persons who want their loved ones back need to look for some other way to love them while they are apart" (p. xii). Writing a memoir can be a way to love them in their absence. In writing a memoir, we tap into those sometimes unexplored "places in our hearts where we hold their legacies" (Attig, 2001, p. 47).

What Will My Family Say or Think?

I respond to those fears with two words: Just write! Forget about what Aunt Lucille is going to say, at least, in this draft. Write! After the publication of Alexandra Styron's memoir of her father, William Styron, *Reading My Father*, some of her father's fans took exception with her perspective. Edmond Miller (2011), in a letter to *The Wall Street Journal*, protested a review of the memoir: "Grant Ms. Styron her insider's perspective, and grant her whatever interpretation of the facts she makes at this point" (p. A14). In a sense, the memoirist has the floor.

Sue Miller, author of *The Story of My Father*, initially feared that writing a memoir would heighten her sense of loss. To her surprise, she found meaning in the process. "I *liked* it. I liked doing the research, finding out about the disease. I like remembering my father, searching for the words to call him, even to call up in his illness. It comforted me. It excited me" (2003, pp. 166–167). Miller reflects on the experience, "As I wrote, as I held up bits and pieces I'd gathered to make the memoir from, I learned from them. I changed, and my understandings of things changed" (p. 168). Moreover, "I've called him up over and over and in a variety of ways as I thought and wrote this memoir. And he's come to me over and over, and more clearly" (p. 171). A grieving client of yours might have a similar experience. Miller discovered that "by the making of the story, and by everything that changed in my understanding of him and of myself as I made it, that I have been, as the writer that I am, also controlled" (p. 171).

Joan Didion survived the deaths of her husband and only child within 12 months by recognizing that writing offered an environment in which she could

> attempt to make sense of the period that followed, weeks and then months that cut loose any fixed ideas I had ever had about death, about illness, about probability and luck, about good fortune and bad, about marriage and children and memory, about grief, about the ways in which we do and do not deal with the fact that death ends, about the shallowness of sanity, and life itself. (2007, p. 7)

Didion's interaction with her memories led to a bestseller and a Broadway adaptation of the memoir. As I sat in a darkened theater in New York City and watched Vanessa Redgrave's stunning performance in the role of Didion, I understood that the writer had opened a door for some readers, and theater goers, to think and reflect, and perhaps, to talk about their losses. A client's memoiring might have a profound impact on another griever or a whole host of other grievers. A griever's memoir begins with the first word of the first sentence of the first paragraph of the first page.

A Story for the Road

Arthur, age six, was slowly eating his breakfast when his mother scolded that he was going to be late for school. He looked up and smiled at his mother leaning in her bathrobe against the door. He had no idea that would be the last time he would see her. Hours later, when he returned home from school, he found his father sobbing hysterically. Learning that his mother had died after he left for school, Arthur sat down beside his father, put his arm around him and said, "Don't cry, Daddy. As long as we have each other, we'll be all right." Since Arthur's father worked on the grounds crew of a Richmond park, the family lived in a house on the property. The grieving boy often wandered to the tennis courts to watch games and practices. Finally one player invited him onto the court to hit tennis balls and, as they say, the rest is history (Ashe & McNabe, 1995, p. 50).

Arthur Ashe rose to the top of the professional tennis world but at a price. He did not seek psychological assistance with his long suppressed grief until just before he died in February 1993. One wonders what his life might have been like, had he and his family received help earlier (H. I. Smith, 2004b).

Meaningful Memoirs Worth Exploring

Given the number of new memoirs published annually, creating a list of meaningful memoirs is challenging. Moreover, given the memoirs published by small independent, regional, or academic presses, or self-published, requires that any list be fluid. The memoirs that have enhanced my understanding of bereavement include the following:

> Barkin, Laurie. (2011). *The Comfort Garden: Tales From the Trauma Unit*. San Francisco, CA: Fresh Pond Press.
>
> How does a psychiatric nurse have a personal life as wife and mother and work at San Francisco General Hospital where 60% of nurses have been attacked or assaulted? How does one transition after a long shift in a psychiatric ward? How does a caring nurse deal with the loss of a medical institution she had grown to love when new management charts a new direction that discounts the contributions of nurses? This memoir has much to say about professionals taking care of themselves in contemporary managed, or "mangled," care.
>
> Brady, Sally Ryder. (2011). *A Box of Darkness: The Story of a Marriage*. New York: St. Martin's Press.
>
> After you have been married to a man for 46 years, and four children, you assume you know him. Brady began discovering "secrets" after her husband's death that led her to ask: Who was this man? She frames a riveting question: "What do I know that I didn't know I knew until now?" (p. 6).
>
> Buckley, Christopher. (2009). *Losing Mum and Pup: A Memoir*. New York: Twelve Press.
>
> Within a 12-month span, writer Christopher Buckley experienced the deaths of his mother and his father, famed

conservative pundit William F. Buckley. Although an only child, the relationship of son and parents was complicated and in no way could the Buckleys be considered your "typical mom and dad." After William F. Buckley died at his desk, bloggers begin spinning that he had suicided. Christopher learned that he had to share the ritualizing of his famous father with a wide cast, many of whom were equally famous or powerful political figures. Moreover, Christopher, at age 55, had to wrestle with the word *orphan* and the absence of a sibling with whom he could share his parents' deaths.

Cain, Hamilton. (2011). *This Boy's Faith: Notes From a Southern Baptist Upbringing: A Memoir.* New York: Crown.

How many nonfinite losses can an individual juggle? This memoir is structured around an individual's loss of the security of a religious framework, that is, the Southern Baptist fundamentalist faith. That abandonment leads to estrangement and restructuring of family connections. Cain and his Jewish wife have a child born with significant medical challenges that negates a normal childhood.

Caldwell, Gail. (2010). *Let's Take the Long Way Home: A Memoir of Friendship.* New York: Random House.

Two individuals daily walking their dogs initiate a friendship that evolved through many ordinary moments of life. One does not expect the younger friend to die first. Caldwell's memoir traces the development of the friendship as well as life after and life "without *us.*"

Clark, Mary Higgins. (2002). *Kitchen Privileges: A Memoir.* New York: Simon & Schuster.

Famed romance writer Mary Higgins Clark writes about her husband's early death and her mother-in-law's death moments later at his bedside. Dual deaths rebooted memories of her father's death when Clark was a child. This book is a wonderful door opener for therapeutic conversation, especially if the griever likes romance novels.

Clift, Eleanor. (2008). *Two Weeks of Life: A Memoir of Love, Death, and Politics.* New York: Basic Books.

> This memoir examines the overlapping last 2 weeks of the author's journalist husband and Terri Schiavo. Two questions predominate: How do we handle the decisions made necessary by a person's dying? What do we do when the dying individual cannot express wishes or confirm decisions? This memoir offers insights from a reporter who covered Schiavo's death and simultaneously experienced her husband's dying.

Crittenden, Lindsey. (2007). *The Water Will Hold You: A Skeptic Learns to Pray.* New York: Harmony Books.

> This memoir has two threads: the search for meaning in the faith one has formerly practiced, prompted by a brother's death, which led to a significant restructuring of the family. With the deaths of her elderly parents, and the ending of an intimate relationship, Crittenden becomes a single parent of an adolescent nephew.

Daily, Art, and Daily, Allison. (2010). *Out of the Canyon: A True Story of Loss and Love.* New York: Harmony Books.

> Life can change in a second. After a hockey game Art Daily was driving home with his wife and sons when a boulder fell from a mountainside and crushed their vehicle. Daily's wife was killed instantly and his two sons soon died in a hospital; he was unscratched. How does—how can—such a bizarre act of nature change one's life? How does one begin over following such tragedy? Enter Allison, a visitor to the area, who had survived a divorce and a brother's suicide death. Out of great suffering and loss, two mourners create a future together.

Dann, Patty. (2007). *The Goldfish Went on Vacation: A Memoir of Loss (and Learning to Tell the Truth About It).* New York: Trumpeter.

> This memoir offers insight into grief and survival from a wife and mother through the physical decline and death of a brilliant husband (who spoke seven-languages). How do

you explain death to a child and care for yourself? This memoirist chose goldfish as an analogy.

Davis, Patti. (2004). *The Long Goodbye*. New York: Knopf.
  Ronald Reagan's one-time estranged daughter constructs a stunning memoir about her father's descent into Alzheimer's. The book focuses on how a splintered family declared a truce to concentrate on what was best for the former president. She concludes, "The only way through grief is through it. There are no shortcuts, no detours."

Didion, Joan. (2007). *The Year of Magical Thinking*. New York: Knopf.
  This memoir is focused on surviving the unexpected deaths of husband and only child within one calendar year. Writing was Didion's attempt to "make sense" of the experience "that cut loose any fixed ideas I have about death, illness" and life itself. Didion learned what many grievers have learned: "Life changes fast."

Doty, Mark. (2007). *Dog Years: A Memoir*. New York: HarperCollins.
  Doty's third memoir focuses on the death of a partner from AIDS and the death of Arden, the beloved dog that kept him company—and sane—during his partner's illness and after his death. Grief is not a wise time to take on a puppy but Doty did. This memoir examines the interaction of dogs and grieving guardians.

Goldman, Ari. (2003). *Living a Year of* Kaddish: *A Memoir*. New York: Schocken.
  The day after Ari's 50th birthday, his father died. The son, according to Jewish tradition, must pray *kaddish* three times daily. The memoir chronicles how through this ritual a nonobservant son honors both parents (his mother had died 4 years earlier) and how faith provides resources to thoughtfully navigate the loss.

Goolrick, Rick. (2007). *The End of the World as We Know It: Scenes From a Life*. Chapel Hill, NC: Algonquin Books of Chapel Hill.

A profoundly disturbing memoir of a child in a prominent Southern family molested by his father and subsequently warned by his grandmother, "You must never tell or something bad will happen to our family." Unrelenting emotional pain from an unspeakable grief triggers alcoholism and cutting episodes long after the deaths of his parents.

Gordon, Mary. (2007). *Circling My Mother: A Memoir*. New York: Pantheon.

In this memoir, a well-known literary giant examines the life of her mother: a devout traditional Catholic, an alcoholic, a polio survivor, and a survivor of a dysfunctional family. Gordon's Jewish father, who died when she was 7, is also examined. Gordon's memoir explores the meaning of the phrase "family of origin."

Hadas, Rachel. (2011). *Strange Relation: A Memoir of Marriage, Dementia, and Poetry*. Philadelphia: Paul Dry Books.

Rachel Hadas, and her composer husband, George Edwards, had a wonderful life together, until he was diagnosed with early-onset dementia at age 61. What proved most troubling was the loss of conversation and the shared enjoyment of each other's creativity. Hadas grieves through poetry—her own and poems from established poems she reads differently now.

Hall, Donald. (1998). *Without: Poems*. Boston: Houghton-Mifflin.

A collection of poems chronicling the last illness and death of Jane Kenyon, Hall's wife, a well-known poet. Hall writes out of active bereavement. The spouses shared offices, which complicates his mourning when working. This memoir explores the significant role of familiar place in mourning.

Hall, Donald. (2008). *Unpacking the Boxes: A Memoir of a Life in Poetry*. Boston: Houghton-Mifflin.

While this memoir focuses on Hall's career as a poet, the long chapter, "Grief House," offers a stunning account of the death of his wife and his role as her caregiver. Hall is remarkably vulnerable in disclosing his sexual yearnings as a widower and describes the impact of the death on their dog, Gus.

Harris, E. Lynn. (2003). *What Becomes of the Brokenhearted: A Memoir.* New York: Anchor Books.

The celebrated, gay, African American novelist tells the story of how the child born into poverty, graduates from the University of Arkansas, and "blows" through a series of well-paying jobs while trying to find himself and come to terms with his homosexuality. Less than a year after he meets his biological father, he dies. He navigates a string of friends dying during the AIDS epidemic. Finally, he has to grieve for a career lost to drinking and partying. Through therapy, he begins writing authentically.

Homes, A. M. (2007). *The Mistress's Daughter.* New York: Viking.

How does a relationship change after discovering your mother was the mistress of a famous man? After Homes becomes well known as a writer, someone discloses her biological father's identity. The father has conflicting feelings about now acknowledging his daughter. The memoir offers incredible insight into the effort to discover the identity and narrative of a relationship between her unmarried biological parents. This memoir offers no "and they all lived happily ever after" ending.

Hotchner, A. E. (2010). *Paul and Me: 53 Years of Adventure and Misadventure With My Pal Paul Newman.* New York: Doubleday.

This memoir chronicles the close friendship and business partnership of writer A. E. Hotchner and the actor, Paul Newman: a relationship that lasted more than half a century until Newman's death. It details the development of Newman's Own Salad Dressing, a prank that morphed into a major commercial venture that has raised $300 million for charities and funded Hole in the Wall, a summer camp for children. Particularly insightful are disclosures about the grief following the death of Newman's son Scott after a drug overdose.

Jennings, Kevin. (2006). *Mama's Boy, Preacher's Son*. Boston: Beacon Press.
How does a sensitive child live with a conclusion that his wish for a birthday present resulted in his father's heart attack and death? In time, he learns that his minister father had a pattern of marital infidelity (thus their sudden moves). Then, given the baggage of grief, how does the son disclose homosexual orientation? Who would have predicted that his widowed mother would, in time, become an AIDS activist?

Kamen, Paula. (2007). *Finding Iris Chang: Friendship, Ambition and the Loss of an Extraordinary Mind*. New York: Da Capo Press.
Celebrated author Iris Chang's suicide at age 36 left a hole in a lot of hearts, especially her friend Paula Kamen. In this investigative memoir, a close friend searches for answers to why brilliance and professional success could not save her friend.

Karbo, Karen. (2003). *The Stuff of Life: A Daughter's Memoir*. New York: Bloomsburg.
A brilliant memoir of a daughter navigating the last months of her father's life. She comes to discover and grapple with the reasons that she is so much like her father.

Krasnow, Iris. (2006). *I Am My Mother's Daughter: Making Peace With Mom—Before it's too late*. New York: Basic Books.
Krasnow's mother is a survivor of the Holocaust. Krasnow, after her father's death, has to deal with her mother's coma as a consequence of an amputation of a leg. How does conflict between mother and daughter during adolescence influence an opportunity to make some sort of peace at the end of life?

McCracken, Elizabeth. (2008). *An Exact Replication of a Figment of My Imagination*. New York: Little, Brown and Company.

Stillbirth is a common but disenfranchised grief. Many individuals assume that it happens to other people. Elizabeth McCracken found herself in rural France awaiting the birth of a long-desired baby. The memoir chronicles her longings for a child, the waiting, then the discovery that the fetus had died. She chronicles the following 12 months waiting for another baby's birth. How does one await a child's birth aware of what can go wrong in the last weeks of a pregnancy? How does one remember the first baby? In this memoir a baby dies, a baby lives, and a couple balances the reality of having two children in their hearts.

Miller, Sue. (2003). *The Story of My Father*. New York: Knopf.

In 1988, the novelist Sue Miller found herself caring for her father, an Alzheimer's patient, although feeling that she was the least constitutionally suited of her siblings for such responsibility. She watched her father—a minister and brilliant professor of history—struggle as the disease took away his sense of time, history, meaning, and livelihood. Miller ponders the variable nature of memory and tries to weave a faithful narrative from the threads of a dissolving life.

Moore, Honor. (2008). *The Bishop's Daughter: A Memoir*. New York: Norton.

Honor Moore, a poet, thought she "knew" her father—a prominent Episcopal bishop of New York and an activist. After his death, a former partner of her father's contacts her and thus she discovers her father's closet. The memoir examines two lives at the intersection of public and private.

Nuland, Sherwin B. (2003). *Lost in America: My life with my father*. New York: Alfred N. Knopf.

The defining experience of a Yale surgeon and prize-winning author was the death of his mother when he was 8 years old and the extended family's conclusion that his father was incapable of caring for him. Everything changed

because he was sent to live with family members who provided the incredible educational opportunities that led to
his distinguished career. How does one resume relationship with a banished father?

Orr, Greg. (2002). *The Blessing: The Memoir*. San Francisco, CA:
Council Oak Books.

This memoirist accidentally shot his brother while hunting.
In a dysfunctional family that did not talk, Orr grieved—
and continues to grieve—alone.

O'Rourke, Meghan. (2011). *The Long Goodbye: A Memoir*. New
York: Riverhead.

Unmothered may not be a word in the dictionary, according
to O'Rourke, but it should be. An amazing memoir of
her mother's dying at age 55 and being blindsided by the
intensity of the sorrow. Her grief was complicated by marrying and divorcing in the same year.

Rice, Condoleezza. (2010). *Extraordinary, Ordinary People: A
Memoir of Family*. New York: Crown/Archetype.

The accomplished diplomat was an only child growing up
in racially segregated Birmingham. After her best friend
was killed in the bombing of the Sixteenth Avenue
Baptist Church, her parents committed themselves to
facilitating their daughter's survival and potential in a
hostile environment; their sacrifices provided many
opportunities. How does someone in the public eye as an
academic and diplomat grieve the death of her mother
and father?

Rieff, David. (2008). *Swimming in a Sea of Death: A Son's Memoir*.
New York: Simon & Schuster.

This investigative memoir examines the illness and death of
the author's mother, novelist Susan Sontag. Rieff examines what it means to fully confront the death of a celebrity mother in a death-denying culture. What made his
mother willing to try every possible medical treatment?
How did her desire to live impact a son's bereavement?

Seel, Pierre. (1995). *I, Pierre Seel, Deported Homosexual: A Memoir of Nazi Terror* (J. Neugroschel, Trans.). New York: Basic Books.

Seel, as an adolescent during the Nazi occupation of France, was placed on a police-maintained list of homosexuals. Eventually, he was arrested and sent to a concentration camp where he was raped, tortured, and assaulted. After liberation by the Russian Army, he had to rebuild his life in a postwar world. He chose to abandon his silence to speak out for the recognition of 800,000 homosexuals put to death by the Nazis.

Selwyn, Peter A. (1998). *Surviving the Fall: The Personal Journey of an AIDS Doctor.* New Haven, CT: Yale University Press.

Decades after his father's death (when the memoirist was 2), as an AIDS specialist Selwyn interacts with many IV drug users who are going to die at a young age. In listening to their narratives, he reexamined his understanding of his father's "accidental" death. Through a vigorous search for the truth, Selwyn discovered that his father suicided.

Silen, Jonathan G. (2006). *My Father's Keeper: The Story of a Gay Son and His Aging Parents.* Boston, MA: Beacon Press.

Many adult children have an anxiety: What will happen when I become the parent and my aged parent(s) become the child? Silen's relationship is complicated because he, an only child, is gay, has a partner, and does not live in the same city as his parents. The memoir addresses the partner's participation in caregiving and how geographic distance creates demands on the son's time and energy that challenge the intimate relationship.

Smith, Gordon. (2006). *Remembering Garrett: One Family's Battle With a Child's Depression.* New York: Carroll & Graf.

This memoir chronicles the grief of a prominent political family with a mentally ill adolescent, Garrett, who in a moment of despair, suicided. Smith, blaming himself for some of his son's crisis, pondered resigning his U. S. Senate seat. However, he discovers a way to create good from this tragedy: The Garrett Lee Smith Memorial Act, which provides federal funding for mental health care and suicide prevention for adolescents.

Spring, Janis Abrahms (with Spring, Michael). (2009). *Life With Pop: Lessons on Caring for an Aging Parent.* New York: Avery.

The death of one parent, or stepparent, alters the relationship with the surviving parent, even when the adult child is a therapist. For 5 years, wanting a rich, meaningful life for her father, she transitioned her father into an assisted-living facility. Soon Spring was wrestling with her father's eroding physical and mental decline. How does one balance one's own needs and a professional career with increasing demands of her father's care?

Stepanek, Jeni, and Linder, Larry. (2009). *Messenger: The Legacy of Mattie J. T. Stepanek and Heartsongs.* New York: New American Library.

How does a single parent/doctoral student integrate the death of three children and manage life with a surviving child who will die from a rare medical trait she passed to him? Life gets interesting when her brilliant son Mattie's poetry reaches bestseller status in *The New York Times.* Every day offers some element of medical challenge. This memoir has a great deal to say about living, rather than existing, with a terminal medical diagnosis.

Trillin, Calvin. (1993). *Remembering Denny.* New York: Farrar, Straus, Giroux.

Over the years, friendships change and people lose contact. One day a writer reads the newspaper obituary for an estranged friend. He gathers a group of shared friends to attend a memorial service only to discover what none of them knew the deceased, a distinguished diplomat, was gay.

Trillin, Calvin. (1996). *Messages From My Father.* New York: Farrar, Straus, Giroux.

This readable memoir by a distinguished author offers a particular insight into an immigrant father who nurtured keen expectations that his son "would not be like the old man."

Trillin, Calvin. (2006). *About Alice*. New York: Random House.
Alice, Trillin's wife, had long been a presence in his published writing. How does an author—and readers—grieve her absence? In this brief memoir, Trillin, as a widower, weaves a tapestry of a relationship that ended when she succumbed to heart failure as a consequence of radiation treatment for cancer.

Vonnegut, Mark. (2010). *Just Like Someone Without Mental Illness Only More So: A Memoir*. New York: Delacorte Press.
Doctors are "supposed" to be psychologically healthy. What if you are the number one pediatrician in Boston, the son of a famous author, and you have experienced your fourth psychotic breakdown? Vonnegut concludes, "None of us is entirely well, and none of us are irrecoverably sick."

Wickersham, Joan. (2008). *The Suicide Index: Putting My Father's Death in Order*. Orlando, FL: Harcourt.
The memoirist asks a question: How does an adult child "make sense" of a father's suicide? And how does she survive the bureaucracy of death, police, and pathologists? As she puts the death "in order," she has to deal with a mother who outlives him and unexpected financial consequences. She discovers one cannot always put a period after a suicide.

7

Using Borrowed Narratives

A picture is worth a thousand words.

Sometimes, a picture stimulates a thousand words. Some iconic pictures have long lives and jump-start many conversations. Stories and pictures go together like a horse and carriage, in the words of the Broadway musical.

Organizing the Narratives

What good is a borrowed narrative if you cannot retrieve it? Admittedly, you could wing it and tell the portion of the story that you remember. However, will the story have the impact you want? The difference is like that between a skeleton and a full body. It is important to be able to readily access the story in case you should be challenged about your accuracy. Perhaps you have experienced doing a presentation and having someone in the audience believe he knew more than you.

Hamilton (2008) insists that the element in biographical research is "careful recordkeeping" (p. 69). You must accurately credit material you quote in speaking, writing, or other resources that influenced your interpretation or understanding of a specific event. This is nonnegotiable. The *Publication Manual of the American Psychological Association* is clear: "Whether paraphrasing or quoting an author directly, you must credit the source" (2001, p. 120). Moreover, your work is a contribution to the field and literature in thanatology and social sciences. "Direct quotations must be accurate. ... The quotation must follow the wording, spelling, and interior punctuation of the original source, even if the source is incorrect" (2001, p. 172), in which case you use *sic.* "Any direct quotation, regardless of length, must be accompanied by a reference citation that, if at all possible, includes a page number" (2001, p. 121).

Admittedly, many clinicians find such guidance rudimentary, but in the pressure of time, errors are made that can prove embarrassing and compromise the integrity of the work and your reputation. Frank (2011) raises issues about overenthusiasm for quotations from public or historical figures. It is tempting to borrow the quote from a secondary source. Nevertheless, "Painstaking faithfulness to primary documents is one of the shibboleths of academic professionalism" (p. 9). It is too easy to borrow a quote, or the essence of a quote, which you have "read numerous times in what appears to be authoritative works" (p. 9). Frank warns that some writers in the field of "pop" American history are on "a sacred mission to rescue history-as-legend from the corrosive influence" of academia (p. 9). Consequently, words are being put in the mouths of the Founding Fathers for ideological advantage. One can almost hear Franklin or Jefferson responding, "I *never* said that!" The time to create good citations is at the beginning of the project.

Photocopies

Two great technological advances for scholars and writers are the photocopy machine (the researcher's "friend") and the scanner. I moan remembering the old days of filling out three-by-five index cards for possible citation.

Now, when I appropriate material from books, I photocopy the pages of text I want, the title page and, often, the copyright page. I am generous with photocopy expenditures because I consider photocopies an investment rather than an expense. I would rather have an extra photocopy or two than be frustrated because I overlooked something (particularly when I tried to save money at presidential libraries that charge 20 or 25 cents per page; more if staff do photocopies).

Make sure that page numbers have been photocopied. Sometimes, in rushing to photocopy or given the size of the book and the limitations of the copier's reduction process, the page number or a critical line of text may be cut off. That may prove to be the page number needed to meet APA standards accurately.

When you quote directly from a book or article, the exact page of the citation is required. Some famous writers may get away with eliminating page numbers but you cannot. An inquiring reader should be able to locate the book, journal, or document and find that page with a minimum of difficulty.

Pagination can change in editions or from hardback to paperback editions and in a revised edition. Editions published in other countries may have different pagination, even different titles. Investing extra moments at the time of photocopying can save you a great deal of time retracing your steps when preparing your manuscript for publication.

An "extra" photocopy may be as valuable a second or third time you read it. You may have photocopied for a particular quote or story, and later discovered that the third paragraph from the bottom of the page is equally useful.

A reader may question the accuracy of your citations—especially if several sloppy endnotes have been noticed. Readers may be curious if there is more to the story. They may wonder if you deleted a sentence or phrase that changed the quotation or suggested another interpretation, or may wonder if you have deliberately misinterpreted a source to support your point of view.

For example, Mary Lincoln did not use her maiden name, Todd, after marrying Abraham Lincoln. A reader might protest: "But I see Mary *Todd* Lincoln everywhere." Or "It is in large letters on the cover of Jean Baker's classic, *Mary Todd Lincoln: A Biography*." Yes, while many authors use Mary *Todd* Lincoln, I rely on Catherine Clinton, the eminent Mary Lincoln scholar, who authored *Mrs. Lincoln*. If I use Mary "Todd" Lincoln, a reader may conclude that I have not read, or consulted, Clinton's "definitive" biography.

Readers familiar with historical figures bring a bias to their reading. Barbara Bush, First Lady, 1989–1993, is respected and admired. Anything that questions her image—such as the fact the day after her 4-year-old daughter Robin died at Sloan-Kettering Hospital in New York City, Bush played golf—could raise the ire of readers or a listener, as I learned after a presentation in Houston. I had correctly cited Bush's account of the incident in *Barbara Bush: A Memoir*.

I had, however, misinterpreted her intention. Yes she did play golf that day. Because she had spent weeks in a hospital room with her dying daughter, family members thought she needed some exercise before heading home to Texas. That confrontation with a clinician who admired Bush has made me more careful using facts. So, here is what Bush wrote about the incident:

> The day after Robin died, George and I went to Rye [New York] to play golf with Daddy, at his suggestion. As we drove out on the parkway, I was shocked that the leaves were at the peak of their fall beauty. I remembered realizing life went on, whether we were looking or not. I also remember changing my shoes in the ladies' locker room and seeing a childhood friend, Marilyn Peterson. We talked briefly, and I did not mention Robin. I wondered later if she thought it was strange that we were playing golf the day after our baby died. I, for one, was numb. (B. Bush, 1994, p. 45)

If I deleted, or overlooked, "I, for one, was numb" from the citation, the narrative changes. When rechecking this quote for inclusion in this chapter, I found something that I had overlooked in my original reading. Mrs. Bush mentions a friend awkwardly consoling her, "At least it wasn't your firstborn and a boy at that." How did Barbara Bush respond? "I was speechless" (B. Bush, 1994, p. 46). George H. W. Bush explained that, in their grief, they had to make allowances for other parents hunting for words to verbalize their condolences. The Bushes learned "to be patient" (B. Bush, 1994, p. 46) with would-be consolers.

That short narrative slice might be valuable to a griever who is angry with someone who has said something outrageous. In the Grief Gatherings I lead, that quote is a good way to start a discussion: What is the most insensitive thing that has been said to you? That narrative slice could be a bridge for further conversation and exploration: Why do people say such things? Is there a way to respond to individuals that educates them on how their words sound?

Readers have a right to weigh a presenter's or therapist's interpretation or slant on the facts or even the order of those facts—especially if they intend to use your edition of the narrative. Nothing is more humbling, after the publication of an article or book, than receiving a reader's e-mail, phone call, or letter pointing out that you were sloppy or, worse, mistaken! Some readers may conclude that if you were repeatedly sloppy with particular details, your work is not trustworthy.

Identify the Location of the Original Source

When photocopying materials, I write on the first photocopy where I found the material: the Kansas City Public Library, Central Branch, the University of Kansas, or the John F. Kennedy Presidential Library in Boston. That detail will simplify the search if I need to eyeball or fact-check a detail. Since libraries have different editions of books and reference materials, the pagination may be different in hardback, revised, or paperback editions.

Storing Photocopies

"Where did I file that photocopy?" That question has dashed across my brain too many times! When writing on the Barbara Bush golf episode, I pulled my Barbara Bush file and found the photocopy. I did not have to interrupt the flow of writing significantly to head into the "rabbit hole" to locate the quotation. On other occasions, unfortunately, I have spent more time than I care to admit searching for a "prodigal" citation.

I organize photocopies in individual manila files tabbed by the subject of the research, that is, B.B. King, Condoleezza Rice, Mackenzie King, William Brennan, Albert Einstein, and so forth. In my master files, U.S. presidents have a red file; first ladies, a yellow file. Sometimes a particular photocopy belongs in two places. A duplicate photocopy or a sticky note, "See Bush, Barbara file," are practical solutions.

Files multiply like guppies. With my two major subjects, Eleanor Roosevelt and Harry Truman, I subdivided materials into multiple folders. Some are "issue" files: Mrs. Roosevelt and African-American issues, Mrs. Roosevelt and the Holocaust, or Mrs. Roosevelt and labor issues. I maintain subsubject files for her relationships with individuals: Eleanor and Elinor (*sic*) Morgenthau, for example, where I filed material about the elegant eulogy Mrs. Roosevelt offered when her close friend died. Information on Eleanor's prolonged dying is filed in Eleanor and David Gurewitsch (her longtime primary physician and friend).

Nothing frustrates me more than wanting to cite a narrative and being unable to retrieve it in a timely manner. A moment now may save minutes later.

Paying Attention to Citations in the First Draft

The time to cite a footnote—even a familiar quote, even if it slows the writing process—is the first time you use it. When using a direct quote in the first draft, I highlight the direct quotation in purple and sometimes bold. I insert brackets at the end of a direct quote and note the author's name, year of publication, and page number(s) such as "[Henry, 2002, p. 76]."

This is critically important when citing authors who have written multiple books on a particular subject like Eleanor Roosevelt, as have Joseph Lash or Blanche Cook. Within the brackets I abbreviate the first name when I am using Roosevelt family members: J. Roosevelt (James), or E. Roosevelt (Eleanor).

As I rewrite, through numerous drafts, moving paragraphs, sentences, or sentence fragments within the chapter or to other chapters, it is essential that the basic citation accompany the quotation so that I know it is a direct quote and I know the source. In the first draft, I also cite ideas, because in editing, I may conclude that I need a direct quote to strengthen the point. If I use an idea about Lincoln from Burlingame (2008) in early drafts, I include page numbers that I will eventually eliminate if I do not directly quote from this source.

Benjamin Franklin quipped: "An ounce of prevention is worth a pound of cure" ("The Electric Ben Franklin," n.d.). Dr. Franklin's advice is applicable when citing sources. I have wasted too many hours trying to track down quotes for accuracy and for citation. Unfortunately, on some occasions, I have had to abandon a particular quotation.

Check and Verify Dates

In reading about the end of World War I, many readers know that November 11 was the day hostilities ceased. The date is captured in the memorable phrase: "on the eleventh hour of the eleventh day of the eleventh month." Even a typo may detract the serious reader.

For some historical persons, birthdates and dates of death are not precise or known. While writing on Francis "The Swamp Fox" Marion, the revolutionary hero, I e-mailed the Library of Congress for assistance and learned that there is no definitive date of birth for Marion. To appear younger, some celebrities alter their year of birth.

Translating Facts Into Story

Although a story may not benefit a griever, having read the narrative may cause you to be more sensitive to the issues the client is presenting. How does a clinician translate facts into attractive narrative?

Begin by Telling the Story Aloud

I practice stories aloud. In early run-throughs, I stumble over key words, phrases, or transitions. The ear hears the story differently than the eye reads it. Some stories work well in print but are less effective in verbal settings; some stories can be rather dull in print but come alive with the tone of voice and pauses. In a text format, a reader can go back and reread; the listener does not have that advantage. To communicate the narrative effectively, you may need to add or shrink unnecessary details.

Polishing the Story Through Rehearsal

Stories ripen through rehearsal. Rehearsing the story is like a pianist rigorously practicing the scales or an athlete stretching before competition. In each retelling, the story sinks deeper into the storyteller's consciousness and may, over time, prompt questions. Make this commitment, "I will tell no story publically before its time." You might benefit by rehearsing a story with a colleague and asking, "What did you hear in that story? What confused you?"

A borrowed narrative is not simply a string of words. It is an accumulation of particular words, punctuated by passion, timing, detail, and rehearsal. The clinician must translate facts into a compelling story. Stories ripen through repeated telling, sometimes focusing on a different facet. Have you laughed when a friend has said, "Now stop me if you have heard this story before?"

Support Narratives with Photographs

A picture is worth a thousand words, particularly in the age of PowerPoint. In a presentation on Martin Luther King, Jr., I could point out that he was arrested 17 times and that an arrest in the South could be life-threatening for African Americans in that day. I could mention King's arrest for attempting to testify as a character witness for Ralph David Abernathy at a trial in Montgomery, Alabama. However, if I use a picture of King being booked in Montgomery, Alabama, which captures his hands held behind his back and his body being slammed against a counter at the jail, that picture is worth more than a thousand words.

I can share stories about Martin Luther King, Sr.'s, grief at his son's funeral. Showing a picture of King, Sr., being led out of that funeral gives the story impact. If I am talking about the stoic calmness of Coretta Scott King at the funeral, I enhance that narrative with a picture of her sitting calmly on the front pew of the Ebenezer Baptist Church where she heard her husband preach many times. Someone in an audience, or a griever, may store that picture in escrow for future use when they are experiencing grief firsthand. Indeed, many note that Mrs. King modeled another way for African Americans to grieve that challenged the traditions—and stereotypes—of emotionally overwhelmed African American grievers.

Thanatologists and grief educators have access to resources unimaginable just a few years ago. You can find great pictures using Google Images. I may browse picture after picture and invest more time than I intended, but often I am rewarded with the "Yes!" image. I also learned that although I have Googled images of Martin Luther King, Jr., on previous occasions, *this* search may produce an image that I have not seen, a picture that drives home powerfully what I want to communicate.

WhiteHouse.gov offers pictures of the presidents and first ladies. For presidents since Franklin D. Roosevelt, their presidential libraries are repositories of photos that can be downloaded and used with proper credit, generally without charge. Many Internet image providers charge or watermark their photos, which detracts from their impact. Snagit is a helpful computer software that allows you to capture any picture on the screen, scan, and save in picture files for future use.

Pictures also have secondary threads. For example, a particular photo captures how young Martin Luther and Coretta Scott King were when they joined the Montgomery bus boycott in 1955. If I talk about that January night in 1956, when the King's parsonage was bombed while he was preaching at a rally, I note that his first concern was for the safety of Coretta and their baby, Yolanda. If I show a picture of Coretta holding the baby, his anxiety becomes more apparent.

Recently, after a presentation on multiple homicides in the extended King family, an African American in the audience approached me. "I am from Atlanta. I knew the Kings but I have *never* seen some of those pictures! Where did you get them?" Admittedly, it does take time to find the right picture but that picture may initiate a significant conversation.

Using Photos in Clinical Settings

Pictures can be valuable in one-on-one settings. You might show the picture and ask the client: "What do you see in this picture?" If you use a photo of a stoic Coretta Scott King at the funeral, you might ask: "What does Mrs. King's body language communicate to you?"

If I am commenting on the grief of President and Mrs. Calvin Coolidge following the death of their son Calvin Jr., I show two photos. The first photo is the Coolidge family taken in the summer on 1923 (before the death). Then I show a picture of the four stoic Coolidge survivors in late summer, 1924. I ask the griever, "What do you see in these pictures?" Sometimes I borrow a phrase from Kenya, "What leaps out at you in this picture?"

Someone may respond: "Why does President Coolidge have a black cloth around his left sleeve?" I then explain the armband, worn to signify the individual is in mourning, is a funeral symbol that has been discarded in a grief-lite culture. Historically, males wore the armband as long as a year, just as females wore black clothing for that period.

Photos in Your Office

Pictures of historical grievers may enhance an office or waiting room. A particular picture might prompt the question, "Why do you have *that* picture of Eleanor Roosevelt?" Eleanor Roosevelt, I would explain, was no stranger to death and grief. She experienced 20 significant deaths other than her husband's death (H. I. Smith, 2007). That response might prompt the griever's curiosity or initiate a question in the future. I might follow-up with one of Mrs. Roosevelt's quotations, "You must do the thing you think you cannot do!" (E. Roosevelt, 1960, p. 30) or another of her grief-related quotations, "I have the habit of doing things I have said I will do" ("Mrs. Roosevelt in Peril," 1933, p. 1).

Zinn (2003) suggests that history is made up of stories of ordinary people who have had a part in the making of history, personalities that historians often overlook. I believe that history also has stories of ordinary—and some extraordinary—individuals who faced the dragons and harnessed grief before they became known. Condoleezza Rice (2010) captures that reality in the title of her memoir of her parents, *Extraordinary, Ordinary People: A Memoir of Family.*

A framed picture of Condoleezza Rice might invite a conversation that jump-starts a story about the role of the bombing of the Sixteenth Avenue Baptist Church in Birmingham, Alabama, on September 15, 1963. Although Condoleezza was one mile away in her father's church, she felt the blast of the bomb.

If presenting on the impact of grief on children, I often begin by telling a story without disclosing that Dr. Rice is the subject of the narrative. I use a PowerPoint image of her at age 6 and ask, "Does anyone know who this girl is?" After a moment, I advance to a picture of a smiling Secretary of State Condoleezza Rice. Giving the picture a moment, I follow-up by asking, "So, what is the future of a child-griever you are counseling? Might she be a future Dr. Rice?"

PowerPointing and Narratives

A borrowed narrative is only a string of words organized around a group of facts until it is harnessed. I have experienced many PowerPoint presentations that were well grounded in theory and practice but not in presentation technique. During one lecture in Hanoi, an American presenter did not use one picture to support the text, thereby missing an opportunity to enhance her time before an audience of Vietnamese nursing and medical staff. As many in the audience waited for the translation, pictures could have enhanced the theory the speaker was sharing.

In January 2010, I lectured on grief to 100 student nurses at Bach Ma Hospital in Hanoi. Some could "read" the English in the PowerPoint, and a few could understand portions of my English. I kept reminding myself, as a Southerner, that my speech patterns are challenging to translate and that I talk rapidly. Although I had a brilliant translator (who held an MD and PhD), communicating concepts like death and grief is subject to linguistic, cultural, and the listener's personal interpretation. I had one instructional trump card. In preparation for the lecture, I researched the life of Ho Chi Minh whose mother died in 1901 from complications of childbirth; Ho was 10 years old at the time of her death (Duiker, 2000). So committed was he to Vietnamese nationalism, he never married. As I closed my presentation I used a series of pictures of and quotations by Ho Chi Minh that surprised and pleased my audience. Students wanted to know how I, an American, knew about "Uncle Ho" as he is commonly called in Vietnam. I used his words, "Look wide and think deep" (as cited in Nguyen Dy Nien, 2008, p. 194) to apply to grief. Ho Chi Minh learned the power of storytelling from the village blacksmith who befriended him. Around the forge, at night, as villagers gathered, Ho heard versions of borrowed narratives that focused on "the glorious achievements of warriors long dead like Le Loi and Mai Thuc Loan, who had fought to protect their homeland against invaders" (Duiker, 2000, p. 24). He also heard the stories of contemporaries who were fighting the French colonialists. Then he used those stories to drive home his belief in an independent Vietnam.

A borrowed image in a PowerPoint presentation is not used like a caboose on a train. An effective PowerPoint presentation is an appealing collage of concepts and words, punctuated by passion, timing, detail, and *enhanced* by photographs.

The Power of a Picture as a Bridge

A picture may capture an audience's attention to shift a focus in a presentation (especially for those participants who are multitasking rather than solely paying attention to a lecture). Presenters, even with the best or newest data and insights, today have to engage and hang on to audiences.

Grievers need well-rehearsed and photo-enhanced stories of other grievers who have faced loss. Many grievers know Jackie Kennedy as a widowed single parent. I can use an image of her as the young wife of an ambitious U.S. senator to mention the anguish she experienced when her father died. Thinking Jack Bouvier something of a hypochondriac, she did not respond immediately to the call from the hospital, "You need to come *now*." That hesitancy—something she long regretted—was driven by a fact: she arrived after her father died.

I might use a picture of a smiling Jackie Onassis to raise the issue of unimaginable futures. I might use an image of Mrs. Kennedy sitting with her grown children, Caroline and John, at a Kennedy Library function. I contend that when first images of her as a widow were taken she could not have imagined that life would ever be good again. Perhaps individuals in the audience cannot imagine a good future. A photo image might plant a seed of hope.

I could compose a "photo album" of pictures of Mrs. Kennedy that supports her grief grid (see Chapter 10). A young widow may find this set of images a "thread" that makes hope more believable.

The Last Pictures in Eleanor's Marriage

Sometimes, I use two images of Eleanor Roosevelt. First, a smiling Eleanor arriving at the Sulgrave Club on April 12, 1945, for a benefit; the second is Eleanor, in black, following the pallbearers carrying Franklin D. Roosevelt's flag-draped casket into the White House on April 13, 1945. I ask the griever to notice her body language captured in the image. Then I ask what the participant thinks might have been going through her mind at that moment in time.

Soon after she arrived at the Little White House in Georgia, Eleanor learned that Lucy Mercer Rutherfurd, the woman Franklin had promised to give up in 1918 to avoid a divorce, had been with him in Georgia for 3 days. Eleanor soon discovered that Franklin and Rutherfurd had been together on several occasions, even in the White House in her absence, and that Anna, the Roosevelts' daughter, had "facilitated" the meetings (Swift, 2004).

To catch a glimpse of the train bearing the body to Washington, millions lined the rail right-of-way from Georgia to Washington. Eleanor spent the night looking out the window at those people. Over those long hours, she reviewed her life with Franklin and assessed his impact on those citizens. That experience was like that many spouses or partners feel in the immediate hours after a death.

One week after the president died, Eleanor moved out of the White House, which had been their home for 12 years, convinced that her life was over. Early one morning, a young reporter from *The New York Times* stopped her on the sidewalk. "What's next, Mrs. Roosevelt?" Eleanor briskly responded, "The story is over" and walked away (Lash, 1984, p. 123).

In reviewing photographs of Eleanor following her husband's death, I think that she thought that her "story was over." She told a granddaughter that no one would remember her in 10 years. She grappled with questions widows commonly face: Who am I now? What am I free to be? What am I free to do?

Eleanor, like many widows of that time period, especially given the number of war widows, believed that her influence had been contingent on her relationship to Franklin as *Mrs.* Franklin D. Roosevelt. Generally first ladies have months to prepare for transition to private life; Eleanor had days.

Harry Truman, whose competency was questioned by many, including Eleanor, knew that he needed her support as he began shouldering incredible burdens in leading a postwar society. Despite her initial protests that she knew nothing about diplomacy, Truman appointed her to the first U.S. delegation to the United Nations in 1945. Eleanor, in that post, kept the world remembering the commitment Franklin made to lasting peace through a world organization, the United Nations.

She was FDR's primary rememberer. As a widow, she found ways to lead wary and weary diplomats—and governments—to what was then unimaginable: a Universal Declaration of Human Rights signed on December 10, 1948. She used her widowhood for the betterment of humankind and, in the process, emerged on her own as *Eleanor* Roosevelt.

In presentations I often link two pictures of Eleanor: the widowed Eleanor in black and a smiling Eleanor holding an oversize copy of the Universal Declaration of Human Rights. I conclude that the future found Eleanor while Eleanor defined and shaped her future.

Discriminate When Using Photos

The purpose of a borrowed photo image is to support a borrowed narrative. Some individuals use photographs like a teenager learning to drive a stick shift—a blur of rapidly passing photos. When you zip through images, someone in the audience may still be thinking about a previous slide, and miss the point you want to share. Flashing pictures too quickly or too slowly or using too many pictures can sabotage the points you want to make in your presentation.

Some questions to consider when borrowing photographs to complement narratives in a PowerPoint presentation are:

Why this picture?
Why this image at this point in the presentation?
What size should the picture be when projected on the screen?
Does the photo complement or distract from the content (if there is content) of the slide?

An interested griever may do his own Internet search looking for more pictures of Eleanor Roosevelt or more pictures of a griever of interest, or he may spend invest time sifting for clues in the photos.

When PowerPoint Is Counterproductive

The increased sophistication of PowerPoint technology tempts a presenter to overuse or rely on the bells and whistles, particularly dancing animation or fade-ins and fade-outs, and unusual script fonts or color combinations. The clinician designing a presentation must always consider the audience's perspective. Does this image enhance the narrative or distract? The PowerPoint that would be effective with university students in Death and Dying 101 might be distracting in a presentation to a group of widows.

Font Size Counts

Your well-prepared PowerPoint may be seen differently in different room formats, especially with florescent lighting or lots of lighting or windows, which bleach the screen. Consider the appropriate font size for a presentation. DeBourgh (2008) recommends 32-point font (36 as the ideal for major points; 32 for subtext; 44 for titles). You may have, at the last minute, a setting change for your presentation, perhaps from a small room to a larger one. I followed a brilliant psy-chobiologist's data-overloaded presentation on the impact of grief on brain chemistry. The presenter sabotaged himself by using the wrong font selection (6 pica!), which no one could read either on the screen or on the handout. Moreover, many slides had too many words. The evaluations were less than positive.

Be Cautious of Overcontenting a Slide

Some slides may be so wordy that they are counterproductive. DeBourgh (2008) offers this guidance on content: "Be brief, use short phrases" rather than sentences. Some presenters want few(er) slides to minimize the transitions; however, if the presenter crams too much content into the slide, effectiveness is sabotaged. The wise presenter "fills in details verbally in the presentation." DeBourgh urges presenters to use emphasis options, such as italics or bolding, sparingly.

In a recent continuing education experience, I was seated toward the back of the room. I noticed the presenter had dramatically enhanced a quotation from a colleague of mine by using bold and large font. However, the attribution at the bottom of the slide was unreadable. I wish that my colleague's name, at least, could have been highlighted because some thought the quotation was the presenter's.

Use Color Cautiously

PowerPoint offers a tempting palette of colors to highlight points. Many presenters choose colors that do not magnify well. Some colors—red, black, blue—enhance but other colors fade out on a screen. DeBourgh (2008) notes: "Use a high-contrast font color. Light text on dark background—white on blue; or dark text on light background— blue on white. Avoid yellow and green as font colors. Use red for emphasis, and only on high-contrasted black or white backgrounds."

Anticipate Technological Snafus

The Boy Scout motto, "Be prepared!" is wise guidance for presenters. Count the ways that a technical "malfunction" can happen:

1. The technician is not present to assist.
2. The bulb in the LCD blows.
3. The power cord does not reach an outlet.
4. Someone trips over the power cord.
5. The introducer reads every detail in your curriculum vitae.
6. The screen is bleached by a florescent light (or series of lights) or spotlights.

These, coupled with announcements and introductions that go on forever, elevate anxiety in a presenter.

I survive such experiences by being prepared. Technological malfunctions happen. Plan for them. Be relieved when they do not happen this time! Unfortunately, tech-nightmares can significantly diminish your time for presentation and ruffle presentation skills, as you have to leap over slides racing against the clock. Remember: A tech-crisis is not the time to pitch a fit in front of an audience, which will encourage the storytelling skills of members of the audience!

Never let it be said of you, "No PowerPoint, no presentation." Audiences appreciate presenters who handle technical difficulties calmly and remain focused on the audience rather than the technology. Unfortunately, as a result of poorly responding to technical issues that have eaten into my time to present, I have imposed the equivalent of "cerebral whiplash" by dashing through slides in a "hang on" manner. If you insist on showing all 126 content slides in a 60-minute presentation, you may have to eliminate questions-and-answers from the audience, and you eliminate a learning opportunity for you and for the audience.

Where Did the Image Come From?

Attribute your slides. If you did not take the photograph or sketch, attribute. Make sure the attribution on the screen is in readable font. Make certain of the accuracy of the photographer's names and institutions, that is, Associated Press, *The New York Times*, and so forth.

Reading the Slides

Do not read your slides word for word to any audience. Too many presenters stand with their backs to the audience (which can limit amplification) while reading the slides, especially long quotes. Effective presenters highlight or call attention to key words or phrases, especially if the audience has been given the material in a handout.

Be Cautious Sharing PowerPoints and Pictures

I have been surprised by the number of individuals who request my *whole* PowerPoint presentation—one that I have spent hours preparing. I decline. First, the PowerPoint is my intellectual property. Second, the PowerPoint can be used verbatim. Richard Gilbert reminds, "It also could bite you if the person misrepresents or miscredits the source and excuses it by saying that this is the way he got it from you" (personal communication, July 16, 2011). I have been willing, on occasion, to e-mail a few content slides but not pictures or drawings.

PowerPoint Development as Rehearsal

Time spent preparing, re-editing, or refining a PowerPoint is not wasted time. I consider it rehearsal time. More than once I have discovered ideas that work in my head are ineffective in PowerPoint format.

Even if I have used a particular PowerPoint presentation before, I need to make sure it communicates effectively to the current audience.

Be Sensitive

Diversity is a significant reality that needs to be considered in every presentation. The presenter must be diversity sensitive in selecting images to include in PowerPoint. In a presentation to funeral directors on dysfunctioning families, I deliberately used African American, Korean, Chinese, and Hispanic images, and balanced the number of images of women, older and younger, and included images of gay and lesbian persons. After the first session, a participant suggested, "You might want to take a closer look at your PowerPoint." I asked why. He lowered his voice and said, "All your images of African Americans depicted negative behaviors."

I groaned and returned to my hotel room and carefully evaluated the slides. Diversity is in the eye of the beholder. Knowing one person had been concerned, I reworked the PowerPoint. In the repeat presentation, more than half of the audience was African American. I was glad for the participant's comment. If I had presented the original PowerPoint I could have lost my audience long before image 20.

Remember: Participants have evaluation forms in their hands. You want the program planner to read, "Have this speaker back."

Finding Valuable Photographs

Borrowable photographs are a few clicks away in resources such as Google Images. Online photographic archives and sources are constantly expanding. WhiteHouse.gov offers pictures or sketches of the presidents and first ladies. Moreover, basic computer programs can enhance images.

Enlist Friends to Critique PowerPoints

Do your friends who read widely know of your interest in being more diverse in your PowerPoints and presentations? If so, as a person of color, they may offer insights from their perspective. Issues of ethnicity, family practices, or religious beliefs would also benefit from scrutiny. Friends may start you in the direction Gregory DeBourgh calls "a good steer."

For one presentation, I borrowed insights on grief from Judaism. Before the presentation, I reviewed those slides with two Jewish colleagues. Viewing a pivotal slide, one asked, "Where did you get that? I have never heard of that!" I pointed to the citation and my friend said, "I am going to check into that."

Second, a colleague may place a particular fact in context or challenge a perception of misuse. When I wrote and lectured about the grief of Albert Einstein, my limited understanding of science was a barrier. A colleague I consulted found her appreciation for Einstein as a grieving human stretched by our conversation. "Wow," she smiled, "that's a different side of Albert Einstein!"

Research Grievers in Your Local Community

Grievers need stories of others who have faced, survived, even thrived in circumstances similar to the grief they are navigating. Paradoxically, the wilderness of another griever may become, through narrative, an oasis of insight and inspiration. While writing this book, I was invited to speak on Bess Truman to a women's group in Kansas City where Mrs. Truman is legendary. What could I say that individuals in the audience did not know? Because I had researched Mrs. Truman's grief grid, I presented highlights of her life through the prism of her accumulated grief. Thus, the audience gained an enhanced awareness of her stress during the 1944 and 1948 campaigns when she feared that the press or her husband's political opponents would expose her father's suicide. Sometimes one can find borrowable stories close to home.

Revisit Your Stories

To effectively borrow grief narratives, the clinician revisits the stories. In the repeated use of the story, details may have been eliminated, compressed, or become threadbare. I have often talked about Eleanor Roosevelt packing the family possessions and moving out of the White House in 7 days—despite the Trumans' insistence she take her time. In my repeated telling, however, I overlooked an amazing narrative slice.

Eleanor, while packing her husband's possessions, found a small painting of FDR by Elizabeth Shoumatoff, the same artist who was painting Franklin's image at the time of his stroke; Lucy Mercer Rutherfurd had commissioned the painting. Eleanor realized, that at some point, Rutherfurd had given Franklin the painting. Although a bittersweet discovery, Eleanor instructed an aide to send the painting to Rutherfurd. That may be a lesson some griever needs to know and borrow.

Conclusion

I find meaning in a scene in *The Godfather*, where Marlon Brando, as the grief-stricken Mafia godfather Don Corleone whose son has been shot to death in an ambush at a tollbooth, walks into the embalming room at the funeral home. Weeping as he views his son's corpse, he moans, "Look what they have done to my boy! I don't want his mother to see him *like this*." He instructs the undertaker, "I want you to use *all* your powers" to restore him.

That should be a presenter's standard: To use all our powers to ensure that a borrowed narrative is not simply a string of words and images but a creative accumulation of particular words, punctuated by passion, timing, and detail.

A Story for the Road

Too many individuals cannot own their grief. That 29th day of August 1942, as the Royal Family crowded into the chapel at Windsor Palace for the Duke of Kent's funeral, many eyes darted toward King George VI. He later acknowledged having attended many funerals in that sacred setting and admitted that "none have moved me in the same way" (Aronson, 1993, p. 91). That day in that place King George VI, at rituals for his brother, did not have the luxury of crying. No British king had ever been seen weeping, at least in public (Swift, 2004) and George would not rupture that long tradition. Nor could he look to fellow mourners for condolence. "I did not dare to look at any of them," he later confessed, "for fear of breaking down" (Swift, 2004, p. 91). In fact, instructions had come down from Mary, the aged queen dowager, reminding the family of the "imperatives of duty" (Swift, 2004, p. 91), and tradition to preserve the image of monarchy. Her admonition reduced to two words: Buck up! I wonder if George VI ever found a moment to express his grief of losing his younger brother.

8

Borrowing for Loss of Animal Companions

Princess Kitty's death broke my heart. I don't how long it takes to fix a broken heart.

Karen Payne, grieving pet owner (as cited in Martin, 1996, p. 8B)

With great love comes great grief. If love weren't so strong, the intense grief and sorrow at the time of the animal companion's death wouldn't be so wrenching.

Betty Carmack (2003, p. 5)

Lyndon Baines Johnson, president of the United States (1963–1969), loved dogs. He wanted Yuki in the family portrait at Luci Johnson's White House wedding, but Lady Bird vetoed his decision: "That dog is *not* going to be in the wedding picture!" (Rowan & Janis, 2009, p. 119). Johnson kept the cremated remains of one dog, LBJ, on top of the refrigerator until the cook threatened to stop preparing meals in that kitchen. Johnson bonded with his two beagles, Him and Her. In 1964, a storm of protest from animal lovers erupted after a photo appeared in newspapers of Johnson holding up Him by the ears. In November 1964, Her died after swallowing a stone; Him died in June 1966, after being struck by a car while chasing a squirrel in the White House driveway. Days after the death, J. Edgar Hoover, head of the Federal Bureau of Investigation, arrived at the White House with a "replacement" beagle which Johnson promptly named J. Edgar.

In a society that actively discourages publically expressed grief for pets and rituals to honor the relationship, to many, the reasonable response seems to be to "replace" the deceased animal companion. Halpern-Lewis (1996) recalls,

> What works for some, does not for others. Despite the advice of family and friends to get another dog right away, I recognize a need in me to truly grieve Colleena before I can offer love to another. For a moment, I still hear Colleena's purposeful gait in the silence, and her wet nose against my cheek when I wake in the morning. (1996, p. 1)

Millan (2008), an animal trainer, calls immediate replacement unhealthy. "To me, this is totally against the order of Mother Nature, no living thing is instantly replaceable" (p. 277). Millan laments parents who rush out to buy a new puppy after a child's dog dies. He cautions, "you bring a dog—adult or puppy—into a household that is heavy with the weight of mourning, you are bringing that dog into a toxic situation" (p. 278). Replacement, for some, is a bypass to avoid the emotional demands of grief. On the other hand, J. Johnson writes,

> Some people have great comfort in getting another dog right away. We realized our Old English Sheepdog wasn't going to be with us much longer so we got a "back-up" puppy, of the opposite sex. Bailey gave Windsor new life. We introduced them gradually but would not have needed to. It was instant love and when Windsor did die, we had the tremendous comfort from a wet nose that was also grieving. (Personal communication, August 1, 2011)

The Prevalence of Animal Death

Currently, some 72.9% of American households have pets (American Pet Products Association, n.d.). Packman, Carmack, and Romen (in press), in a large study of owners and continuing bonds with pets ($N = 3705$), found 96.7% "almost always" considered their pet a family member. Bill Hoy, a respected thanatologist, wrote after his dog Pirate died, "She wasn't like a member of the family; she *was* a member of the family" (2010, p. 1). Identification of the animal as a family member may be the barrier to respectful condolence by some—especially those who have never had, let alone lost, an animal companion.

Some individuals have more emotionally intimate and meaningful relationships with animal companions than with spouses, partners, children, or friends. Halpern-Lewis (1996) notes, "The ties that attach people to their pets are often extremely strong, based on unfailing loyalty and a genuine need to be needed. How many relationships are that pure and unselfish" (p. 1). Because of the emotional investment in caring for a pet, especially for those living alone or whose adult children live some distance, the daily presence of the pet strengthens the "bandwidth" of the bond. Not surprisingly, many have higher expectations on veterinarians for "miracles" to restore or prolong an animal's life (Parker, 2005, p. 1B). More people are buying medical insurance for their pets.

Recognition of Grief Following Animal Loss

Grief following the death of an animal companion is increasingly recognized by clinicians (Carmack, 2003; Donohue, 2005; Keenan, 2008; Ross & Baron-Sorenson, 2007) because, as Titcombe (2001) observes, "We are beginning to acknowledge the strength of the bond between people and their pets, and the pain endured when that bond is severed" (p. 40). Yet the grief for animals may be discounted, ridiculed, or ignored by family members, friends, and coworkers—often the individuals the griever expected to offer comfort or, at least, sensitively acknowledge the loss. Because pet loss remains socially disenfranchised (Doka, 1989) both owners and clinicians need borrowed narratives for navigating this grief. Clinicians who have never had a pet or had a pet die will have difficulty fully receiving narratives of a beloved animal companion's loss. Thus, exposure to and reflection upon borrowed narratives of grief following the death of companion animals may stretch the clinician's awareness of pet-related grief issues.

Millan (2008) suggests that death is a reality humans "share with elephants, with ants, with horses, with whales, with fleas, and of course, with dogs." Simply, "When it comes to the end of life, we are all in the same boat" (p. 273). Chris Raymond, editor of *The Director*, published by the National Funeral Directors Association, challenged the disenfranchisement: "By volume, I shed more tears following the death of Pops then I did following the death of some people I have loved and lost" (2005, p. 6). In the assessment of Halpern-Lewis (1996), we have a clear and simple explanation of this unique grief journey, "the caliber of the relationship and the meaning one has in his/her life ... whether they be made of flesh or fur" (p. 1). Pet loss, observed Jean Haley "makes [owners] come to terms with their own mortality and realize that nothing is forever" (1997, p. C-9). Catherine Johnson raises a fascinating point:

> I am wondering if there is a "safety" aspect for the griever expressing grief over the death of an animal because it is not as "scary" as delving into the grief morass when a parent or spouse dies—a morass they fear they will never be able to climb out of. (Personal communication, August 1, 2011)

Titcombe (2001) expands on this theme:

> In some ways, I believe the loss of an animal can be even more difficult than the loss of a person. Pets supply us with unconditional love and acceptance, they are integral to our daily lives, with us through good times and bad, and depend on us for everything, even to make the decision when to end their lives. It is only natural to mourn the loss of such a trusting and faithful companion. (p. 40)

Grievers who have had other losses may be ambushed by the intensity of loss following an animal companion's death, especially if the animal was critical in adjusting to a previous loss. Wallie Freeburgh eulogized Trixie, his dog, as the one who "helped me get through a traumatic time in my life, because my wife had just left me. ... Trixie related to me like another human being" (as cited in Harlow, 2003, p. B4). Perhaps, Trixie was the last "linking object" to his ex-wife or to a period of his life. J. Johnson recalled that a teen in a support group said, "I cried more when my dad's dog died than when my dad died—she was my closest link to my memories of him" (personal communication, August 1, 2011).

Ways an Individual Can "Lose" a Companion Animal

Although death is the focus in this chapter, individuals can "lose" a pet in other ways. I remember the day my paternal grandfather sent the visiting grandchildren to fish on a neighboring farm. What was wrong with the pond by the barn where we always fished? Hours later when we returned from fishing the neighbor's pond, we found the barn empty. Granddad had sold his horses! Although they were not my horses, I no longer had access to horses and I grieved for that change.

Revisiting that day was triggered by reading Haag's (2011) account of her relationship with John Kennedy, Jr. After his baby brother Patrick died, a grieving president-father arrived with a puppy, Shannon, as if the pup would distract the children from the grief. John told Haag that when he was a toddler, at times, his mother, did not know whether to scold him or the dog for messes or for sweets disappearing from the table.

> He laughed when he told the story. But his mood darkened when he told
> of another Shannon, the one he loved best, the one who was irascible.
> He had been away for part of the summer, and on his return, he found
> that his mother had given the dog away. "I didn't even get to say good-
> bye" he said sadly. (2011, p. xvii)

This narrative tidbit of a loss John experienced a quarter century earlier, deeply moved Haag. Its inclusion in her memoir moved me.

Moving Away

Given the mobility of Americans, animals may be unable to accompany the owner in a career transition. While writing this chapter I received an e-mail from a friend:

> Cute Beautiful Male Hyacinth Macaw parrot is ready for sale to any
> caring and loving home where he will be spoiled with all his needs and
> passions. He is very playful, registered, well tamed, good health, has all
> of his papers, current vaccinations. … since I am leaving the country
> and have no one to take good care of him, I decided to sell him.

Whether a move is across the nation or the world, individuals have to consider how the pet will adjust. What is best for the animal? In late 2000, the Clintons, preparing to leave the White House, decided their dog Buddy would go to their new home in New York, but Socks, the cat, would be given to Betty Currie, President Clinton's secretary (K. Jones, 2009).

For some older adults, moving into a retirement community or assisted living with restrictions on pets forces the decision. The loss of daily contact with pets may complicate adjustment to a new living environment, especially if the individual believes the decision was forced or made under pressure, perhaps following the death of a spouse.

Losing the Animal Through a Divorce or the Ending of a Relationship

Given that animal companions are de facto children in some relationships, the custody of the pet may be litigated and subsequently complicate any settlement. To some divorcees, the loss of a pet compounds the grief over the loss of the marriage.

Having an Animal Stolen

When an animal is stolen, it is an ambiguous loss because of uncertainty about what happened to the animal. Has the animal been harmed, sold, or mistreated? Killed? Many are anxious: Is my animal being cared for or receiving care like I provided? Lord, Wittum, Ferketich, Funk, and Rajala-Schultz (2007) note that owners are far less likely to get their dogs back if they believe the dog has been stolen.

Watching the Animal Lose Capacities or "Getting Old"

One troubling aspect of a relationship with a pet is the inevitable changes of aging, which are heightened in some breeds. Katz (2011) captures this reality:

> Everyone has to make their own decisions, but I do not believe dogs were put on earth to suffer, or to live impaired lives in which they cannot function as dogs—moving freely, eliminating outside, and being free of pain.
>
> When my Lab Stanley was stricken with heart disease he could barely walk to his food bowl, could no longer take a single step toward

his beloved red and blue balls, and gasped for almost every breath. I saw
he could no longer live the life of a healthy dog. . . . (pp. 29–30)

One grieves for what the animal can no longer do; some owners
grieve while watching beloved pets attempt the familiar. Conflict may
arise when one family member is in denial, or not in daily contact
with the animal, or if that individual has not been "friendly" to the
animal or has been quick to point out negative behaviors.

In recent years, decisions have become more complicated due to
the advances in veterinary science and owners' increased expectations.
Some care decisions can be financially and emotionally challenging.
Haley (1994) observed: "Human beings who acquire a companion dog
set themselves up for a certain spell of suffering if they truly intend to
keep the dog for life and not just for Christmas. Even if no problems
occur, the dog will die before his or her person" (p. C-5).

Serial Animal Loss

Pet enthusiasts have, over the years, lost several companion animals.
Carmack (2003) names the dogs no longer present in her home:
Rocky, Puccini, and Sunshine. Congalton (2000) addresses this issue
in *Three Cats, Two Dogs: One Journey Through Multiple Pet Loss.* This
latest death may reboot grief from previous losses, particularly those
that were un- or underacknowledged. By creating a grief grid to assess
previous pet losses, the clinician and client may better appreciate
the accumulative grief for companion animals. Unfortunately, some
decide not to have another pet to avoid another grief experience.

Animal Runs Away

Sometimes an animal disappears without explanation. The owner
may search vigorously, posting signs, offering rewards, walking or
driving slowly through neighborhoods calling for the animal. How
long before accepting, to the degree it can be accepted, that one will
not hear scratching at the door or a familiar bark again? This can
be a dual-loss when animals are lost in fires, hurricanes, tornadoes,
and floods.

Having to Euthanize the Animal

The relationship with a companion animal is elevated by euthanasia, which for many owners is fraught with ambiguity and anticipatory grief, particularly if they do not have a ritual to honor the pet's life. Carmack comments:

> This is the absolutely hardest thing that pet parents do and there is nothing comparable to that in their life so many have never been prepared to do such a huge thing. This is such an important aspect of end of life decision-making and has such potential for wrenching guilt and self-doubts afterwards. Those self-doubts and second guessing can keep one in grief that is more intense and longer. (Personal communication, August 1, 2011)

Each year some 7 million animals are euthanized (Peters, 2009). Anticipatory grief is complicated by the question: Am I doing the right thing? Whose best interests are at work here? Long after the decision, the thought may linger, "*Did* I do the right thing?" A grieving client may seek a second opinion: "Do *you* think that I did the right thing?" Jean Haley (1994) notes that some questions hang out in the heart of the grieving owner. "A melancholic seed lies dormant in those of us owned by dogs: What will it be like when this good old friend goes to sleep forever? You don't want to think about it at all. But you do. The longer the dog ages, the more insistently the question nags" (p. C5).

Admittedly, treatment options for pets can be prohibitive—an issue that troubles individuals on fixed incomes, especially if the treatment will not significantly enhance the pet's life. Coming to the decision may be contentious with spouses or family members. M. Thomas (1998) asks: "But where do you draw the line? Do you spend $1,000 to save a geriatric cat? Sorry, Chester, it's been swell, but I can't afford to invest that much money if you're only going to be around for another year at most. The bottom line is, you are a cat, not one of us" (p. 26).

Grief may be complicated if the decision is not mutually agreed upon. Some conclude, afterward, that they let the animal down by not pursuing aggressive treatments or resisting suggestions to euthanize. Others believe that delaying the decision increased the pet's suffering.

Self-disenfranchisement occurs when an owner denies or hides feelings, particularly in front of the veterinarian, with whom she or he may have a long relationship. Titcombe (2001), a veterinarian, notes, "Many clients apologize to me for their tears, as they say their final good-byes to their animal companions. Why is it that we, as a society, don't accept grief over the loss of a pet the way we do over the loss of a human companion?" (p. 40).

John Altevogt (1998) describes his stress:

> I took him to the vet to be euthanized, wrestling over whether to stay with him. I reasoned that he would get upset if he sensed that I was leaving. But, really, I didn't want to lose it in front of the vet or his staff, so I left. But I look back and see how easy it was for me to take a beloved friend to have him killed, and I wonder whether I was really interested in Bobo's well-being or my own. (p. B-7)

Clinicians would do well to explore when the client's uses *killed*.

Unmarried or unpartnered adults have to be *the* decider. One unmarried woman e-mailed me:

> Last week I had to put my 10½ year old cat down. It was the hardest thing that I ever did. … Am I making too big of a deal concerning this? I talked to a friend about this today and she said I needed to stop whining about this and get over it. "Death happens."

Animals Other Than Dogs and Cats

Grief following the death of an animal companion is subject to misinterpretation, misunderstanding, and even ridicule. Certainly, it is not uncommon for a griever to hear, "*It* [the animal] was *only* a dog!" (The use of *it* devalues the pet and the grief.) Some resist fully enfranchising grief for other pets, particularly exotic animals. E. Mitchell (2005) retorts, "Our level of mourning isn't determined by species but by genuine feelings. The dictionary defines a pet as 'an object of affection,' 'particularly cherished or indulged' and 'being a favorite'" (p. F2). Humans have an incredible ability to have ferrets, rabbits, gerbils, and snakes as pets. So, why does species matter? Eileen Mitchell wrote in the *San Francisco Chronicle* about the death of her bird:

I wanted to cry but couldn't muster the tears. I wanted to call someone but didn't want to disturb anyone. After all, it wasn't as if a human had died. A bird's death wasn't worth inflicting on anyone that shrill, heart-gripping ring of a wee-hours phone call. (2005, p. F2)

Mitchell describes returning to work, a hurdle for many pet grievers.

The next day I returned to work, puffy-faced and swollen-eyed. Word had spread that my pet bird had died, and my co-workers were kind and sympathetic. Although sad, I had to admit I felt a tad foolish. This was, after all, not a human being I was mourning but "just" a bird. (p. F2)

Some readers, no doubt, scoffed over breakfast, "She's carrying on about a *bird*! Lady, get a life!" Other readers, however, well familiar with pet loss, were moved by her story. This borrowed narrative in a newspaper may have been placed in escrow for future use and caused some readers to be far more sensitive.

Borrowed Narratives From Presidents

If only Mitchell had known of diary entries by Rutherford B. Hayes, U.S. president, 1877–1881, who wrote:

Our mocking-bird, a fine singer, died last night. We had him in Columbus in 1876 and took him to Washington where he sang in the White House during our four years there, and returned with us in March, 1881, and sang his best in rivalry with the uncaged songsters of Spiegel Grove. (August 27, 1881)

When America was primarily an agrarian culture, individuals had different relationships with animals, particularly those that were involved in farm production or were raised for eventual sale or slaughter. Hayes grieved deeply following the death of Grim, his greyhound, who was hit by a train after the family returned home to Ohio. "The death of Grim has made us all mourn. He was a great ornament to our home, and comfort to all of us." Grim was buried in the family cemetery near Hayes's two favorite horses, Old Whitey and Old Ned. Hayes concluded his letter, "Some natural tears have been shed over him, and you will be sad as your mother was and is" (Rutherford B.

Hayes to Fanny, March 5, 1885, Diary, IV, pp. 196–197). After newspapers published the story of Grim's death, the Hayes' family received hundreds of condolence letters.

Theodore Roosevelt grieved after his horse, Rain-in-the-Face, drowned in the confusion of disembarking in Cuba during the Spanish American War. Admittedly, he secured another horse for his legendary charge with the Rough Riders up San Juan Hill but it was not Rain-in-the-Face (Scott Miller, 2011).

Pets and Estate Planning

Increasingly, what will happen to pets is a consideration in estate planning (Hirschfeld, 2008, 2010). Leona Helmsley, hotel magnate and entrepreneur, received significant postmortem publicity—and criticism—for leaving Trouble, her Maltese, some $12 million ("Helmsley Has Last Word," 2007, p. A1). Television personality Bob Barker, a longtime animal rights activist, has structured the major part of his estate not only to care for his animal companions following his death, but to endow programs in animal legal rights at eight of the nation's leading law schools and for a center for animal rights at his alma mater, Drury University (Barker & Diehl, 2009; Keck, 2007).

Public Identification With Well-Known Animals

John Grogan achieved some notoriety for his stories, newspaper columns, and books (and eventually for the movie) about his relationship with Marley, a rambunctious Labrador retriever. Grogan (2005) received more than eight hundred responses to his column on the death of Marley.

Ten days before George and Laura Bush were to return to private life, their cat India died in the White House. (The public better knew their Scottish terriers, Barney and Miss Beasley.) The Bushes had India since their twin daughters were age 9. Sally McDonough, Laura Bush's spokeswoman, reported that the First Family is "deeply saddened" since "India was a beloved member of the Bush family for two decades. She will be greatly missed" (Gillman, 2009).

Responses to the deaths of pets can become political fodder. In 1997, Bill Clinton named a puppy "Buddy" for his great-uncle who died earlier that year. Buddy was struck and killed by a car near the Clinton's residence in Chappaqua, New York. One letter to the editor of *The Kansas City Star* took issue with a radio commentator's joking about Buddy's death. Lena Kalicak wrote, "Family members and pets are too precious to us all to be made fun of" (2002, p. B6). Larry Roth branded radio hosts' comments "a condemnation of anyone who has lost a pet through an accident" (2002, p. B6).

An incredible outpouring of public grief occurred when Barbaro, the winner of 2006 Kentucky Derby, had to be euthanized following injuries in the Preakness weeks later. Gretchen and Roy Jackson, Barbaro's owners, after exhausting treatment options, confessed, "You could go on forever. But we didn't want to see him on life support. We wanted to be sure he would have a quality life, too" (Curry & Denk, 2007). Given the widespread television and cable coverage of sporting events—and replays of major sporting events—this death touched many lives.

Issues for Children Following Pet Loss

For some children, the loss of a pet is the first exposure to dying and death. Many adults recall having a "funeral" for a beloved cat, dog, goldfish, turtle, or bird. Corr (2003–2004) points out that pets, as friends, playmates, and sources of unconditional love, help children learn responsibilities for caring for another living creature. Thus, children look to parents, teachers, or other adults for recognizing their grieving and for permission to feel their grief. That may be facilitated by the adult saying, "I remember when my dog died" and sharing details of the experience. Many adults seek to "rescue" children from the grief. Grogan (2005) recalls his experience as a father with young children:

> Seeing them grieving—their first up-close experience with death—deeply affected me. Yet, it was only a dog, and dogs come and go in the course of a human life, sometimes simply because they become an inconvenience. It was only a dog, and yet every time I tried to talk to [my children] about Marley, tears welled in my eyes. (p. 274)

Grogan explained to his children (and, indirectly, to his readers) that is was okay to cry and "that owning a dog always ended with this sadness because dogs just don't live as long as people do" (p. 274).

Not surprisingly, an adult's response to an animal's death may link to the death of a childhood pet, especially if that grief was disenfranchised. Patti Davis (2004) recalls that her father, Ronald Reagan, kindly responded to the death of her goldfish.

> He and I scooped it out of the aquarium and gave it a funeral. My father tied sticks together to form a cross, which he placed on the tiny grave; he gave my fish a brief eulogy and described to me the clear blue waters it would be swimming in up to heaven. I could see the water—blue as the sky, endless, and teeming with other fish, none of whom would eat one another. I became so enchanted with this vision that I felt sorry for my other fish, condemned to the small, unnatural environment of the aquarium, with its colored rocks and gray plastic castle. (p. 8)

Ronald Reagan was stunned by Patti's conclusion, "Maybe we should kill the others!" Reagan turned the experience into a "teaching moment," explaining that "in God's time, the others would go too" (p. 8). As her father was dying, Davis revisited this narrative slice:

> I go back to childhood to retrieve the stories that once made me feel better, hoping they still have the same effect. I became less certain as I got older. When did I stop imagining a green-and-blue paradise on the other side? When did fear throw in shadow? I need to return to the stories in order to let my father go. (p. 8)

Animal Companions and the Afterlife

Questions about the afterlife and pets concern many owners. Wise clergy and clinicians show hospitality to pet owners' concerns for animals' future. A griever may raise the issue with a clinician because she is reluctant to seek counsel from a religious authority. Increasingly, as animals have been recognized as family, questions have grown about heaven and reunion with pets. If sense making (Currier, Holland, & Neimeyer, 2010) and storytelling (Humphrey, 2009) are important following human death, pet loss presents challenges to sense making to be navigated. Carmack (2003) urges grievers to remember, tell, and share stories because your story permissions another's. Susan Chernak McElroy notes: "Settle down gently and let these finely told stories scurry through your head and take up lodging in the inner chambers of your heart, where all true learning and healing must come home to rest" (2003, p. xv).

The Christian Century reported in 2006 that 43% of Americans believe pets go to heaven; 93% go even if owners do not ("Faithful Fido," 2006). Many grievers and clinicians have found the "children's" books by Cynthia Rylant, *Dog Heaven* (1995) and *Cat Heaven* (1997), meaningful. Rylant closes *Dog Heaven* with reassuring words: "Dogs in Dog Heaven may stay as long as they like and this can mean forever. They will be there when old friends show up. They will be there at the door" (p. 26). Carmack (2003), from extensive clinical experience addressing religious concerns following animal companion loss, notes, "For many, reconstructing their world means holding on to the belief that they will be reunited with their beloved animal companion. Looking forward to being together again is a hope that gives meaning to life" (p. 117).

Buddemeyer-Porter, author of *Will I See Fido in Heaven?* insists, "Until they [grievers] actually believe their pets are in heaven, they can't have any comfort" (as cited in Briggs, 2001, p. G2). Some clinicians may acknowledge that while the afterlife is an unknown to them or belief in an afterlife is alien, the issue is significant for many grieving the death of a companion animal.

In 2003, two religious leaders faced off on the issue in *The Kansas City Star.* Father Patrick Rush, then Vicar General of the Roman Catholic Diocese of Kansas City, dismissed the concerns, "I believe that we will all be so overwhelmed with God's love that we won't relate to our now-favorite puppy, or python or parakeet as a special pet" (Rush, 2003, p. H-1). The Reverend Duke Tuffy, the leader of a large community of faith in Kansas City, countered Rush's conclusion: "All life forms are God's sacred creations. ... What is heaven without puppies, kittens or the magical melody of a songbird? So rather than hoping our pets will be in heaven, perhaps we should be hoping we will" (Tuffy, 2003, p. H-1).

Mike Thomas, a columnist for *The Orlando Sentinel*, received an outpouring of letters and e-mails after writing a column on the death of his beloved cat, Chester. "It seems that, indeed, there is a cat heaven. A couple hundred readers told me so after I wrote about our dearly departed Chester a week ago." Thomas quoted from Paulette Carollo's letter: "I will be seriously mad if I get to heaven and am not joined by all my furry children. Then it wouldn't be heaven. It would be assisted living. And that would be hell for me." Constance Clover contends, "If God gives us pets to love and companionship while we are on earth, why would he not extend that benefit to us in the hereafter?" (Thomas, 2004, p. B-1).

Thomas sought out the opinion of two religious leaders. Billy Graham responded: "God will provide us with everything we need to be happy in heaven—and if animals are necessary to make us completely happy there, then you can be confident that he will arrange for them to be with us" (as cited in Thomas, 2004, p. B-1).

The Reverend Jim Henry, a key leader in the Southern Baptist Convention, concedes, "There is nothing in the Bible to tell us" that owners will be reunited with beloved pets. However, "since God is a loving Father, it could just be another of the serendipitous for us on the other side!" (as cited in Thomas, 2004, p. B-1). Niki Benrikis Shanahan, author of *There Is Eternal Life for Animals*, asserts, "All of the animals will go to heaven. They are sinless. Every creature that was created was created for eternity" (as cited in Briggs, 2001, p. G2).

Whether one believes in eternal life for themselves or their pets, the death of a companion animal has spiritual implications. Two friends who take their faith quite seriously announced the death of their cocker spaniel in an e-mail: "If you are reading this I pray you're not thinking, 'she was just a dog,' for our Jenni was much more to us. Please remember us as we grieve." From *The New Zealand Prayer Book* I borrow a prayer that some grievers find valuable. "When all we are and everything we do are called into question, grant us dignity and direction, grant us patience" (Anglican Church of Aotearoa, New Zealand and Polynesia, 1989, p. 583).

The Timing of a Pet's Death

Timing is a critical factor in grief of death of a companion animal. Any loss juxtaposes with other life-changing or life-challenging events. George H. W. Bush, U.S. president 1989–1993, was defeated for reelection in November 1992. Two weeks later, his mother, Dorothy Prescott Bush, died. In January 1993, after George and Barbara Bush moved to Houston, Barbara had concerns about how her husband would handle the transition. She recalls: "April 6—What a year it has been. Today we are sick at heart. Our gallant, funny, awkward Ranger Boy died. He had to be put down. He was riddled with cancer. ... George didn't need this now" (B. Bush, 2003, p. 13). Later, in writing *Reflections: Life after the White House*, Barbara Bush revisited that sad day.

> I felt so sorry for George. He loved Ranger and got such pleasure walking, playing, and laughing with and at him. He and Don Rhodes, our dear friend who has been in our lives for almost forty years ... truly mourned Ranger's death. George had been so brave about losing the election and then the death of his wonderful mother, who died shortly afterward. But he couldn't hide his feelings about Ranger. I believe Ranger's death allowed him to vent his accumulated grief over the three losses. (Bush, 2003, p. 14)

Bush, as a mother who had a 4-year old daughter die, was sensitive how some readers might take her words. "I am not in any way comparing Ranger's death to that of George's mother, but just saying that this was the straw that broke the camel's back" (B. Bush, 2003, p. 14). Bush commented to friends, "I think he let Ranger be sort of the tunnel of mourning. You can't cry, if you're a man, over an election. You can't cry over your mother, I guess. But Ranger's death devastated George" (as cited in Kilian, 2002, p. 204).

How might that narrative slice be used meaningfully with a griever?

A Link to Our Own Grief and Mortality

Insight from a borrowed narrative may be a door opener for conversation with a client. On February 10, 1864, a disgruntled former employee set fire to the White House stables. After the fire alarm sounded, Abraham Lincoln bounded from bed and raced across the yard, leaping over a fence, and tried unsuccessfully to break open the stable doors to rescue the horses and ponies. Lincoln had to be restrained by soldiers. Finally, an officer led Lincoln back into the

White House. The pony of Willie, Lincoln's deceased son, died in that fire as well as a pony belonging to his surviving son, Tad. The president was observed weeping afterward at a window in the East Room (R. L. Miller, 2008, p. 339). Tad Lincoln threw himself on the floor and "could not be comforted." John Hay remarked that it was one of the few times as a presidential aide he heard the president speak directly of Willie in comforting Tad (Stimmel, 1928, pp. 37–39).

What Pet Death Can Teach Us

Life changed unexpectedly for Betty Carmack, a professor of nursing emeritus at the University of San Francisco and pet-grief specialist, while on vacation in July 1978. Before heading home, Betty, Rocky— her 10-year-old-dachshund—and a friend, Bill, were enjoying a leisurely rafting ride on the Trinity River. The current pulled their raft along a thicket of low branches, which knocked them into the water. Carmack struggled as Bill kept her afloat and she kept Rocky afloat.

> At some point in the struggle, I simply could not physically hold on to Rocky and continue to hold on to branches or try to swim. … I do remember letting go of his collar and seeing him float down the river with his little head above the water. This is my last image of him. I never saw him again, and I never learned what happened to him, but I think that most likely he drowned. (Carmack, 2003, p. 2)

Carmack reflects, "Rocky's loss taught me how deeply we grieve for our loved animals, the intensity of pain, the length of time it can last, and how one's life can be forever changed" (p. 3). Carmack ran ads in the local newspaper and posted a reward. Through that experience she learned "grief for a companion animal matters" and she had to grieve in a world "that reminds us repeatedly that grief for an animal doesn't count as much as grief for a person" (p. 3). The first anniversary and subsequent anniversaries evoked great sorrow for her. Yet, "Within the next three years, I had started my pet loss counseling practice, seeing clients individually as well as in pet loss support groups" (p. 3). Standing on the muddy banks of the Trinity River, Carmack could not have imagined that good would come out of this loss. Over the years, others borrowed her stories to find their own story. Years later, Carmack collected her stories and the stories of many others and organized them into *Grieving the Death of a Pet*, a resource many grievers have found valuable.

Conclusion

How will grievers feel actively and adequately permissioned? Comfort and support may come packaged in a borrowed narrative. Carmack (2003) suggests we integrate our grief through rituals and memorials. It is not a ritual for an animal but rather a ritual for a *particular* animal. This gives the pet parent an opportunity to be creative and sensitive. "Rituals have the ability to focus, center, and call us and convert something painful into something less painful" so that planning and participating "in a memorial can be a transformative step" (Carmack, 2003, p. 99). Clinicians should ask: "How have you memorialized your pet? Did you have a formal ritual?" If not, the clinician may identify resources that can assist the client in planning a ritual or memorialization. Katz (2011) comments, "Perhaps it is time for this particular form of grief to come out of the closet and into the open" (p. xxii). That permissioning can be accomplished, with your help, one client at a time.

A Concluding Narrative

An animal's death may be linked to a previous death or significant loss. Elliott Roosevelt revealed that his mother had been dry-eyed at the funeral rituals for Franklin D. Roosevelt in April 1945. However, he witnessed a different response when Fala, the president's beloved Scottish terrier, died in April 1952, 7 years after FDR. Although clearly FDR's dog, and although initially given to Daisy Suckley (FDR's cousin), Eleanor requested that Fala be returned to her. Elliott, who accompanied his mother to FDR's grave for Fala's internment, recalled, "She had not wept at Father's burial, but the tears came this day. I had never seen her openly give way to grief before. … In lamenting the end of the Scottie, Mother wept for his master" (as cited in Lash, 1984, p. 382).

This narrative of Eleanor Roosevelt illustrates a point well made by Constance Mucha: "You will and must grieve. Your choice is when and how" (2006, p. 18).

PART II
A Sample of Borrowed Narratives

9

A GRIEVER NAMED NELSON

I do not have words to express the sorrow, or the loss I felt. It left a hole in my heart that can never be filled.

Nelson Mandela (as cited in Maharaj & Kothrada, 2006, p. 158)

Nelson Mandela, one of the world's most revered elders, is no stranger to grief. Few leaders on the world stage have so frequently navigated this densely populated, persistent "valley of the shadow of death" (Psalm 23:4). How, I wonder, has his grief load not killed him? However, Mandela worried about his elevation to "sainthood" in the minds of many.

One issue that deeply worried me in prison was the false image that I unwittingly projected to the outside world; of being regarded as a saint. I never was one, even on the basis of an earthly definition or a sinner as a saint who keeps trying. (Mandela, 2010, p. 410)

An Early Loss Experience

Born in South Africa in 1918, Mandela first experienced grief when his father, Gadla Henry Mphakanyiswa, died in 1927. Nine-year-old Nelson's belongings were immediately packed, and his mother escorted him to the home of a chieftain who, under tribal tradition, would now rear the boy. In a sense, Mandela lost his father and mother, as well as his home.

While a law student in 1944, Mandela married Evelyn Mase, a nurse; 3 years later, in 1947, their first child Makaziwe was born but failed to thrive. "From the start," Mandela recalled, "we feared the worst" (Mandela, 1994, p. 106). The medical techniques that "save" babies today were but fantasies then, particularly in Third World South Africa. Through long nights as the couple cared for the little one, the mysteriousness of the disease troubled Evelyn. After 9 months, Makaziwe died. Mandela recalls, "Evelyn was distraught, and the only thing that helped temper my own grief was trying to alleviate hers" (p. 107). The death of this child would have a lingering impact on Mandela. David James Smith quotes Mandela's late-life reflections on the loss:

> Way back in the 1940s I lost a nine month baby girl. She had been hospital-ized and had been making good progress when suddenly her condition took a grave turn and she died. I managed to see her during the critical moments when she was struggling desperately to hold within her body the last sparks of life which were flickering away. I have never known whether I was fortu-nate to witness that grievous scene. It haunted me for many days thereafter and *still provokes painful memories right up to the present day* [emphasis added]. (2010, p. 79)

That disclosure was written five decades after the baby's death. Many who have lost a child would nod in agreement when reading Mandela's recollection.

In July 1947, Anton Lembede, 33, Mandela's close personal friend and political ally in the Youth League, died suddenly, which set-back the league's fledging challenge to apartheid. A repressive South African government jailed Mandela for his political activism. During one jail term, Evelyn took their two surviving children and moved out of their home. In March 1958, Evelyn and Nelson divorced after years of escalating conflict over her religion and his political activism. Mandela concedes, "My devotion to the [African National Congress] and to the struggle was unremitting" (2010, p. 206) but a passion Evelyn did not share. "I could not give up my life in the struggle" to end apartheid, "and she could not live with my devotion to something other than herself and the family" (p. 208).

In 1964, Nelson was convicted of crimes against the state and sen-tenced to life in prison. For more than two decades, Mandela survived solitary confinement within the notoriously inhumane South African prison system. In the summer of 1968, the government allowed Nasekeni Fanny, his aged mother, and three other family members to visit. Near the end of their time together, Mandela realized that he would never see his mother again.

Several weeks later, after having worked all day in a limestone quarry, an exhausted Mandela returned to his cell. A prison guard delivered a telegram: Mandela's mother had died (Meredith, 2010). Mandela ruminated over his treatment of her, specifically how little he had done for her financially. He indicted himself for his neglect and questioned his judgment in abandoning his law practice, which would have provided a generous income to care for her, all in order to pursue political activism. Immediately, as the oldest son of a widow under tribal tradition, he requested permission to attend her funeral. The request was denied. He recalls his mental anguish: "For a few days I spent moments in my cell which I never want to remember" (Mandela, 2010, p. 171).

The Arrest of Winnie Mandela

In May 1969, his wife Winnie, a social worker he had married in 1958, was arrested by security police. Mandela noted, "There was nothing I found so agonizing in prison as the thought that Winnie was in prison too" (2010, p. 446). Two months later, on July 13, 1969, Nelson received a one-sentence telegram: Matiba Thembekile "Thembi," Mandela's oldest son, aged 25, the father of two, had died after a motorcycle accident. Mandela juggled overlapping grief. He comments:

> What can one say about such a tragedy? I was already overwrought about my wife, I was still grieving for my mother, and then to hear such news. ... I do not have words to express the sorrow, or the loss I felt. It left a hole in my heart that can never be filled. (1994, pp. 446–447)

In a letter to Irene Buthelezi, Mandela described the darkness he experienced upon learning that his firstborn son had died.

> Suddenly my heart seemed to have stopped beating and the warm blood that had freely flown in my veins for the last 51 years froze into ice. For some time I could neither think nor talk and my strength appeared to be draining out. (2010, p. 174)

Grief and Tribal Tradition

Tribal tradition required Mandela to be with his family to ensure his son's proper burial (just as it had been the tradition for him to supervise the burial of his mother months earlier). Again authorities ignored his request to supervise the arrangements and attend the funeral. Mandela recalled, "My heart bled when I finally realized that I could not be present at the graveside—the one moment in life a parent would never like to miss" (2010, p. 172). He wrote his ex-wife, uncertain that she would receive the letter. "I did my best to comfort her and tell her that I shared her suffering" (p. 447). Mandela grieved for the young boy who had promised in the courtroom at the end of his father's trial, "I will look after the family while you are gone" (p. 447).

Again, fellow prisoner-friends made their way to Mandela's cell to offer condolences. One remembered finding Mandela tightly wrapped in a blanket, as if "to keep his pain inside him" (Maharaj & Kathrada, 2006, p. 159). Mandela wrote his ex-wife and the two siblings of the deceased:

> I write to give you, Kgatho and Maki, my deepest sympathy. I know more than anybody else living today just how devastating this cruel blow must have been to you for Thembi was your first born and the second child you have lost. The blow has been equally grievous to me. In addition to the fact that I had not seen him for at least sixty months, I was neither privileged to give him a wedding ceremony nor to lay him to rest when the final hour had struck. (Maharaj & Kathrada, 2006, p. 160)

Mandela left unsaid his resentment that Thembi had never visited him in prison, although he lived a short boat ride across the water from the Robben Island prison. If his 74-year-old mother had traveled to visit him, what was his son's excuse?

Mandela appealed to his jailers to consider "this request more humanely than you treated a similar application I made barely ten months ago." Mandela later reflected that a "humanitarian" response by the government "would have gone a long way in softening the hard blow and painful misfortune of an imprisoned man losing a mother" (p. 160).

Mandela pointed out that the government had approved applications from other prisoners to attend funerals; thus, the rejection was personal. Mandela penned words of condolence to his younger son Makgatho in late July 1969, again without guarantee that his letter would get past prison censors.

Mandela wrote a third letter to his young daughters, Zeni and Zindzi—a letter they never received—acknowledging his deep regret that neither he nor Winnie had been allowed to attend the funeral. He concluded, "Perhaps one day Mummy and I will be able also to visit the grave" (2010, p. 164). As a father he attempted to "take away" the children's latest grief:

> But now that he is gone, we must forget about the painful fact of his death. Now he sleeps in peace, my darlings, free from troubles, worries, sickness, or need; he can feel neither [feel] pain nor hunger. You must continue your schoolwork, play games and sing songs. (Mandela, 2010, p. 164)

Mandela conceded, "This year has been a bad one indeed for us, but happy days will come when we will be full of joy and laughter." He closed the letter,

> What is even more important is that one day Mummy and I will come back and live happily together with you in one house, sit at the table together, help you with the many problems you will experience as you grow. (Mandela, 2010, p. 164)

Mandela's daughters were adults before that hope was realized. One guard recalls witnessing Mandela's grief following his son's death:

> In his eye I could see the sternness I was to recognize when he struggled to maintain self control. It was a distancing from me and from others, and in some ways his face receded into a fixed expression, tight lines around the mouth. Those lines went deeper the more he worried ... or [the more] angry he became. At that time [when the guard delivered the telegram] he simply said, "Thank you, Mr. Gregory," and walked away. (Meredith, 2010, p. 304)

In 1988, Mandela developed tuberculosis and, after initial treatment, was housed under less stressful conditions. Finally, under pressure from world leaders, he was released from prison on February 11, 1990.

Freedom

Freedom presented new challenges within both of Mandela's families. In 1993, Mandela separated from Winnie; their divorce was finalized in 1996. Ironically, the children thought they would have their father back but discovered they had to share him with the nation. In April 1994, the prisoner of Robben Island was elected president of South Africa.

As he aged, Mandela experienced more losses. Thoko, his daughter-in-law, suicided in 2002 (D. J. Smith, 2010, p. 187). In May 2003, Mandela was devastated when Walter Sisulu, his trusted friend and colleague in the long fight against apartheid, died; later that year Zondi, another daughter-in-law, died. On April 30, 2004, Nelson's first wife, Evelyn Mase Mandela Rakeepile (she had remarried), died. Mandela attended her funeral to support their children.

The Death of Makgatho Mandela and Zenani Mandela

On January 6, 2005, Makgatho, Mandela's son, died from complications of AIDS. In an act of enormous political courage, Mandela called a press conference and acknowledged the cause of death hoping to challenge the stigma then attached to AIDS-related deaths in South Africa.

On June 10, 2010, Mandela's great-granddaughter, Zenani Mandela, died in an automobile crash on her way home from the opening concert for the World Cup. The car in which she was riding was struck by an intoxicated driver. Mandela, 91, planned to attend the World Cup's opening game, the first ever on African soil, but cancelled saying that it would be "inappropriate … to personally attend." He promised that "he would be with the fans in spirit today" (as cited in Frayer, 2010).

Implications for Clinicians

Why is Nelson Mandela's grief narrative important? Given the global awareness of Mandela, his grief resume is both interesting and believable. Krugman (2007) insists that "historical narratives matter" because they offer potential insights for adaptation in our grief. Thus, the narratives of other grievers can be helpful in several ways.

Borrowed Historical Narratives Offer Insights for Reflection

Taylor (2005) contends we seek wisdom in stories as we try to figure out our own unfolding story. This is particularly true for individuals juggling multiple losses who find strength in Mandela's repeated exposure to loss. Your client may conclude, "If Mandela got through his string of losses, maybe I can too."

Mandela in his grief probed the narratives of the experiences of others. In prison he focused on reading biographies. "It is possible," he noted, "that if I had not gone to jail and been able to read and listen to the stories of many people … I might not have learned these things" (Cohen & Battersby, 2009, p. 164) or had such a well-stocked reservoir of narrative to draw upon.

Age Is Too Commonly Disenfranchised

In this culture, condolence seems rationed when the deceased was elderly or ill. Mandela clearly responds: "Death is a frightful disaster no matter what the cause and the age of the person affected" (Mandela, 2010, p. 170). Given that Mandela is over 90, he has had to carry a large number of antecedent losses. That grief, however, was not supported by a strong belief in reunion in an afterlife. "In a sense," Nelson noted, "I felt cheated by Walter [Sisulu]. If there be another life beyond this physical world, I would have loved to be there first so that I could welcome him" (Kathrada, 2004, p. 369).

Honor Friendships Strengthened Working on a Common Cause

In the long fight against apartheid, Mandela invested deeply in friendships and imagining shared visions of a vibrant future for South Africa. Mandela found the death of his colleague of 50 years, Oliver Tambo, troubling. He shared his sorrow with their mutual friend, Ahmed Kathrada, "As much as I respected him as a leader, that is how much I love him as a man. When I looked at him in his coffin, it was as if a part of myself had died" (Mandela, 1994, p. 600). Kathrada declared his admiration for the triumvirate: Mandela, Oliver Tambo, and Walter Sisulu. He grieved for the passing of two legs of that stool.

Kathrada, a fellow prisoner with Mandela, notes that aging had demanded that Mandela "come to terms with the loss of many friends and family members over time" (2004, p. 363). One factor in the death of his friends was the greater "loss to Africa" as models of resistance died. When their mutual friend, Walter Sisulu, died, Mandela confessed, "Xhamela is no more. May he live forever! His absence has carved a void. A part of me is gone" (p. 363).

Loss Impacts Family Narratives and Dynamics,
Particularly With Multiple Marriages

Children of a first marriage, or other marriage or relationship, sometimes require assistance in sorting through grief because issues that led to a divorce of parents may never have been fully processed. The circumstances of a divorce, in itself, can create a grief that needs to be explored with clinicians. Creating or having another family may cut back on time to spend with children or money to spend on children from a previous marriage; this reality can fuel resentment. Moreover, some of these adult children may have issues because they have little or no say in the funeral arrangements. Even divorces and remarriages that happened a long time ago may never have been thoroughly examined (Balaswamy & Richardson, 2001; Rushton, 2007; Smith, 2006). Settling the estate can complicate the grief, particularly if there is a perception of partiality in the distribution of personal effects between children from different marriages.

A Clinician Might Follow the Guidance of Bonanno (2009) to
Explore With Clients, "How Could This Have Been Worse?"

After highlighting Mandela's losses, a clinician might ask, "What would it be like to be unable to attend the funerals of your loved ones? Are there responsibilities that you would not get to fulfill?"

Further exploration in the Mandela narrative offers insights on how to deal with grieving children and stepchildren. Admittedly,

Mandela attended his first wife's funeral—widely covered by the media—to support their children. Increasingly, in this society, individuals face questions about attending memorials for previous spouses and in-laws. How does one decide to attend or not attend, and how does one communicate that?

Mandela Narratives Remind Clinicians That Incarceration Can
Heighten Family Stress and Estrangement, and Complicate Grief

Given the 2.8 million individuals who are incarcerated in U.S. prisons and jails (Bureau of Justice Statistics, 2011), Nelson's appeal for permission to attend the funeral is significant. States and the federal government have varied policies and procedures for permitting prisoners to attend funeral rituals for family members. The reality of Mandela's imprisonment and the futility of his request to attend funerals may be meaningful to a prisoner who is unable to attend or to that prisoner's family members. Moreover, the clinician must consider that some families have more than one member in prison. Mandela was imprisoned for human rights issues. Shame issues might surface if a family member was imprisoned for rape, murder, assault, or theft. Fortunately, today a video or a cyber "attendance" may be arranged.

The Honesty of Mandela's Feelings Might Open Up a Client

Mandela discloses his mental state following his mother's death: "For a few days I spent moments in my cell which I never want to remember" (Mandela, 2010, p. 171). What might your grieving client never want to remember? Cohen and Battersby (2009) point to the need for "interrogating the memory" (p. xvi) in order to diffuse its impact on grief. The client's efforts to block those feelings, to bypass them, or to anesthetize them will complicate the integration of the loss.

Mandela, during a visit to his former cell, reflected that those years had given ample opportunities "to think about one's own life—including the mistakes made and having time to read the biographies of great people was a transformative experience" and taught him "to respect even the most ordinary people" (Cohen & Battersby, 2009, p. 164).

The clinician might initiate a conversation: "I want to share something Nelson Mandela said of his prison experience." The clinician would either read or let the client read: "It is possible that if I had not gone to jail and been able to read and listen to the stories of many people ... I might not have learned these things." (Cohen & Battersby, 2009, p. 164) The clinician then could ask the client: "If you had not had the experience of grief—which can be a type of prison—and read and listened to other grievers, what might you not have learned?"

Twenty-seven years in prison shaped Mandela into a more sensitive individual. The clinician might ask: "What might you borrow from Mandela's grief that would make you a more sensitive individual?" The old counseling cliché insists that you either get better or bitter. Mandela chose to get better.

A Story for the Road

After being notified of his son's death, Mandela stretched out on the bunk in his cell, telegram in hand. He would later comment that a prison cell is "the last place where a man stricken with sorrow should be" (Mandela, 2010, p. 162). He lost track of time and ignored fellow prisoners who looked in on him. Finally, Walter Sisulu, his closest friend, entered the cell and knelt beside the bed. Nelson handed him the telegram. Mandela later remembered: "He said nothing, but only held my hand. I do not know how long he remained with me. There is nothing that one man can say to another at such a time" (p. 447). Clinicians may share this narrative slice with individuals who protest, "I don't know what to say." Often there is nothing to say, but, like Sisulu, show up.

There are times when experienced therapists may have no words of wisdom and need to realize that witnessing another's pain is sufficient.

10

A GRIEVER NAMED JACQUELINE

Oh, Jack, there's only one thing I could not bear now—if I ever lost you.

Jackie Kennedy to John F. Kennedy, August 1963
(as cited in Andersen, 2000, p. 63)

Although known as a presidential widow, Jacqueline Kennedy Onassis experienced a wide palette of grief largely unexplored by biographers. Her grief as Mrs. Kennedy can only be understood by assessing the previous losses she had experienced.

The Grief Grid of Jacqueline Bouvier Kennedy

Birth of Jacqueline Bouvier	1929 (July 28)
Parents divorce	1940
Janet, mother, marries Hugh Auchincloss	1942 (June 21)
Jackie marries John F. Kennedy	1953 (September 12)
Near death of John F. Kennedy following back surgeries	1954 (October); 1955 (February)
Miscarriage	1955
Death of Arabella, neonate	1956 (August 23)
Death of John Vernon Bouvier, III, father	1957 (August 2)
Stroke of Joseph P. Kennedy, Sr.	1961 (December)
Death of Patrick Bouvier Kennedy, son	1963 (August 9)
Death of John F. Kennedy	1963 (November 22)
Death of Robert Kennedy, brother-in-law	1968 (June 6)
Marries Aristotle Onassis	1968 (October 20)
Death of Joseph P. Kennedy, Sr.	1969 (November 18)
Death of Alexander Onassis, stepson	1973 (January 23)
Death of Aristotle Onassis, husband	1975 (March 15)
Death of Hugh Auchincloss, stepfather	1976 (November 19)
Death of Janet Auchincloss Rutherfurd, half-sister	1985 (March 13)
Death of mother, Janet Auchincloss Morris	1989 (July 22)
Death of Jacqueline	1994 (May 19)
Death of John, Jr.	1999 (July 16)

Her Parents' Divorce

For Jacqueline Bouvier, her parents' divorce in 1940, after 12 con-
flicted years of marriage, was a significant loss. In the Bouviers'
social and religious circles, divorce was scandalous, particularly if the
"dirty linen" got news coverage. Pictures of Jackie and Lee, her sister,
appeared in *The New York Times* with stories chronicling her father's
financial dealings and infidelities. Not only had Jackie witnessed her
parents fighting, she was a pawn between them—and remained so.

Leaming (2001) insists that Jackie "never really recovered from
the newspaper accounts of her parents' divorce" (p. 14), especially
given the stigma she felt at the private school she attended. When
her mother married Hugh Auchincloss, a wealthy Standard Oil heir,
Jackie became the stepdaughter who "had no money;" she felt looked
down on by children from the "blue bloods" of old money families
in Newport, Rhode Island. Moreover, the Catholic Church excommunicated her mother for remarrying. Jackie spent her adolescence
"mourning for an absent parent" (p. 6), that is, the flamboyant dashing Black Jack Bouvier, in whose eyes Jackie could do no wrong (and
Janet could do no good!).

Marriage Into the Kennedy Family

Jacqueline Bouvier's marriage to Senator John Fitzgerald "Jack"
Kennedy, and into the Kennedy family, was jointly managed by
Jackie's mother and Joseph P. Kennedy, Sr., who turned it into a lavish
production labeled "the Wedding of the Year." Jack Bouvier's determination to walk his daughter down the aisle infuriated Janet. The night
before the ceremony, Janet had Bouvier sequestered in a nearby hotel
with family members acting as "handlers" to make sure he did not get
drunk; Bouvier became unpredictable with a few drinks. Although he
had not been invited to the rehearsal dinner or preceremony parties,
early on September 12, 1953, Bouvier was ready to be father of the
soon-to-be-famous bride.

For 90 minutes before the ceremony, the phone conversations
between Janet and the family members "guarding" Jack became more
intense. Janet kept calling hoping that her ex-husband was drunk

but his handlers had hidden the alcohol and kept him away from the hotel bar. When told that he insisted on coming to the church, Janet screamed, "We don't want him at the wedding even if he had only a couple of *sips*." Janet snarled that if the handlers allowed Jack to get to the church, there would be a scene. Finally, Janet threatened, "Don't you dare bring him. If you do, Jackie and I will never speak to you again" (Davis, 1966, p. 192).

Jackie was stunned not to find her father waiting at the church door. Davis (1966), her cousin, recalls, "But she could do nothing; Jackie was no longer her own master. She had become an unwilling pawn of her mother's animosity toward Jack Bouvier (p. 193). The 600 guests inside St. Mary's Catholic Church (and thousands outside) saw a poised, smiling bride on her stepfather's arm.

John F. Kennedy Battles for His Life

John F. Kennedy had never been a healthy individual. In 1946, Sir Daniel Davis, a British physician who had treated him and officially diagnosed him as having Addison's disease, privately predicted that he would not live a year. After a bone graft in his back (he had been injured during World War II) his compromised immune system resulted in a serious infection at the site of his surgery. Ghaemi (2011) reports that the senator went into a full coma and was administered the last rights while Joseph P. Kennedy and Jackie "watched helplessly" (Ghaemi, 2011, p. 161). His illness created anguish for the then vice president of the United States, Richard Nixon, who anxiously visited Kennedy's secretary to ask if the reports of Kennedy's illness were true. A Secret Service agent heard Nixon say, "That poor young man is going to die. Poor brave Jack is going to die. Oh, God, don't let him die" (p. 161).

Two months later, John F. Kennedy was released, although his medical condition was reportedly worse than before the surgery. The metal plate surgeons had placed in his back repeatedly became infected and was finally removed. After studying Kennedy's medical records, Ghaemi (2011) describes the consequences of the surgery: "an open hole in his back, large enough to fit a man's fist up to the wrist, drained pus for six months. Every night, his new wife would clean the open wound" (p. 161). For more than 7 months, Kennedy was depressed. One friend later said, "We came close to losing him. I don't just mean losing his life. I mean losing him as a person" (citing Giglio, 2006, p. 378, as cited in Ghaemi, 2011, p. 161). This was one of Kennedy's seven hospitalizations between 1953 and 1957 (Ghaemi, 2011, p. 162).

The Death of Arabella

The death of baby Arabella Kennedy in July 1956 was triggered by "exhaustion and nervous tension" following Jackie's participation as something of a "prop"—the candidate's photogenic young pregnant wife—at the Democratic National Convention (Andersen, 1996, p. 168). Although Jack lost the vice presidential nomination, his efforts thrust him onto the fast track for the presidential nomination in 1960.

After a week consulting on postconvention strategy with his father, Kennedy and a group of male companions flew to Greece to relax while cruising the islands, that is, partying. After Jackie went into premature labor, her life was endangered; the senator was unreachable. Finally Robert, her brother-in-law, told Jackie that the baby died but did not disclose that he had made burial arrangements. *The Washington Post* headlined the drama, "Senator Kennedy on Mediterranean Trip Unaware that His Wife Has Lost Baby" (Andersen, 1996, p. 168).

When Kennedy's party boat sailed into Genoa, Italy, he learned of the baby's death. Tensions escalated dramatically during a phone conversation when Jackie insisted that he come home. Andersen (1996) reports, "Whether in shock or just unimaginably callous—most likely a little of both—Jack told his wife that he did not intend to cut short his cruise" (p. 168). His insensitivity angered Jackie. Finally, his pal George Smathers challenged Kennedy: "You'd better get your ass back there right away if you plan on staying married—or getting to the White House" (Andersen, 1996, pp. 168–169).

By the time Kennedy arrived at his mother-in-law's home in Newport, where Jackie was recuperating, neither Jackie nor her mother were in a mood for "kiss-and-make-up." Jackie blamed the Kennedys' "hectic pace of life" and frantic overscheduling for the miscarriage.

She refused to move into their new house with the nursery she had decorated.

The death of Arabella raised questions in the family about Jackie's ability to have a child—a critical issue for Roman Catholics and for Joseph Kennedy's public relations machine. Jackie felt "judged" by the Kennedy women who "speculated behind her back that the highborn Miss Bouvier was of too delicate a constitution to bear a child" (Andersen, 1996, pp. 168–170). Moreover, during the search for John Kennedy, her sister-in-law Patricia Lawford gave birth to a baby and 2 weeks later sister-in-law Ethel Kennedy gave birth to her fifth child.

Soon rumors swirled about a possible divorce, which seemed plausible to those who knew of the couple's growing estrangement. Syndicated columnist Drew Pearson broke the story; *Time* followed featuring "rumors" that Ambassador Kennedy had offered Jackie $1 million to stay with his son; Jackie was "an asset" (H. Smith, 2004a, p. 38) the family needed. Ironically, out of this crisis, Jackie and her father-in-law developed a close bond. (She spent Thanksgiving after the assassination at the family compound to comfort him.)

The Death of Jack Bouvier

Almost 1 year after Arabella's death, Jack Bouvier became ill. The family had long considered him something of a hypochondriac alcoholic and a social embarrassment. Jackie visited her father in a New York City hospital, but concluding that he was not seriously ill, returned to Hyannis Port. On August 3, 1957, Bouvier, "riddled with cancer," lapsed into a coma and died. Although notified of his deteriorating condition, Jackie and Senator Kennedy arrived too late to say good-bye. Bradford (2000) reports that while "Black Jack's death was the worst emotional shock of her life so far," Jackie "took charge, dry-eyed" (p. 112), managing details for her father's funeral—which drew less than two dozen mourners, counting former girlfriends—at St. Patrick's Cathedral. He was buried next to her grandparents in East Hampton. Jack Bouvier's death "signaled the passing of an era in Jackie's life" (p. 111). Four months later, Jackie gave birth to Caroline. If only her father, she lamented, had lived to see his granddaughter.

Jacqueline Kennedy as First Lady

John Kennedy was elected president in 1960 by a margin of 114,673 votes (Spoto, 2000, p. 145). The public, after 30 years of grandparents in the White House—the Roosevelts, Trumans, Eisenhowers—fixated on the young family, particularly 3-year-old Caroline and baby John. Jackie resisted the term "First Lady," which she thought more appropriate for a horse. She declined to meet with White House visitors or engage in traditional activities like teas and hand-shaking receptions that did not interest her. Jackie focused her attention on the children and three projects: renovating the White House furnishings for historical authenticity, raising the "tone of entertainment" by inviting legendary artists to perform at the White House, and by supporting artistic and cultural endeavors ignored or neglected by previous administrations (Mayo, 1996). Through Jackie's persuasive lobbying, the White House was designated a museum to protect the art and antiques she and curators acquired. On Valentine's Day 1962, 46.6 million viewers–75% of the nation's television audience—watched Jackie's live tour of the renovated White House (H. Smith, 2004a, p. 255).

Joseph Kennedy's Stroke

On December 18, 1961, a shift occurred within the family when Joseph Kennedy, the patriarch who controlled the purse strings and was Jackie's major supporter, financier, and defender within the Kennedy tribe, suffered a massive stroke. H. Smith (2004a) observed, "For Joseph Kennedy, long accustomed to power and control, the fate of being trapped speechless inside a largely immobile body was especially cruel" (p. 249).

The Birth of Patrick

Leaming (2001) termed Jackie's pregnancy in the summer of 1963 "a national event" (p. 271). A baby had not been born to a First Family in 80 years; with luck the baby might be born *in* the White House. On August 9, while vacationing on Squaw Island in Massachusetts, Jackie went into labor and gave birth to Patrick Bouvier Kennedy at nearby Otis Air Force Base. Patrick, 5 months premature, was air-lifted immediately to Massachusetts General Hospital in Boston; Jackie never got to hold him.

For 2 days, the nation—and the world—waited; masses were said for the baby, and reporters stalked the hospital corridors for stories. When the 2-day-old died in his father's arms on August 9, of complications of hyaline membrane disease, seemingly the whole world grieved with the young parents (H. Smith, 2004a).

Patrick's death was front-page news. *The Kansas City Star* ran this headline, "Kennedy baby dies at Boston hospital; president is at hand." An editorial in *The New York Times* (1963, p. 16) noted:

> The sorrow borne today by President and Mrs. Kennedy touches the entire nation. Theirs is the deep personal loss no words of sympathy can assuage; theirs is the added burden of having no privacy in their grief, for they must endure their family tragedy before the eyes of the world.

Citizens from all levels of society deluged the grieving First Family with condolence messages. John D. Rockefeller III, expressed his hope that "you would take comfort from the fact that you already have two wonderful children and also that you are still young" (J.F.K. Personal Papers, Death of Patrick, 1963, JFK Presidential Library). One telegram was particularly meaningful to the president, given his commitment to the space program: "The length of a life cannot be a measure of either its value or its effect on many people. All of us extend our sincerest sympathy in this time of bereavement," signed, The Astronauts (Astronauts to President Kennedy, n.d., JFK PPP, Box 498, JFKPL).

President Kennedy abandoned his schedule to spend the greater part of the last months of his life with Jackie, Caroline, and John, Jr., out of the public eye.

The Trip to Texas

The splintered Texas Democratic Party needed Kennedy to heal their wrangling before 1964 when he would need Texas' electoral votes to retain the White House. Jackie's decision to campaign with him that long weekend was seen as proof that she was "over" Patrick's death.

That decision resulted in an iconic niche for Jackie in American narrative. The images of her standing numbly in a blood-splattered dress as Lyndon Johnson was sworn in, and stoic as she walked with the Kennedy brothers and world leaders in procession to the funeral Mass were seen around the world. *The New York Times* commented, "Grasping the hands of her two children on the steps of St. Matthew's Cathedral, she presented to the world a portrait of regal serenity and resolute strength" (as cited in Klemesrud, 1968, p. 4E). Millions watching the services on television asked, "How can she be so strong?"

Jackie's Life After the White House

One indication of Jackie's perception of her future became evident 3 weeks after the assassination. Friends Ben and Toni Bradlee, spending a weekend with Jackie, predicted she would marry again and, maybe, have more children. Days later, in a note thanking the couple for the children's Christmas gifts, Jackie wrote, "You must know that I consider my life to be over. And I will spend the rest of my life waiting for it really to be over" (Bradlee, 1995, p. 262). In 2003, the papers of Father Richard McSorley, who served informally as a confessor to Jackie in the months after the assassination, were released. Clearly, Jackie was suicidal and thought her children would be better off with Robert and Ethel Kennedy. In April 1964, she lamented, "I don't know how God could take him away" (CNN, 2003). She told Father McSorley, "I know I won't ever get over it, but I am getting better at hiding it from my children" (*CBS News*, 2003). In late July, she wrote to the priest, a Jesuit at Georgetown University, to explain how she was implementing his spiritual guidance:

> I am trying to make all the efforts you said I should make. It doesn't get a bit easier. If you want to know what my religious convictions are now, they are to keep busy, to keep healthy so that you [I] can do all you [I] should do for your [my] children, and to get to bed early at night so that you [I] don't have time to think. (CBS News, 2003)

Initially, Jackie moved into a leased a home in Georgetown until the constant tourist crawl outside the house heightened her concern for the normalcy of Caroline and John's childhoods, and for their personal safety. She purchased a high-rise apartment in New York City and terminated the children's nanny, Maude Shaw—a decision that distressed the children. That spring the Gallup Poll named Jackie "the most admired woman in the world" (Mayo, 1996, p. 228).

Jackie focused her attention on her children and launching the John F. Kennedy Presidential Library in Boston. She also raised money for Robert Kennedy's 1964 Senate campaign in New York. Jackie was a natural. Who could resist her requests for donations to the campaign and to the library?

The Greek Bearing Gifts

Meanwhile, Jackie spent more time with Aristotle Onassis, the Greek shipping magnate, on whose yacht she had recuperated following Patrick's death. When the Kennedys learned marriage was in the air, Ethel and Joan were dispatched to convince Jackie not to marry him. When Jackie resisted, they pleaded that she not marry until after the November election. "Negative publicity" triggered by a wedding, they contended, "would irrevocably damage Bobby's chances for the presidency" (Heymann, 2009, p. 156). Jackie dismissed their premise that she "owed it" to the Kennedys to put "the family's priorities" ahead of hers.

Robert Kennedy's Assassination

Hours after winning the California presidential primary, Senator Robert Kennedy died of gunshot wounds on June 6, 1968. A distraught Jackie flew to Los Angeles to be with the family. Heymann (2009) insists she wanted to be with Robert since their secret affair had ended when Robert decided to seek the presidency.

Because Robert was a de facto father for Caroline and John, Jr., his death impacted both significantly. Fearing the political climate, Jackie imagined that her children could be harmed or be the next Kennedy to die (Spoto, 2000, p. 236). Onassis's wealth and obsession with security offered an opportunity for a "secure and safe" (p. 235) future for her and the children.

On October 20, 1968, 40-year-old Jackie married Onassis. "How could she!?" raged columnists, headline writers, and citizens on the street. Klemesrud (1968) wrote in *The New York Times*, "It was almost as though an American legend had deserted her people. She had become, instead, a living breathing woman, choosing for her husband a man old enough to be her father" (p. 4E). When Nancy Tuckerman, her close friend and former social secretary, challenged Jackie, "you're going to fall off your pedestal!" the former First Lady retorted, "That's better than freezing up here. You don't know how lonely I've been" (Mayo, 1996, p. 228).

The question, "What does she see in him?" prompted pragmatic answers: Onassis offered her unlimited financial resources, travel on the family-owned airline, the isolation of a primary residence on a private Greek island, and, most important, a large security force to keep threats away. Simply, Onassis's wealth offered her a way to end her reliance on Kennedy trust funds and achieve financial independence (J. H. Davis, 1996).

But how could she "abandon" her grief for the martyred president to marry a divorced man? Roman Catholics could not marry divorced individuals without an annulment. Bradford (2000) summarized the reaction, "Public reaction was uniformly hostile worldwide, from top to bottom of the social spectrum" (p. 337). In short, "The Queen had abdicated" (p. 337). Leaming (2001) contends that the media harangued Jackie for tarnishing the president's memory with its implication "that she had sold herself. How could she possibly have married this toad of a man" (p. 359)?

Overnight, Jackie's persona as "Camelot's martyr" disintegrated (O'Neill, 1968). Americans had expected her, in time, to "move on," but not this far! Others argued Jackie was entitled to happiness "wherever" she could find it. Rose Kennedy publically supported this perspective: "Jackie deserved a full life, a happy future." Although Rose had some "doubts," when Jackie called, "I told her to ... go ahead ... with my loving wishes" (R. F. Kennedy, 1974, p. 483).

Conservative Roman Catholics claimed Jackie was challenging the church's doctrine on the sanctity of marriage. Rumors swirled that Jackie would be excommunicated (like her mother). Finally, Cardinal Richard Cushing of Boston, the longtime Kennedy family friend, blasted her critics: "This idea of saying she's excommunicated, that she's a public sinner—what a lot of nonsense! Only God knows who is a sinner and who is not. Why can't she marry whoever she wants?" (Cutler, 1970, p. 357).

Years later, Bradford (2000) identified Jackie's desire for freedom as the motivating factor:

> She wanted to be free, emotionally and financially, from the hard-core Kennedys, free (temporarily at least) from the burden of being a slain hero's widow, the high priestess of the cult, whose behavior must conform to the worshipper's demands. And she wanted her children free of them too; free of the financial bonds that tied her heirs to the Kennedy fortune, free of the political legacy stemming from old Joe's ambition, the presidency of the United States. (p. 334)

"Jackie O"

As "Jackie O," she recharmed the world. Over time, the marriage unraveled because of her lavish spending, personality differences, and Aristotle's continued relationship with his mistress, Maria Callas. The marriage was challenged by grief within the Onassis family following the deaths of three family members. In January 1973, Alexander Onassis, 24, was killed in a plane crash. An emotionally distraught Aristotle, suspecting foul play, could not attend the funeral (Birmingham, 1978). In October 1974, Tina, Onassis's first wife—married to his shipping rival, Stavros Niarchos—died under mysterious circumstances (as had her sister who had been married to Niarchos). Onassis's daughter Christina, who wielded great influence within the family, had lost an aunt, a mother, and a brother in a short period. Someone, she reasoned, had brought a curse on the family.

Although Jackie tried to maintain a friendly relationship with her stepdaughter, Christina concluded that Jackie was "the Angel of Death." Would her father be the next "victim"? Aristotle initiated legal explorations to divorce Jackie, despite warnings from attorneys that the prenuptial arrangement could not protect his sizeable assets (Birmingham, 1978, p. 196).

During the winter of 1975, Onassis's health declined rapidly. Jackie took her turn at his bedside until unpleasant exchanges with Christina and others elevated the stress. Finally, Jackie flew home to her children in New York City. When Onassis died on March 15, 1975, Jackie's critics relished disclosing that the "pampered" wife was thousands of miles from her "poor" husband's deathbed.

After 2 years of intense legal negotiations, Jackie relinquished her widow's rights to inherit the majority of Onassis's estate and settled for $20 million to add to the estimated $10 million John Kennedy had left in trusts—significant sums in 1963 and 1977 (Birmingham, 1978).

Life After Aristotle

In 1975, Jackie stunned the country by joining the editorial staff of Viking Press as a consulting editor, becoming the second presidential widow to take a job (Mrs. Eleanor Roosevelt was the first); later she moved to Doubleday. She explained to one friend, "I have always lived through men. Now I realize I can't do that anymore" (Lawrence, 2011, p. 4). While some expected her job to be cosmetic, Jackie immersed herself in learning the craft of editing. As an editor, she guided more than 100 books into print and helped launch the careers of many young writers (Kuhn, 2010).

She protectively nurtured Caroline and John Jr. Following Caroline's marriage, she relished her role as mother-in-law and then after the birth of Caroline's children, as grandmother. At the time of her death on May 22, 1994, Jackie had lived since 1982 with financier Maurice Tempelsman, a married Jewish father of three. Although they had been romantically involved since the late 1970s, the relationship flourished below the media radar screen (Bradford, 2000). Tempelsman skillfully managed Jackie's money; at her death the estate was valued at more than $43 million ("Jacqueline Onassis Estate," 1996)

Just as people were puzzled by her marriage to Onassis, many wondered, "Why Tempelsman?" Bradford (2000) theorized that Jackie cherished the emotional stability he offered her. "For the first time in her life, she had a man upon whom she knew she could rely; a man for whom she was absolutely and forever number one" (p. 419). Kuhn (2010) contends that Tempelsman loved her and gave her "ample space to be the woman she'd always wanted to be" (p. 92).

Janet's Alzheimer's

The relationship between Jackie and her mother had, through the years, been "difficult." Jackie's stepbrother, Louis Auchincloss, concluded that Janet significantly rescripted the family narrative. Given her expectations for upward mobility for both of her daughters, maternal warmth was absent. Auchincloss recalled Janet's frequent temper tantrums that resulted in her striking Jackie, but moments later "cooing like a dove" (Kuhn, 2010, p. 230) as if nothing had happened.

When her mother was diagnosed with Alzheimer's, Jackie established a $1 million trust fund to provide for her care (Pottker, 2001) and "took a generous amount of time from her schedule to spend with her mother" (p. 308). Jackie included her mother in family gatherings, even though Janet was often confused. At the dedication of the John F. Kennedy School of Government, Janet asked Jackie, "Who was John Kennedy?" (p. 309). At Caroline's wedding to Edward Schlossberg, she kept asking whose wedding it was.

Janet had always wanted a grandchild named after her. When Caroline gave birth to her first child, Jackie insisted, however, she be named Rose, which Pottker (2001) notes was a slap in the face to Janet. Janet's health deteriorated after a fall. As Jackie left to attend Rose Kennedy's 99th birthday she received a "time was short" call. Although Janet had been excommunicated, a Roman Catholic priest offered her the last rites. Janet died at age 81.

The Death of Jacqueline Bouvier Kennedy Onassis

As Mrs. Onassis, Jackie had always guarded her figure, aware of the ever-lurking paparazzi. After a fall from a horse, her health rapidly declined. In January 1994, she was diagnosed with non-Hodgkin's lymphoma. Faced with the fragility of health, she told historian Arthur Schlesinger, Jr., "I have always been proud of keeping so fit, I swim, I jog, I do my push-ups, and walk around the reservoir—and now this suddenly happens" (Lawrence, 2011, p. 261). Jacqueline Bouvier Kennedy Onassis, 64, died on May 19, 1994, never having lost her ability to command the world's attention. John Jr. broke the news the following day, saying "She was surrounded by her friends and her books and the people and things she loved. She did it her own way and on her own terms, and we all feel lucky for that" (Kuhn, 2010, p. 4). To be certain his phrase, "She did it her own way and on her own terms" raised speculation on the details of her death.

Some Implications for Clinicians

Psychiatrist Richard Isay, in *Commitment and Healing*, insists that "a loving relationship over time can transform anyone's life" (2006, p. 3). Isay's contention is demonstrated in Jackie's relationship with Tempelsman. At last, Jackie had someone who was committed to her, someone in whose eyes the sun rose and set.

Given the significant number of second and subsequent marriages and nonmarital intimate relationships in contemporary American culture, elements of Jackie's narratives offer resources for clinicians and for individuals navigating the reassessment of relationships.

Who Am I Now?

A common question for widows is, "Who am I without [name or relationship]?" Jackie was, in Norman Mailer's words, "the Prisoner of Celebrity" (Lawrence, 2011, p. 1). Her years on the margin of public interest were longer than her marriages. As a widow she faced the question: What do I do with me in the years ahead (or in the years remaining)? What Lawrence labels "the third act of Jackie's saga" (p. 5), as editor, went without recognition until two biographers closely examined her work and impact: Lawrence (2011) and Kuhn (2010). The latter subtitled his book, *Her Autobiography in Books*. Jackie once said, "If you produce one book, you will have done something wonderful in your life" (Lawrence, 2011, p. 1).

One indication of her re-creation of herself is her devotion to her authors. Long after she had left her office at Doubleday for the last time, as she was dying, she continued to work on Antony Beevor's manuscript on postwar Paris; both author and editor recognized that the ending of the manuscript was not right. Beevor was stunned when she faxed a suggestion for fixing it that worked (Kuhn, 2010).

Jackie worked to exercise her soul by shepherding the book making of others. She offered many authors the break they needed. Once asked why she championed expensive books that would never become bestsellers, she insisted, "Every once in a while you have to do something for the soul" (Kuhn, 2010, p. 283).

Jackie's observation has enormous potential in grief counseling. The clinician can share the quotation with a client and ask: "What are you doing for your soul?"

Legacy Making

Jackie invested enormous time and energy into protecting and expanding John Kennedy's legacy through a presidential library that would be more than displays of memorabilia and a repository for books and papers.

She told Jann Wenner, one of her authors, that his manuscript on John Lennon needed work. She discerned that his grief following his friend John Lennon's death was keeping him from finishing his manuscript. From her grief experience, Jackie challenged him:

> It helps people who mourn to be able to do something for the cause of the fallen, not to have let them die in vain. Even though you may feel a deep weariness and despair, you mustn't abdicate a leadership that has meant a great deal to mankind. (Kuhn, 2010, p. 268)

Through her fascination with words, ideas, and images, she championed individuals like African American novelist Dorothy West and helped create a new genre by publishing children's books by Carly Simon. Jackie helped institutionalize the work of Joseph Campbell, particularly his understanding of myth.

Jackie chose the hard work of turning manuscripts into books and writers into authors. Kuhn (2010) describes "the Cinderella or fairy godmother effect" that Jackie had on writers and colleagues. Jackie as "den mother" prodded and protected a cadre of writers she thought had futures in the literary world.

Affirmation of the Griever

"Can I survive this death?" is a menacing question many grievers confront. Jackie survived and thrived. When Stephen Spender asked Jackie what her greatest accomplishment would be, she answered, "I think that my biggest achievement is that after going through a rather difficult time, I consider myself relatively sane" (Lawrence, 2011, p. 256). The clinician might borrow that question and ask, "What will your greatest achievement be?"

A Story for the Road

As an editor, Jackie invested time lavishly on her authors. Mike D'Orso recalls overhearing his 7-year-old daughter talking to someone on the phone. Her answers were crisp: "Fine … Second Grade … Playing with my dolls," until apparently, the caller asked to speak to "your father." "Daddy, it's the dead president's wife" (Kuhn, 2010, p. 69).

Kuhn concludes,

> That was the paradox of Jackie's fame: she lived for three decades after her first husband, married another man, edited dozens of books, and collaborated with scores of writers but she remained famous for having been the wife of JFK. (2010, p. 69)

11

A GRIEVER NAMED CORAZON

Sometimes life does not proceed as you expected it. You must deal with the circumstances you're in.

Corazon "Cory" Aquino (as cited in Simon, 2009)

I am not embarrassed to tell you that I believe in miracles.

Corazon "Cory" Cory Aquino (Stewart & Sindayen, 1987, p. 27)

In 1983, who would have predicted that a Filipino housewife, living in a Boston suburb, would later grace the cover of the January 5, 1987 issue of *Time* as "Woman of the Year"? Three years after the assassination of Benigno Aquino, her husband, Corazon "Cory" Aquino's "People Power" movement toppled Philippine dictators Ferdinand and Imelda Marcos. The story of a "miracle-believing" courageous widow stepping into a husband's shoes contains much to borrow.

Terror Management Theory

Terror management theory contends that the control of death-related anxiety is "the primary function of society" and a significant motivation in human behavior (VandenBos, 2007). Following the assassination or attempted assassination of a head of state or leader of a political movement, individuals must defuse heightened death anxiety (Norenzayan, Dar-Nimrod, Hansen, & Proulx, 2007). Such upheavals produce psychological, social, religious, and financial instability within a nation and, given globalization, far beyond borders drawn on maps (Weise et al., 2008). Or it may resurrect hope. How can individuals manage death anxiety to step forward to face challenges, seemingly, with no fear for their own lives? (Norenzayan et al., 2007). Corazon Aquino offers a case study of one who did.

The Background: Benigno vs. Ferdinand

The enmity between Benigno Aquino and Ferdinand Marcos—and their influential families—ran long and deep (Burton, 1990). Aquino, because of his meteoric rise, was deemed "the wonder boy of politics" ("Aquino, Benigno," 1989, p. 77). Many, including the Marcoses, assessed Aquino, the young Filipino senator, as capable of unseating them in the 1973 presidential election. Not surprisingly, when Marcos declared martial law on September 23, 1972, Aquino was among the first of 6,000 activists, journalists, and politicians arrested. Corazon Aquino (from hereon referred to as Cory) "who had only known a life of ease and affluence" (Haag, 1999, p. 426) was distraught with no idea where her husband was being held or under what conditions. In April 1975, when ordered to stand trial before a military tribunal, Ninoy (Benigno Aquino's family nickname) refused, citing his rights under Philippine law to be tried in a civilian court. When he went on a 40-day hunger strike, Cory organized prayer meetings for his safety (Komisar, 1987, pp. 41–42).

In November 1977, when a military tribunal sentenced Ninoy to death for murder, subversion, and possession of illegal firearms, the conviction and the proceedings evoked international outrage. Ninoy suffered systematic inhumane treatment in solitary confinement; he lost weight fearing his food was poisoned; he could not sleep because a neon light burned in his cell 24 hours a day. Cory was his only link with the outside world. Eventually, the Aquinos were allowed weekend conjugal visits even though cameras monitored the cell and Cory had to endure humiliating nude strip searches before and after each visit. Still Cory ingeniously smuggled messages—sometimes memorized, sometimes concealed in tampons—and she recruited Catholic nuns to disseminate Ninoy's messages through their social networks. Finally, an enraged Marcos ordered Ninoy moved to an undisclosed location, placed in a small cell with only a steel bed frame and no mattress, and to be kept naked and denied his eyeglasses (Komisar, 1987, p. 39).

Seven years in solitary confinement took a psychological and physiological toll on both Aquinos, especially because Ninoy's heart problems went untreated. Cory described this period as her "first great suffering." "If we are to be real Christians," she reminded friends, "we have to accept suffering as a part of our life" (Komisar, 1987, p. 41). If Jesus suffered—a key component in Filipino Catholic theology—then the Aquinos must suffer. "Prison," Cory later reflected, "brought out a whole new set of values for both of us" (Stewart & Sindayen, 1987, p. 32). During her husband's imprisonment, Cory mined strength from her spiritual tradition, attending Mass daily and praying to the Blessed Mother. Ninoy extracted a promise that she would "be strong" and never let the children see her cry or cry in public. Whatever happened, Cory must never beg Marcos for his release. Survival meant exhibiting no "display of weakness" (p. 39).

Benigno Aquino's Conversion

In prison Ninoy experienced a religious conversion. Initially, he had repeatedly asked God what terrible crimes—especially compared to Marcos—he had committed to deserve such harsh treatment. He questioned a god who ignored rampant injustice and political corruption. Honoring his Catholic tradition, particularly during Lent, Ninoy contemplated the sufferings of Jesus. Compared to Jesus' sufferings, he concluded, how could he complain? Ninoy "offered up his life," "picked up his cross"—in the language of Catholic spirituality—to follow Jesus wherever it led. Ninoy believed the Blessed Mother had visited his cell to strengthen him. Chua-Eoan (1988) contends that renewed Christian faith sustained him through physical and psychological abuse, and reduced his death anxiety.

In May 1980, with economic pressure by the Carter Administration intensifying, Marcos released Ninoy to have heart surgery in Houston, cognizant that if Ninoy died in prison he would be hailed as a martyr. After the successful surgery, for 3 years, Ninoy was a fellow at Harvard's Center for International Affairs and at MIT's Center for Southeastern Asian Studies. Under the cover of academia, he plotted strategies for challenging the regime. In May 1983, in New York City, Ninoy met with Imelda Marcos who invited him to return to the Philippines with her, promising a "lucrative" government position. "Together you and I," she wooed, "will be invincible" (Komisar, 1987, p. 48). He declined. Imelda offered to set him up in a business in the

United States that would make him wealthy. Ninoy rejected what he considered a bribe. Finally, Imelda threatened, "we will not be able to control even our friends" (p. 48) if you return to Manila. Although the Aquinos acknowledged Ninoy could be injured if he returned, they doubted, in the gaze of world media and the numbers of Filipinos praying, that he would be killed. When his elderly mother questioned his safety, Ninoy dismissed her concerns. "Why," he asked, "would they kill me, make a martyr out of me" (Komisar, 1987, p. 49)?

Going Home to Manila

In August 1983, Ninoy gave up his comfortable life in Boston to return to Manila. Not necessarily to challenge Marcos, Haag (1999) argues, but to serve as an intermediary between the opposition and the regime. Aquino's last written statement, declared,

> I have returned on my free will to join the ranks of those struggling to restore our rights and freedoms through nonviolence. I seek no confrontation. I only pray and will strive for genuine national reconciliation founded on justice. ("Aquino, Benigno, " 1989, p. 78)

Although many friends considered the challenge to Marcos suicidal, Cory quietly supported the decision. Before his departure, Ninoy bragged, "Isn't she a remarkable woman? If it were some women, they would be crying and begging me not to go home. But she hasn't said a word" (Haag, 1999, p. 428).

That August Day

On August 21, 1983, Aquino and his entourage boarded China Air 811 for Manila. During the flight he quietly prayed the Rosary. Before boarding he had written "in case ..." letters to Cory and to each of his five children. On the final approach, Aquino slipped into a lavatory to put on a bulletproof vest. As the plane landed, family members and 20,000 joyous supporters waited outside the airport to welcome him home (Chua-Eoan, 1988, p. 28).

As soon as the plane's door was opened, uniformed soldiers rushed on to escort Ninoy off; his friends were ordered to remain seated.

Eleven seconds later, on the steps leading to the tarmac, Aquino was shot in the head. His bleeding body was thrown into a van that sped away (Komisar, 1987).

Widowed in Boston

Half a world away in Massachusetts, Cory could not sleep. As she prayed the Rosary, she anxiously awaited her husband's call that he had arrived safely. At 2:30 A.M., a Japanese news agency called seeking confirmation that Ninoy was dead; calls from United Press International and the Associated Press followed. By 3 A.M., friends filled the home offering condolences as Cory and her children knelt "to pray the rosary and ask our Blessed Mother to help us" (Burton, 1989, p. 143). At dawn, the Aquino family drove to a nearby church to pray. Afterward, Cory conducted television interviews and talked by phone to reporters around the world. Fearing that the Marcos regime would impose a news blackout, Cory called family in Manila to ask, "Do the people know?" She learned that soon after her husband's corpse had been delivered to their bungalow, crowds lined up to view the body, pray, and offer condolences to his mother.

Twenty-four hours later, Cory and the children landed in Manila. En route home, Cory noticed thousands waiting alongside the road, a line that eventually stretched 2 miles (Komisar, 1987). When Cory arrived at her home wanting to spend private time with her husband's corpse, she realized that would inconvenience those waiting in line. She wanted as many people as possible to see Ninoy's body which

> lay in the coffin, still bloodied, his face marked by bruises and a gaping hole made by the bullet that tore through his chin. He was wearing the same bloody clothes he had on when he fell. His family believed that soldiers must have battered him in the van to make sure he was dead. (Komisar, 1987, p. 8)

The body had not been washed, groomed, or dressed, nor had cosmetics been applied, as per instructions from Dona Aurora Aquino, his mother, who declared, "I want the Filipino people to see what they have done to my son" (Komisar, 1987, p. 8).

To accommodate the mourners, the family arranged to move the corpse to their parish church. In oppressive heat and humidity, a procession immediately formed behind the casket and widow. Some 50,000 mourners lined the route singing "Bayon Ko," the anti-Marcos anthem (Komisar, 1987, p. 9). Thousands of mourners filed by Ninoy's open casket (p. 8) including Cardinal Jaime Sin, the head of the Roman Catholic Church in the Philippines, who came aware that his presence would both annoy Marcos and attract coverage and comment by Catholics across the Philippines and the world. Haag (1999) reports that more than 100,000 people paid their respects in Manila (p. 428). The next day, Aquino's body was transported 60 miles to Tarlac, his childhood home and the province where he had been governor; more than 150,000 passed by the open casket (Komisar, 1987, p. 9). Cory turned down numerous requests for her husband's body to be brought to other towns.

Aquino's Funeral Mass

Ten days after the murder, Cardinal Sin celebrated the funeral Mass for his friend. At the end, Cory expressed gratitude for the promises that she and her children would not be abandoned. Most important, Ninoy, she declared, had not died in vain. Political and economic change would come.

Then the widow and her children led 2 million Filipinos on a 20-mile march that took 10 hours. At the grave, crowd control became impossible because so many pushed forward wanting a last look. Finally, an exhausted widow, who had fasted and prayed intensely during the procession, watched the casket lowered into the vault and accepted the Filipino flag that had draped the casket. What now?

Focus on the Widow

Repeatedly, the question was asked: How could she remain so calm? Cory explained that Ninoy "would have expected it" and her faith sustained her. Komisar (1987) offers an alternative view: "Cory had done all her crying in Newton [Massachusetts]. She felt tears might upset her children and make other people uncomfortable" (p. 10). More important, Cory believed, "When you cry, things do not get done" (p. 10), and there was plenty to be done to bring to justice those who had orchestrated her husband's death (Chua-Eoan, 1988, p. 55).

The Need for a Symbol and a Candidate

Oppositionists wondered who could—or would be willing, given the high stakes—to step forward to harness the outrage and to challenge Marcos. When Cory once asked Ninoy who would take his place if he were killed, he confidently replied, "new leaders would emerge" (Komisar, 1987, p. 43). Gradually consensus built around Cory, who as a widow symbolized the consequences of opposing Marcos. When urged to run, Cory protested that she had no qualifications. (However, she had an American college degree, spoke five languages, and had dropped out of law school in 1954 to marry Ninoy.) The widow had no intention of resuming exile in Boston.

The Power of Faith

One cannot understand how Corazon Aquino managed her anxiety without assessing her Roman Catholic faith and spirituality. While pondering a decision to run for president, she conceded, "The tremendous responsibility scares me" (Komisar, 1987, p. 70). Borrowing from the language of her faith, she labeled the decision as "a cross on my shoulders" (p. 70). She turned to her friends who were nuns. In a convent, she begged the Carmelite Sisters: "Pray for me, because I have this very big problem. I need divine guidance" (p. 70). While weighing the decision, Cory experienced a reoccurring dream in which she visited a church and found a casket at the altar. Expecting to find her husband's body, instead she found the casket empty. Cory interpreted the dream to mean that "Ninoy had been reborn" (p. 70) and his mission was now hers. She explained to family members and political confidantes, "We must present someone who has been a victim [of the Marcos oppression]. I may not be the worst," she acknowledged, "but I *am* the best known" (p. 70). Borrowing from the Old Testament narrative of Gideon, she cast "a fleece": She would run if one million

Filipinos signed petitions supporting her candidacy. By November 25, 1985, that goal was exceeded. Her candidacy was boosted when the media captured Cardinal Sin blessing the petitions, a de facto endorsement by the Roman Catholic hierarchy that was lost on no one. At a Mass on her husband's birthday, Cory told supporters, "I will never forgive myself if I live with the knowledge I could have done something and didn't do anything" (Komisar, 1987, p. 71).

The Assassins Are Found "Not Guilty"

Anger erupted after a civilian court, "ignoring eyewitness accounts and damaging testimony," found General Fabian Ver and 25 others not guilty of assassinating Benigno Aquino (Chua-Eoan, 1988, p. 68). This verdict that mocked justice (Bowman, 2000) was the last straw for the widow.

The Aquino children fumed. "Why, do you have to be a martyr like Dad" (Komisar, 1987, p. 68)? Cory sequestered herself on another retreat in a convent praying for her husband, the prospective vice presidential candidate, and individuals she held responsible for Ninoy's death. Afterward, she told her mother-in-law, "I do not think Marcos will let us win. We will try. This is the challenge I cannot run away from anymore" (Komisar, 1987, p. 68).

"The Lady in Yellow" Emerges

Many were surprised by the confidence that seemed to come over candidate Cory. As a political wife, she had always been in the background, preparing food, offering hospitality to her husband's guests, caring for the children (Haskins, 1988), always compliant with the Filipino patriarchal model. Ballsy, her oldest daughter, explained, "But when my father died, everything changed" (Komisar, 1987, p. 59).

The widow Aquino, who dressed in yellow as a symbol of hope, rallied the crowds who turned out to hear her. She united the fragmented opposition despite competing agendas, framing her campaign as a spiritual challenge. Cory drew upon lessons learned in the background while observing her husband and her father, both consummate politicians. Cory's campaign got a boost when an overconfident Marcos called snap elections for February 7, 1986. Large numbers of optimistic voters turned out but violence broke out, and 30 individuals died. When the Marcos-controlled Batasang Pambansa proclaimed him the winner with 53.8% of the vote (Haag, 1999, p. 429), protests of tampering and intimidation, particularly by the army and police, clouded his election.

On Valentine's Day, the Roman Catholic Church publically condemned the election, reminding the faithful that any government that won by intimidation could not be legitimate in the eyes of the church. The nation's Catholic bishops instructed the faithful:

> We therefore ask every loyal member of the Church, every commu-
> nity of the faithful, to form their judgment about the February 7 polls.
> And if in faith they see things as we do, we must come together and
> discern what actions we will take according to the mind of Christ. In
> a creative, imaginative way, under the guidance of Christ's Spirit, let
> us pray together, reason together, decide together, act together, always
> with the end that the truth prevail, that the will of the people will be
> fully respected. (Mercado, 1986, p. 78)

The people rallied behind Cory demanding that the world recognize her election. On February 22, Defense Minister Juan Ponce Enrile and General Fidel Ramos's troops seized key military bases, then issued a mandate for Marcos to step aside for Cory. As protests intensified, especially near the presidential palace, Ramos announced, "What is happening is not a coup d'état but a revolution *of the people* [emphasis added]" (Haag, 1999, p. 430).

Marcos ordered General Ver and the army "to put down" the protests. Ver's column of tanks was stopped physically by thousands of unarmed people kneeling in the streets to pray and protest (Mercado, 1986). The media broadcast images of young mothers with children, nuns, and priests praying fervently; women offering flowers and food to the troops; and the presence of large statues of the Blessed Mother.

After Enrile boldly declared a provisional government, Cory took the oath of office on February 25, pledging a government "in the name of the Filipino people" (Haag, 1999, p. 430). Cory later testified that as she placed her hand on the Bible at the ceremony she felt "the presence of the invisible President," that is, Ninoy (Tatad, 1986, p. 236).

Although Marcos "staged" his own inaugural, tensions escalated until the American Reagan administration offered Marcos safe evacuation and haven in Hawaii. On February 26, jubilant citizens danced as a U.S. military cargo plane airlifted the Marcos retinue from Clark Air Force Base on Luzon Island, Philippines (Komisar, 1987). Admittedly, there were huge political hurdles ahead for Cory. The world, through extensive media coverage, witnessed a courageous widow determined to bring change to her people.

The Accomplishments of Cory Aquino

President Aquino "midwifed" the restoration of democracy in the Philippines through the implementation of a new constitution limiting the powers of the president. Her administration demonstrated concern for civil liberties and human rights, and initiated peace talks with communist insurgents and Muslim secessionists, a decision which angered many backers. Aquino's economic policies restored economic health and confidence, and created a market-oriented, socially responsible economy to attract and reassure foreign investors.

The Promise Fulfilled

Cory survived insubordination within her own administration and several coups. No one doubted her promise: "I only want to be President for one term" (Stewart & Sindayen, 1987, p. 33). In June 1992, General Fidel Ramos, Cory's political ally, was elected president. Cory had led a successful 6-year transition from Marcos to democracy. Haag (1999) insists that "without her leadership, the Philippines could have easily lapsed into chaos and anarchy" (p. 432).

The Last Years

After leaving office, Cory Aquino remained active in the public eye, voicing her views and opinions on political issues. In 2008, she was diagnosed with colon cancer. As the nation prayed, her faith steadied her. "I was prepared to go. I've lived my life. I've been president," she explained to one reporter, "I leave it [my illness] up to God. It's up to Him. But I'm not dying to live long. I never expected to live this long. I am 76 years old and I was widowed at 50" (Ramirez, 2009).

The Role of Faith in Defusing Death Anxiety

Research demonstrates that mortality salience is drawn to certain charismatic political candidates who share the perceiver's political orientation (Kosloff, Greenberg, Weise, & Solomon, 2010). Following threatening events, individuals must manage elevated death anxiety. Because Cory confidently offered hope for "a tomorrow" for her nation, many individuals could believe in a future.

Some individuals become more religious or adapt religiously framed interpretations of the incident-stimulus. Cory "lived" her faith, enjoying a supportive friendship with Cardinal Sin and other key Catholic clergy—relationships significant in a nation that is 85% Catholic (Stewart & Sindayen, 1987).

Some Implications for Clinicians

Few of your clients may follow a spouse into political office, but a widowed client might be faced with saving a family business, challenging injustice, or, like Coretta Scott King, fighting to preserve a husband's legacy. The borrowed narrative of Cory Aquino might inspire your client (H. I. Smith, 2011) and stimulate therapeutic conversation.

One reporter asked: "Wasn't she, a widowed mother of five, afraid that she could be killed?" "If someone wishes to use a bazooka on me," Cory smiled, "it's goodbye. If it's my time to die, I'll go." She repeatedly frustrated security staff by plunging into crowds to shake hands or to listen to someone (Stewart & Sindayen, 1987, p. 27).

Grief in a Global Culture

Citizens of a particular country, for a variety of reasons, live in the United States or elsewhere as expatriates for brief periods like the

Aquinos or for years or generations. Many retain an intense emotional loyalty to their homeland and speak of returning "some day." At the time the Aquinos lived in Boston, 781,894 Filipino citizens lived in the United States; today that number is more than 5 million (Rodis, 2008).

Revolt or political unrest in one's nation of origin can have a tsunami-like psychological impact, particularly if family members, friends, or colleagues still there are potentially threatened or displaced. Cyberlinks offer more ways to stay in touch but may elevate death anxiety. In recent political revolts, however, access to the Internet and social networking has been limited by governments. Around-the-clock news coverage, unsubstantiated reports, or rumors function like a Bunsen burner on an exile's death anxiety.

Clarify

Crenshaw (2007) reminds clinicians that we should focus on the grief "of *this* particular child or adult at *this* specific point in time in the context of present life circumstances" (p. 227) or what Rohr (2011) calls "thisness." Initially, elements in receiving this narrative may confuse the clinician, because, as Tutu (2011) acknowledges, some words or phrases are difficult to translate into English. Intrafamily relationships can be tense if family members align themselves with competing political factions and personalities, or if family members are financially supporting or benefiting from a particular leader or faction.

Sue and Sue (2003) identify three essentials for receiving narratives: the clinician's self-knowledge, respectful communication, and an openness to learning even when one's personal/professional/ spiritual assumptions are challenged. Although I do not believe that Aquino's assassination was "God's will," as Dona Aurora Aquino insisted, I realize that idea is foundational in her assumptive world (and, perhaps, in the assumptive world of many Filipinos). I do value her hope: "Lord, I know that something good will come out of even this" (as cited in Mercado, 1986, p. 13). This mantra, "Lord, you know best" (p. 12) was meaningful as she supported her daughter-in-law and five grandchildren after her son's death.

Some "Economic" Exiles or "Educational" Expatriates Stay Permanently

Some nations rely on remittances its citizens send home to support family members and stimulate local economies, particularly by those Filipinos Cruz (2011) identifies as "transpacific exiles" (p. 6). Given the recent global economic downturn, individuals may grieve that they cannot send home as much money as previously. Thus, counseling may now be a luxury.

Clinicians Need to be Aware That Assassination, Like Terror,
Is Part of the Global Political and Economic Landscape

Assassination and subsequent political and economic reactions may be a definitive element in an individual's or family's narrative. Since 1875, Jones and Olken (2009) have identified at least 298 serious assassination attempts resulting in the death of 59 political leaders on the world stage including King Abdullah I of Jordan (1951), Vietnam President Ngo Dinh Diem (1963), U.S. President John F. Kennedy (1963), Egyptian President Anwar Sadat (1981), Indian Prime Minister Indira Gandhi (1984), and Israeli Prime Minister Yitzhak Rabin (1995).

Fears escalate when religious factors and prejudices are involved in assassination attempts. For example, Rabin was killed in November 1995 not by an Arab but by a radical Jew who did not support negotiations with Arab neighbors. Yigal Amir felt, as he watched Rabin walking toward his waiting car after a rally, that God gave him "the sacred signal." He took several steps, put his gun at Rabin's back and fired. Ironically, Rabin's security agents "did not fire back as they had been trained to do," and that would fuel rumors among Israelis that somehow they were involved (Kurzman, 1998, p. 508).

Failed Assassinations and Coups

Given beliefs about the corruptness of a leader or extent of repression, expatriates grieve because an assassination or coup failed. Politically active exiles, afraid of arrest or having their passport confiscated, cannot go home to be with dying family members, attend funeral rituals, or fulfill family grief-related responsibilities. Religious minorities, educated women, and gay and lesbian persons may face particular threats in returning home. Many grieve being unable to return.

Family members may be angered that exiles do not return. This strain may be heightened when someone is terminally ill, dies unexpectedly, or might have lived if receiving access to American or European medical resources. Given the tradition of burial within 24 hours in many areas of the world, there may be insufficient time for expatriates to return home; some are unable to afford the costs of international flights home.

A national leader, to some degree, becomes an "inescapable presence" in the daily lives of citizens and exiles. Kurzman (1998) describes the effect on Dr. Mordechai Gutman, a trauma surgeon, who worked for more than an hour to save Yitzhak Rabin, the prime minister he loved. "During the operation, I hopelessly looked for something I could fix. ... But I didn't have the guts to declare him dead" (p. 511). Gutman and others in Israel were asking what this shooting would do to the peace process. Would the future of Israel be changed by what happened in this operating room? Sometimes, a government leader is fictive kin. Socialization with other exiles, like the Aquinos in Boston, may be organized around support for, or in opposition to, a leader. Following assassination, one may feel as if a member of the family has died. This was demonstrated in the outpouring of grief following the death of Franklin Roosevelt in 1945, and the assassination of John F. Kennedy in 1963.

Explore the Role of Faith/Spirituality in Grief

Given the impact of religion and spirituality on death anxiety, clinicians must respect the spiritual experience and beliefs of clients. Cory Aquino's Roman Catholic faith and spiritual practices, particularly attending Mass and her reliance on prayer, appealed to and comforted millions who shared that faith. Catholics believe in the intercession of the saints. Cory noted:

> I can't help but remember Ninoy. I cannot resist comparing his death to Good Friday and our liberation to Easter Sunday. I am sure that Ninoy

is smiling at us now from the life after, for truly we have proved him correct: the Filipino is worth dying for.

In the dark days before liberation, I said that I believe God is on our side and that we have nothing to fear. I truly believe that He is not only on our side, He actively intervened and fought by our side. How else can we explain many of the events in the days that just passed?

I pray that He will continue to be by our side in the difficult yet challenging days to come. I am confident that He will not fail us: our cause is just. God is beside us. (As cited in Mercado, 1986, p. 245)

To some readers, that conclusion is troubling. However, it closely resembles what was said following the assassination of Abraham Lincoln on Good Friday 1865 (Burlingame, 2008). Some historians would contend that Lincoln's status was immediately elevated by the application of the word *martyr*.

Cory closed her inaugural speech by linking the political world with the spiritual. She appealed, "Continue praying. Let us pray for God's help especially in these days" (Mercado, 1986, p. 235). Then the crowd softly sang "The Lord's Prayer."

Christian believers disagree on the role of the Blessed Mother; Catholics, like Cory, enthusiastically embrace this construct, especially in response to death anxiety. A Protestant clinician may have to ignore learned skepticism. Francisco Tatad labeled the developments that led to Cory's inauguration "a miracle," explaining:

Cory has been performing as an inspired woman-leader. Another quiet gentle woman, loved by Filipinos, was instrumental in the miracle or victory through nonviolence. She is Mary, our mother.

She took care and made sure that we, her devoted children, who had already suffered for so many years, would be completely delivered from bloodshed. God was actively present during those February days. So was Mary. (As cited in Mercado, 1988, p. 304)

Borrow a Hero

Webb (1999) advocates using "people potential" in counseling; Esme Raji Codell calls this process the "biographical mentor" (as cited in

Young & Bradley, 2011, p. 31). Suppose a client admires or is, at least, aware of the courage of Corazon Aquino. The clinician asks:

> How would Corazon Aquino react in your situation?
> How might Corazon Aquino counsel you?
> What might Corazon Aquino say to you that you would find hopeful?

Conclusion

Corazon "Cory" Aquino, "a woman with no political biography" according to a leading political columnist, and whose place Marcos insisted "was at home" (Chua-Eoan, 1988, p. 71), served as the 11th president of the Philippines, the first female national leader democratically elected in Asia. Her son, Benigno Aquino III, was elected president in a landslide in May 2020 (CNN Wire Staff, 2010).

The Lady in Yellow died on August 1, 2009, and was laid to rest beside Ninoy. A nation and many world citizens mourned a courageous widow who demonstrated that one determined individual can diffuse death anxiety and make a difference. "Tita (Auntie) Cory," as she was affectionately known, is still revered by many Filipinos. The author of the Book of Hebrews pointed to saints "who though dead, yet speak" (Hebrews 11:4). Thus, Cory still has something to say to widows today: Live by the courage of your convictions.

12
A GRIEVER NAMED C. S.

When you starts measuring somebody, measure him right. Make sure you done taken into account what hills and valleys he come through before he got to wherever he is.

Lorraine Hansberry, *A Raisin in the Sun* (1960, p. 145)

C. S. Lewis is one of the "most enduring and often-quoted writers" in the English-speaking world (Mitchell, 1998, p. 7) with more than 200 million books sold worldwide and an estimated 2 million sold annually (A. Brown, Wade Center, personal communication, February 21, 2007). More than 113 C. S. Lewis-related books are currently in print (*The Subject Guide to Books in Print*, 2006–2007, 2006, pp. 10061–10062), something of a paradox because Lewis predicted his books would not be read 5 or 6 years after his death (Dorsett, 1992). Many in the field of thanatology (Ashenburg, 2003; Bowlby, 1980; Corr, Nabe, & Corr, 1997; Hsu, 2002; LaGrand, 2006; Parkes, 1986–1987; H. I. Smith, 2004a; Worden, 2009; Zonnebelt-Smeenge & De Vries, 1998) recognize Lewis's *A Grief Observed* as an important grief narrative. S. M. Gilbert (2006) called the book "one of the twentieth century's classic bereavement texts" (p. 30); Attig (2001) praised the memoir as "one of the most revealing personal accounts of loss and grieving in the English language" (p. 35). *A Grief Observed*, written in old exam booklets immediately following the death of Joy, Lewis's wife, in 1959, is frequently included on recommended reading lists for grievers. Published in 1961 under the pen name N. W. Clerk, ironically, Lewis received copies from friends as gifts of condolence (Walsh, 1976).

Many scholars and readers assume that Joy's death was the dominant grief in Lewis's life. Many would agree with Walmsey's (1998) assessment: "Above all Jack Lewis grieved for the early loss of Joy, the woman who, late in his life, brought him love and happiness and a special friendship, and with whom he spent a few truly joyful years" (p. 7). I disagree. The phrase "above all" discounts the accumulated grief Lewis experienced before he married the American writer; few writers have explored his "historical antecedents" (Worden, 2009, p. 63).

Many clinicians recommend Lewis because of their appreciation of his candor in *A Grief Observed* and shown in *Shadowlands*, the movie portrayal of Lewis's life, which, however, took great liberties with Lewis's life (Dorsett, 2009; Gresham, 2005; Lindskoog, 2001; Neven, 2001). Borrowing wisdom from A *Raisin in the Sun*, to assess Lewis's grief, you have to consider "what hills and valleys he come through" (Hansberry, 1960, p. 145). When taking any individual's grief measure, that is wise guidance.

Antecedent losses shaped Lewis's grief as he wrote *A Grief Observed*. These "other" griefs must be acknowledged to fully appreciate the widower's pain. Some losses that make up his grief grid are unknown, unexamined, or underexamined. Joy's death was, I believe, the last straw—the loss he could not survive. Dorsett (2009) notes, "He was never well after Joy left him [died]" (p. 163). Lewis died on November 22, 1963, the same day as John Kennedy.

The Other Losses of C. S. Lewis

Examining Lewis's grief grid is illuminating.

Birth of C. S. Lewis	1898, November 29
Death of grandfather, Richard Lewis	1907, April 2
Death of uncle, Joseph Lewis	1907, April 12(?)
Death of mother, Flora	1908, August 23
Death of his sergeant, Harry Ayres	1918, April 15
Death of friend, Lawrence Johnson	1918, April 15
Death of friend, Paddy Moore	1918, September 19
Death of mentor, W. T. Kirkpatrick	1921, March 22
Death of father, Albert Lewis	1929, September 25
Death of friend, Charles Williams	1945, May 15
Death of adopted "mother," Janie Moore	1951, January 25
Death of spiritual director, Walter Adams	1951, May 17
Exile from Oxford	1954, Fall
Death of wife, Joy	1959, July 13
Death of C. S. Lewis	1963, November 22

The Early Deaths

C. S. Lewis (called "Jack" by those close to him) identified his family's move into a new home outside Belfast as "the first great change in my life" (1955, p. 9). For Albert Lewis, his father—and therefore for C. S. Lewis—"1907 was a year of unbelievable sorrows" (Wilson, 1990, p. 19). After Flora, C. S. Lewis's mother was diagnosed with cancer, Grandfather Lewis—who lived with the family because of premature senility—was moved out of the home and died. One week later, C. S. Lewis's Uncle Joseph died.

Death 3: Flora Lewis (August 23, 1908)

Lewis's idyllic childhood, Downing (2005) argues, "came to an abrupt end at the age of nine when his mother died" (p. 8) on his father's birthday. Moreover, Flora Lewis's surgery and death occurred in the home and significantly altered the memories of the residence for C. S. Lewis and his brother, Warren (Warnie). C. S. Lewis (1955) reminisced

> the real bereavement had happened before our mother died. We lost her gradually as she was gradually withdrawn from our life into the hands of nurses and delirium and morphia, and as our whole existence changed into something alien and menacing, as the house became full of strange smells and midnight noises and sinister whispered conversations. ... It divided us from our father as well as our mother. They say that a shared sorrow draws people closer together; I can hardly believe that it often has that effect when those who share it are of widely different ages. If I may trust my own experience, the sight of adult misery and adult terror has an effect on children which is ... paralyzing and alienating. (Lewis, 1955, pp. 18–19)

Lewis, attempting to make sense of the death, like many children, blamed himself.

> Perhaps it was our own fault. Perhaps if we had been better children we might have lightened our father's sufferings at this time. We certainly did not. His nerves had never been of the steadiest and his emotions had always been uncontrolled. Under pressure of anxiety his temper became incalculable; he spoke wildly and acted unjustly. Thus by a particular

cruelty of fate, during those months the unfortunate man, had he but known it, was really losing his sons as well as his wife. (Lewis, 1955, p. 19)

Lewis and Warnie, as brothers and best friends, conspired against their father.

> We were coming, my brother and I, to rely more and more exclusively on each other for all that made life bearable; to have confidence only in each other. I expect that we (or at any rate I) were already learning to lie to him. Everything that had made the house a home had failed us; everything except one another. We drew daily closer together … two frightened urchins huddled for warmth in a bleak world. (C. S. Lewis, 1955, p. 19)

Albert Lewis wrote Warnie in boarding school, "It may be that God in his Mercy has decided that you will have no person in the future to turn to but me" (Wilson, 1990, p. 20). That expectation raised profound emotional and religious stress for both boys. How could a merciful God allow emotionally vulnerable boys to be deprived of a mother—given a dysfunctional father who had few graces to offer his sons? Over the years, Albert Lewis refused to alter his daily routines to accommodate anyone. The alienation—and the subsequent anger and guilt the boys experienced for not loving their father—impacted their memories and relationships. Hagman (2001) observed: "Mourning is fundamentally an intersubjective process, and many problems arising from bereavement are due to the failure of other survivors to engage with the bereaved person in mourning together" (p. 25).

C. S. Lewis lamented, "With my mother's death all happiness, all that was tranquil and reliable, disappeared from my life" (1955, p. 21). That seems a bit dramatic. Yet, days after Flora died, Albert sent his sons to a boarding school in England. Thus, within a matter of days, he lost his mother, home, predictable world, independence, and his country. Everything "familiar" disappeared. Gresham (2005) commented, "It is hard to understand how he [Albert] managed to pick what may well have been the worst school in all England" (p. 13). Fifty years later, Warnie dismissed the school as "that hellhole." The headmaster delighted in "flogging the boys for little or no reason. His insane rages were the dominating feature of the school. Jack had been hurled from what could be described as a heavenly existence, directly into a pretty good imitation of hell" (W. H. Lewis, 1982, p. 252).

The headmaster never flogged C. S., but the grieving boy seeing classmates beaten lived in constant fear of being beaten. After legal action for severely beating one pupil, the headmaster was committed to an insane asylum and the school closed. Gormley (1998) concluded that feeling unprotected "under the power of such a brutal tyrant left Jack with an emotional scar for the rest of his life" (p. 20). Forgiving the father who had placed him in that toxic environment was more challenging. The maternal wound shaped C.S.'s future relationships with his adopted mother Janie Moore and wife Joy Davidson.

Death 4: Lawrence Johnson, Friend (April 15, 1917)

During World War I, C. S. Lewis volunteered for the British army and quickly made friends with fellow soldiers. Through spirited late-night conversations with Lawrence Johnson, a student at Oxford, Lewis learned that "argument between two young men could be a source of delight and a cement of affection" (Jacobs, 2005, p. 89), a standard that later shaped friendships with his Oxford peers, the Inklings. In battle, Johnson "was killed by the same shell that wounded me." Lewis wrote his father, Albert, "I can hardly believe that he is dead. I had hoped to meet him at Oxford some day" (p. 89). Indeed, World War I was a blood bath for Lewis and England. Walter (1999) makes the case that the sheer number of deaths overwhelmed and permanently altered British funeral ritualization.

Death 5: Edward Francis Courtney "Paddy" Moore, Close Friend (September 1918)

Lewis's life would have been radically different if he had not roomed at Keble College with Paddy Moore during the summer of 1917, or had the gentlemen not made a pact to "do all in his power to care for and protect the family of his dead friend" if either were killed (Gresham, 1988, p. 40). "All of the subsequent events of Lewis's life until 1951" were shaped by his striving to honor that pledge (Moore, 1990, p. 247).

In September 1917, Lieutenant Jack Lewis spent a leave with Paddy; Janie, Paddy's mother, age 45; and Maureen, Paddy's sister, age 15, in Bristol. With minimal training, Lewis was soon sent to Arras, France, where a corpse-strewn battlefield rebooted "the deadness of his dead mother" (Wilson, 1990, p. 56). Sergeant Harry Ayres devoted himself to making the untested young lieutenant appear competent. "Jack, feeling totally inexperienced in warfare, and inadequate in face of the Sergeant's professional skill" would eventually say that this wise soldier "'turned this ridiculous and painful relation into something beautiful'" (Arnott, 1975, p. 73).

After 60 German soldiers surrendered to a surprised Lewis, Ayres suggested the young officer might have, at least, pulled out his revolver. On April 15, 1918, an English shell exploded killing Ayres instantly and spraying shrapnel into Lewis's leg, arm, face and lung. Lewis was initially evacuated to Liverpool and later to London. Alarmed at the unknown fate of her son, missing in battle since March, Janie Moore came to London to comfort her son's friend, while Albert Lewis ignored repeated requests to come to his son's bedside.

Between 1917 and 1918, in letters to his friend Arthur Greeves, Lewis acknowledged being in love with Mrs. Moore, who was 26 years older and separated from her husband (Bremer, 1998a, p. 300). Some biographers (Bremer, 1998b; Como, 1998; Jacobs, 2005; Wilson, 1990) believe the two had a sexual relationship before or during his convalescence. In September, when Paddy Moore was confirmed dead, Lewis grappled with the implications of their pact. Gresham (1988), Lewis' stepson, concludes: "Jack clearly needed a mother substitute" (p. 40) and Mrs. Moore needed a "replacement" for a dead son. "Mrs. Moore gave Jack the affection and attention he had been missing for years" (Gresham, 2005, p. 59). The relationship was confusing when Lewis introduced her as "Mother." Walsh (1976) explains, "For thirty years he was a kind of son to a kind of mother" (p. 107). The relationship continued long after Warnie thought the promise fulfilled. She was a burden for both brothers as with increasing age, Mrs. Moore became less and less rational and more and more needful of constant, repetitive demonstrations of affection and filial duty on Jack's part, until barely fifteen minutes at a time would pass without some foolish demand interrupting Jack's work. (Gresham, 1988, p. 41)

The responsibility created financial strain because Lewis depended upon Albert's annual allowance of 85 pounds from January 1919 until May 1925. The allowance would have been adequate for an undergraduate but not for one supporting a middle-aged woman and her adolescent daughter. Between 1918 and 1923, Wilson (1990) reports that the Lewis "family" lived "hand to mouth" in nine residences as Lewis did the cooking, shopping, and monitoring of Maureen's schoolwork. To keep the relationship clandestine, Lewis lied to his father, who would never have approved. Moreover, Lewis misled Oxford authorities and risked his academic future by this scandalous "arrangement."

Death 6: W. T. Kirkpatrick, Mentor (March 22, 1921)

The world would never have heard of C. S. Lewis without W. T. Kirkpatrick who prepared the emotionally wounded adolescent for Oxford's entrance exams. Barely surviving the horrors of boarding school from 1914 to 1917, Lewis blossomed under Kirkpatrick's tutoring. Kirkpatrick taught Lewis how to think and to defend his beliefs. Years after Kirkpatrick's death, Lewis assessed his mentor, "I owe him in the intellectual sphere as much as one human can owe another" (Bremer, 1998a, p. 37). In *Surprised by Joy*, Lewis (1955) eulogized, "My debt to him is very great. My reverence to this day undiminished" (p. 148). Kirkpatrick's death challenged the young atheist's thinking (Gormley, 1998). Although "Old Knock" had not believed in an afterlife, Lewis had difficulty believing that Kirkpatrick no longer existed. "I have seen death often and never yet been able to find it anything but extraordinary and rather incredible. The real person is so very different from what is left that one cannot believe something had turned into nothing" (Gormley, 1998, p. 80).

Death 7: Albert Lewis, Father (September 25, 1929)

Lewis identified the summer of 1929 as "the turning point of his whole life" (Wilson, 1990, p. 105). As Lewis, now a tutor, prepared for the fall term at Oxford, his father's health failed. Wilson adds, "Lewis continued, throughout life, to be obsessed" by his father (p. 110). Lewis wrote his friend Arthur Greeves in 1923, of his fear of future mental imbalance based on his grandfather and father's eccentricities and a fear "that the unsatisfactory relations which had existed between himself and his father since early adolescence might somehow mar him for the rest of his life" (Wilson, 1990, p. 111). Albert's unwillingness to come to see Jack escalated the emotional estrangement. Warnie explained that his brother had been "deeply hurt at a neglect which he consider inexcusable" (C. S. Lewis, 1966, p. 10).

Although Lewis dutifully returned to Ireland to nurse his father, he was uncomfortable being in the house. "I have never been able to resist the retrogressive influence of this house, which always plunges me back into the pleasures *and pains* [emphasis added] of a boy" (Lewis, 1966, p. 137). Lewis added, "Every room is soaked with the bogeys of childhood—the awful 'rows' with my father, the awful returnings to school, and also with the old pleasures of an unusually ignoble adolescence" (Lewis, 1966, p. 137). Lewis wrote Greeves,

> you remember from your own experience how horrible one feels when the people who one ought to love, but doesn't very much, are ill and in need of your help and sympathy; when you have to behave as love [would] dictate and yet feel all the time as if you were doing nothing—because you can't give what's really wanted. (Lewis, 1979, p. 305)

Bremer (1998a) observed that "Jack felt a great deal of shame at how he had treated his father. He had lied to him, misled him, and denigrated him" and worked "to understand and deal with his lack of paternal respect" (p. 42). Caregiving gave Lewis an opportunity to see his father differently and to notice "his resemblance to me" (Lewis, 1966, p. 137). Lewis wrote Leo Baker, "I have deep regrets about all my relations with my father (but thank God they were best at the end)" (Jacobs, 2005, p. 111). Convinced by physicians that Albert could linger indefinitely, Lewis returned to Oxford only to receive word that his father's condition had worsened. Although he left immediately for Ireland, he learned upon arrival in Belfast that his father had died. One month after the death, he confessed to Warnie:

> I think the mere pity for the poor old chap and for the life he had led really surmounted everything else. It was also (in the midst of home surroundings) almost impossible to believe. A dozen times while I was making the funeral arrangements I found myself mentally jotting down some episode or other that I wanted to tell him. (Lewis, 1966, p. 138)

Albert's death complicated life for both sons. Warnie had been forced, because of alcoholism, to retire early from the British military. He needed somewhere to live and accepted his brother and Mrs. Moore's offer to live with them, a transition that proved difficult. Moreover, dispersing the contents of their childhood home, particularly the toys, led Lewis to wait until his brother arrived from India because he could not enlist Mrs. Moore's help. "There are ghosts there who wd. not be happy to see her nor anxious to make her happy" (Lewis, 1979, p. 307). Because the brothers were unwilling to give away their toys,

> They packed up their boyhood toys and things they had loved in a large trunk and took it solemnly out into the garden where they dug a deep hole and buried it; with it they buried too the little boys they had once been. Some of the furniture and other things they decided to keep; others they marked to be sold. The house itself was put on the market, and at last they firmly closed the book on all that had been their childhood, turned their backs on it, and went off to catch the ferry to England. (Gresham, 2005, p. 86)

The financial settlement of Albert Lewis's estate did not meet the brothers' expectations. Yet, in time, Lewis, Warnie, and Janie Moore bought a home by pooling resources in a three-party mortgage. Although the house was in Moore's name, Lewis and Warnie could live there for their lifetimes (Bremer, 1998a, p. 44).

Albert's death haunted Lewis spiritually and emotionally. Twenty-five years later, he confessed, "I treated my own father abominably and no sin in my whole life now seems to be so serious." That confession led Wilson (1990) to conclude: "His remorse was perpetual and far-reaching, and it coloured the whole of his memory. Sadness for the way he had felt about the old man blended with a sense that his childhood was irrecoverably lost" (p. 114).

Death 8: Charles Williams, Friend (May 15, 1945)

The unexpected death of Charles Williams, described as "my friend of friends," devastated Lewis (Bremer, 1998a, p. 51). Certainly, Lewis grieved the deaths of several students early in World War II, but this death stunned Lewis. Writing their mutual friend, Owen Barfield, Lewis called the death "the *first really severe loss I have suffered* [emphasis added]" (Lewis, 1966, p. 206). This comment would, to many clinicians, seem peculiar given the previous antecedent losses. The friendship began when Oxford Press, where Williams was an editor, moved to Oxford to avoid the aerial bombings of London. Lewis praised Williams's novel, *The Place of the Lion*, and admired his poetry; Williams admired Lewis's writing. After Williams joined the Inklings, the two writers met at least twice a week from 1939 until 1945. The day after World War II ended, as joy erupted in Oxford, Williams was hospitalized. En route to the Eagle and Child pub for the regular Tuesday gathering of friends, Lewis stopped to inquire about Williams's condition only to be informed bluntly that Williams had died. Lewis stumbled to the Inklings' gathering in a daze to break the news.

Williams' death provoked a significant reexamination of Lewis's understanding of eternal life.

> The experience of loss (the greatest I have yet known) was wholly unlike what I should have expected. We now verified for ourselves what so many bereaved people have reported; the ubiquitous presence of a dead man, as if he had ceased to meet us in particular places in order to meet us everywhere. ... No event has so corroborated my faith in the next world as Williams did simply by dying. When the idea of death and the idea of Williams thus meet in my mind, it was the idea of death that was changed. (Lewis, 1966, p. xiv)

Days later, Lewis expanded on that idea in a letter to an unnamed woman:

I also have become much acquainted with grief now through the death of my great friend Charles Williams, my friend of friends, the comforter of our little set, the most angelic man. The odd thing is that his death had made my faith stronger than it was a week ago. And I find that all that talk about "feeling that he is closer to us than before" isn't just talk. It's just what it does feel like—I can't put it into words. (Lewis, 1966, p. 206)

The admission, "I can't put it into words," sounds odd coming from a best-selling author.

Loss 9: Death of Janie Moore, Companion (January 25, 1951)

The relationship between "adopted son and mother" deteriorated over the years because Lewis could not satisfy Janie Moore's incessant demands. Moreover, due to senility, Moore became difficult "to manage." Lewis requested the prayers of Sister Penelope, "for the old lady I call my mother and live with … an unbeliever, ill, old, frightened" (Gormley, 1998, p. 113). In April 1950, Lewis reluctantly placed the 78-year-old Moore in a nursing home but visited daily until her death.

At the last, according to Bremer (1998a), "she was scarcely coherent and could be very grumpy and blasphemous" (p. 53). Lewis suffered her tongue lashings and prayed for grace to be kind. Her death troubled Lewis because, to his knowledge, she never became a Christian. "Worse," Gormley (1998) notes, "she seemed to resent Jack's faith for creating a distance between them" (p. 113). Lewis had to get used to all the time he now had for himself.

I have lived most of [my private life] in a house which was hardly ever at peace for 24 hours, amid senseless wranglings, lying, backbitings, follies and scares. I never went home without a feeling of terror as to what appalling situation might have developed in my absence. Only now that it is over do I begin to realize quite how bad it was. (Bremer, 1998a, p. 35)

Death 10: Walter Adams, Spiritual Director (May 17, 1951)

Four months after Janie Moore died, Lewis was stunned by the sudden death of Father Walter Adams, his Anglican spiritual director and confessor. For years, Lewis had had intense spiritual conversations with the man perhaps because Adams understood Lewis's complex inner life (Como, 1998). Lewis never replaced Adams as spiritual director or what some term "spiritual friend." Wilson (1990) speculated that certain decisions—accepting the professorship at Cambridge, leaving Oxford, and the romance/marriage with Joy Davidson—might have gone differently if Lewis could have discussed them with Adams. "Without his presence to admonish and guide, Lewis must have felt both a little bereft and, in a sense, liberated" (Wilson, 1990, p. 239).

Loss 11: Leaving Oxford (Fall 1954)

Just as Lewis and Warnie had been "exiled" from their childhood home, over time, Lewis felt estrangement at Oxford, his academic home since 1919. Lewis's fame, the sales of his popular books, and his broadcast lectures on the BBC during World War II strained relationships with faculty colleagues. Some colleagues were annoyed by his public religiosity (Bremer, 1998a; Jacobs, 2005); others harped that Lewis should concentrate on his field of expertise— medieval literature—and leave religion to the clergy or to theological faculty. One doctoral student, Alastair Fowler (2006), opined that Lewis "towered above his colleagues" (p. 108) and that fueled their resentment.

Soon after Janie Moore died in 1951, Lewis was passed over for a professorship that would have freed him from tutorial responsibilities and provided more time to write. He realized that he would "spend the rest of his career as a tutor rather than a professor" (Jacobs, 2005, p. 265). In 1954, when Cambridge offered him a chair of English focusing on medieval and Renaissance literature, Lewis declined although the professorship would have boosted his finances. Money had long been an issue since Lewis gave away a sizeable portion of his royalties to charity (Jacobs, 2005, p. 266). He had to take into consideration how a move would affect his brother.

After J. R. R. Tolkien suggested that Lewis would be happier at Cambridge (Jacobs, 2005, p. 266), Lewis accepted the professorship, living during the week at Cambridge and spending weekends and holidays at the Kilns, his home.

Death 12: Joy Davidson Gresham Lewis, Wife (July 13, 1959)

Against this accumulation of loss, we turn to what many consider his greatest loss: Joy Davidson Lewis. Lewis and Joy, a writer from New York, began corresponding in January 1950 (Lewis, 1982). After she and her young sons moved to England, to escape a bad marriage, Lewis subsidized them. When British authorities denied her request to remain in England, Lewis married her on April 23, 1956. This civil marriage was "a pure formality" (Lewis, 1982, p. 245) to allow Joy and her sons to avoid deportation. After Joy broke her hip and was diagnosed with cancer, Lewis wanted their relationship recognized by The Church of England, which did not permit remarriage of divorced persons; moreover, Joy was twice divorced. Lewis's public stature made any accommodation to the circumstances unlikely. On March 21, 1957, defying church canon, Father Pete Bide married Lewis and Joy. Soon Joy's cancer went into remission and the couple celebrated good times for the next 3 years. Joy died on July 13, 1959, leaving Jack, paradoxically, in his father's position: a widower caring for two boys. According to Austin Farrer, a close friend, Lewis was "almost beside himself by his wife's death" (Farrer, 1979, p. 244). Duncan (2001) comments that while "death was never a stranger" to Lewis, "it was only through the loss of Joy that Lewis was forced to turn inward, to test his faith, and to reveal the insights he gained from his grief to readers around the world. Death, he knew, was inevitable. But his faith in God was a choice" (p. 157).

Lewis followed guidance he had once given Arthur Greeves, "Whenever you are fed up with life, start writing. Ink is the great cure for all human ills, as I have found out long ago" (Gormley, 1998, p. 44). Lewis poured out his grief in short paragraphs in old examination books. Duncan (2001) summarizes the loss:

> What grief did was to wreck havoc. He couldn't control the grief, and that was extremely unsettling for him. The writing out of it was his way of trying to articulate what was going on inside. What he realized is that grief is not a state, it's more like a history. (p. 151)

That angst was eventually published as *A Grief Observed*, under a pen name, N. W. Clerk, because Lewis feared colleagues' reaction.

Although the book sold few copies during his lifetime, after Lewis died the literary executor put his name on the cover and the book became a perennial best-seller.

Implications for Clinicians

Clinicians Deal With Grief Overload

Gilbert (2006b) insists that grievers feel an enormous pressure to hide their griefs. Some, like Lewis, known for their spirituality, find themselves "an embarrassment" (1961, p. 10) in certain settings. Clinicians recognize bibliotherapy and journaling (Corr, Nabe, & Corr, 2006) as useful resources for grievers. Reading another's words in books, articles, poems, newsletters, stories—especially if recommended by a clinician—may lead a griever to conclude, "Ah, *someone* understands." By reading Lewis, individuals might self-enfranchise their grief. Individuals grieving losses other than a spouse's death profit from the awareness that Lewis grieved a string of deaths, which led him to speculate, "I wonder who is next in the queue" (1976, p. 12). Lewis's opus can also be a valuable resource for thanatologists, especially those who identify themselves as Christian counselors. Wilson (1990) commented on *A Grief Observed*, "No one can read the book without being haunted by it. Like everything Lewis published, it is supremely readable, and the experiences it describes are of such pain and such universality that one cannot fail to turn its pages" (p. 285).

Clinicians Should Be Cautious in Using Lewis

Busy scholars and clinicians, aware of the rich trove of quotable material in *A Grief Observed*, may extract selected quotes—a process not unlike seeing a few tourist sites and declaring that one has seen Rome.

Clinicians Need Ways to Recommend Lewis

The clinician may preface a recommendation by saying, "Because this author was so concerned about how this book would be received by colleagues, he published anonymously." Then the clinician might ask,

"To whom are you reluctant to disclose your grief fully?" Or "Lewis was concerned with what his academic colleagues thought. What might colleagues or coworkers think about the way you are handling your grief?" Corr et al. (1997) acknowledge how valuable the book has been to grievers. Although Lewis's original intent was expressing his emotions and puzzlements, he captured grief in such a believable way that "has rung so true with other bereaved persons that his little book provides the normalization and assurance that many desperately need" (p. 252). The clinician might ask for responses to specific quotations from the book.

> I not only live each endless day in grief, but live each day thinking about living each day in grief (Lewis, 1976, p. 9).
> But her voice is still vivid. The remembered voice—that can turn me at any moment to a whimpering child (Lewis, 1976, p. 17).
> An odd by-product of my loss is that I'm aware of being an embarrassment to everyone I meet. At work, at the club, in the street, I see people, as they approach me, trying to make up their minds whether they'll "say something about it" or not. I hate it if they do, and if they don't (Lewis, 1976, p. 10).

Some clients may find permission to write after reading and reflecting on Lewis. If C. S. Lewis can write so vulnerably, perhaps, so can I. A clinician might share this quote, "Ink is the great cure for all human ills, as I have found out long ago" (Gormley, 1998, p. 44).

Conclusion

A Grief Observed is more meaningful if the reader is aware of the string of losses Lewis navigated. The Christian Bible offers this observation, "He still speaks, even though he is dead" (Hebrews 11:4, NIV), which this author contends is an accurate summation of the grief mosaic of C. S. Lewis.

13

GRIEVERS NAMED KING

The King Family's Experience
of Multiple Homicides

God knows, funerals have played a significant role in the story of the King family.

Christine King Farris (2009, p. 124)

Fragility of life is a reality in many contemporary Americans. For too many it is not "if" violence takes a family member but "when." Too many Americans can identify with Dr. Martin Luther King, Jr.'s, sister's observation in the opening quote. Although Dr. King's assassination on April 4, 1968, is a significant thread in America's political, spiritual, and social narrative, his death was only the first of three homicides experienced by members of the King family.

Historical Antecedents of Grief in the King Family

To understand a particular grief one must explore its historical antecedents (Worden, 2009).

Antecedent 1: Dr. King Survives Attempt on His Life

While autographing copies of *Strive Toward Freedom* in a Harlem bookstore on September 17, 1958, Dr. King looked up as Izola Curry thrust an 8-inch Japanese penknife into his chest. Although she tried to escape, several women chased and apprehended her. King, the knife handle protruding from his chest, calmly reassured the crowd, "That's all right. Everything is going to be all right!" (Pearson, 2002, p. 67).

Given segregation, even in the North, Dr. King was transported by ambulance to an all-Black hospital, a decision which proved providential because of the hospital's reputation for trauma care. Fearing that King might die—the knife was nestled between his heart and lung and had nicked the aorta—the police escorted Curry into the emergency room for King to identify. Curry ranted that King was a communist who had destroyed her Roman Catholic faith (Branch, 1988, p. 245).

In his last sermon Dr. King reminisced, "so close was the knife to my heart, that if I had sneezed I would have died." He laughed, "I am glad that I didn't sneeze" (Branch, 2006, p. 757).

Antecedent 2: The Montgomery Bombing

Late on January 29, 1956, Dr. King answered the telephone and heard: "Listen, nigger, we [sic] tired of you and your mess. If you aren't out of this town in three days, we gonna [sic] blow your brains out and blow up your house" (Frady, 2002, p. 45). The next night, when King finished preaching at Montgomery's First Baptist Church, he learned that his home had been bombed. Pastor Ralph David Abernathy waited to tell King until he knew that Coretta and Yolanda, their newborn, were safe. King announced what had happened and asked the congregation to go home peacefully.

Arriving at the parsonage, Dr. King confronted city leaders who had gathered to assess the damage. The mayor promised that everything would be done to bring the perpetrators to justice. When reporters tried to leave, they discovered they were surrounded by between 500 and 1,000 angry Black people (Carson, 1992, p. 179). King stepped out onto the glass-littered porch, motioned for silence, and asked those carrying guns to leave, reminding the crowd that he was totally committed to nonviolence. "I want it to be known the length and breadth of this land that if I am stopped, this movement will not stop. For we are doing what is right. What we are doing is just. And God is with us" (Branch, 1988, p. 166).

Some days Dr. King received more than 40 telephone threats (Carson & Holloran, 1998, p. 160). The bombing convinced King that racists would not hesitate to harm his family. Moreover, King soon worried about attacks by rogue agents within J. Edgar Hoover's Federal Bureau of Investigation (FBI) determined to tarnish his image (Sitkoff, 2008).

Antecedent 3: Incarceration in Reidsville Prison

Dr. King was arrested 17 times in an era when Black males did not always leave Southern jails uninjured or alive; some never made it to a cell or a courtroom (Bullard, 1993). Blacks were arrested on flimsy charges; protest could lead to being beaten and charged "with resisting arrest." On January 26, 1956, police pulled King over "for driving five miles over the speed limit." King was

> ordered out of the car, frisked, promptly bundled into the back of a squad car, and transported to the northern fringes of Montgomery, silent, trembling, his mind suddenly gone empty, to be clamped into the city's murky and reeking jail. A cold fear certainty seized him, he later confided, that he would shortly be sprinted out of the jail and lynched. (Frady, 2002, p. 44)

In May of 1960, Dr. King was arrested for not having a valid Georgia license and auto tags, fined $15, and given 12 months probation. On October 22, after King was arrested while picketing Rich's Department Store in Atlanta, a judge found him in violation of probation and order him jailed. During the night, King was transferred to the notorious Reidsville State Prison (Bennett, 1968). Martin Luther King, Sr., received a tip that Georgia officials were hoping an inmate would kill his son. Coretta Scott King telephoned Harris Wofford, an aide to Massachusetts Senator John F. Kennedy, pleading, "They are going to kill him, I know they are going to kill him" (Frady, 2002, p. 75). On Wofford's advice, Kennedy, battling Richard Nixon in a close presidential election, called Mrs. King. "I want to express to you my concern about your husband. ... I just wanted you to know that I was thinking about you and Dr. King. If there is anything I can do to help, please feel free to call on me" (Bryant, 2006, p. 184).

While Bobby Kennedy aggressively negotiated with Georgia Democratic officials for King's immediate release, news of Kennedy's call spread like wildfire through Black churches across the country the weekend before the election. That contributed, some argued, to Kennedy's narrow win.

The Dance With Violent Death

Dyson (2008) contends that one cannot understand the life of Martin Luther King, Jr., without acknowledging his intense "dance with death." Nor can one understand Coretta Scott King without appreciating that she, too, danced with death. Coretta, growing up in rural Alabama, experienced her parent's home being torched after her father refused to sell his sawmill to a white competitor; 2 weeks later his mill burned (Pope, 2005). After marrying King, Coretta, finishing her master's in music in Boston, was less than enthusiastic when King accepted a pastorate in Montgomery.

Coretta, upon learning of her husband's stabbing in Harlem, prayed, "Lord, if this is the way for him to go, help me accept it." Vivian (1970) adds, "No one saw her shed a tear after that moment" (p. 75) and no one would see her cry at Martin's funeral. Dyson (2008) observes that Martin

> ate, drank, and slept death. He danced with it, he preached it. And he stared it down. He looked for ways to lay it aside, this burden of his own mortality, but ultimately knew that his unwavering insistence on a nonviolent end to the mistreatment of his people could only end violently. (p. 3)

Dr. King preached that individuals "tormented by the fear of death" can be freed only by understanding "that this earthly life is merely an embryonic prelude to a new awakening," that is, God's promised eternal life (Carson & Holloran, 1998, p. 75) captured in the Black spiritual, "Goin' home to live with God."

In 1963, as King and Coretta watched television coverage following John Kennedy's assassination, King predicted to his wife, "This is what is going to happen to me also." Coretta recalls, "I was not able to say anything. I had no word to comfort my husband. I could not say, 'It won't happen to you.' I felt he was right. It was a painfully agonizing silence" (C. S. King, 1969, p. 244). Despite increased threats, King refused bodyguards (McElrath, 2007).

The King Family as Survivors of Multiple Homicides

The term *survivor* is more in line with Dr. King's philosophy of non-violence than the term *victim*.

Homicide 1: Martin Luther King, Jr.

On April 3, 1968, King went to Memphis to march with city sanitation workers protesting substandard wages and inhumane working conditions. That evening at the Mason Temple Church of God in Christ, King prophetically addressed his personal future:

> I don't know what will happen now; we've got some difficult days ahead. But it doesn't really matter with me now, because I've been to the mountaintop. ... Like anybody, I would like to live a long life—longevity has its place but I'm not concerned about that now. I just want to do God's will. And He's allowed me to go up to the mountain. And I've looked over, and I've seen the Promised Land. (Hansen, 2003, p. 206)

Relying on his rhetorical skills, King worked the congregation into a frenzy before exuberantly concluding:

> I may not get there with you. But I want you to know tonight that we, as a people, will get to the Promised Land. And so I'm happy tonight. I'm not worried about anything; I'm not fearing any man. Mine eyes have seen the coming of the Lord. (Hansen, 2003, p. 206)

On April 4, as King and associates gathered on the balcony of the Lorraine Hotel to leave for dinner, a rifle shot ended King's life. The moment was captured in a photograph of King, sprawled on the concrete, bleeding profusely, aides pointing in the direction from whence the shot had come.

Homicide (or Suicide) 2: Rev. A. D. Williams King

Following Dr. King's death, his brother, A. D. Williams King, pastor of Zion Baptist Church in Louisville, moved to Atlanta to support his grieving parents, nieces, and nephews, and become associate pastor at Ebenezer. The emotional toll on the Kings, given the continuous threat of violence to Dr. King, had been exhausting. Daddy King reflected, "There was great anxiety throughout our family. No matter how much protection of any sort a person has, it will not be enough if the enemy is hatred that cannot be turned around" (M. L. King, Sr., 1980b, p. 185).

As heir to a prestigious pulpit that had been in the family for decades, A. D. lavished time on his nieces and nephews. Vacationing with the King children in Jamaica, he left early, promising to see them the next day in Atlanta. At dawn on July 21, 1969, his son Al found the pastor's body at the bottom of the swimming pool in the backyard of their home.

The potential backlash triggered by the death of a second King sibling in 14 months—given the rioting in more than 100 cities in the days following the assassination that resulted in 43 deaths, 20,000 arrests, and $45 million in property damage (Hansen, 2003, p. 209)—weighed heavily on Daddy King. African Americans would not tolerate a homicide of a second King. So, the consensus emerged that A. D.—although a collegiate swimming champion—"drowned." Although the Fulton County Police declared the case closed, many Atlanta residents whispered, "There's more to this than meets the eye, and one day God will judge it all" (D. S. King, 2003, p. 74).

Dexter King, Dr. King's son, recalls, "We hadn't finishing grieving for our father; it was hard to believe Uncle A. D. was gone too" (D. S. King, 2003, p. 75). Alveda, the oldest of A. D.'s five children, did not "agree with the accidental drowning report" and suspected "foul play of some kind or another." Two details troubled her: First, no water was found in her father's lungs. Second, years later, when Alveda and a journalist requested records at the medical examiner's office, there were no notes. According to a clerk, "Dr. Dillion [the medical examiner at the time of both deaths] had a bad habit. He kept it in his head" (D. S. King, 2003, p. 75). Thirty years later, Dexter commented on his cousin's trauma, "I still don't believe she's recovered," then added, "You never recover!" (D. S. King, 2003, p. 75).

Homicide 3: Alberta "Big Momma" Williams King

By 1974, the King family had emerged cautiously into what Christine, sister of Martin and A.D., described as a "different emotional landscape." The Kings found strength in their Christian faith and in the Ebenezer community.

On Sunday June 30, 1974, as worship began M. L. King, Sr., sat in the first row waiting to slip out to catch a flight to a city where he would preach that evening; Coretta was out of town. The other King family members were present except for Dexter, age 11, who had slipped out to buy candy at a nearby store. As Alberta King, M. L. King, Sr.'s, wife, played "The Lord's Prayer" on the organ, the congregation bowed for prayer. Suddenly, Marcus Wayne Chenault, a young Black male screamed, "I am taking over!" and began shooting; worshippers sought cover under pews. Deacons, fearing for their pastor's life, pulled M. L. King, Sr., to safety despite his loud protests that he had to protect his wife. Alberta King later died at Grady Memorial Hospital, as did Deacon Edward Boykin. When Dexter heard gunshots, he ran back to Ebenezer.

For the third time in 6 years a King had died. The King family became prominent members of a select fraternity: individuals who have lost multiple family members through violence. Bernice King, Dr. King's daughter, leafed through photo albums whispering, "Wonder who's next" (D. King, 2003, p. 89)?

Implications for Clinicians

Elements in the King family's bereavement narratives are borrowable for counseling victims of violence and support groups. The Kings, by being well known, offer hope particularly to African American homicide survivors.

Implication 1: Violence in African American Communities

Death is no stranger to African American families who are more acquainted with homicide than Caucasians (Peterson & Krivo, 1993). In 2007, of the 15,831 murders in the FBI Uniform Crime Statistics,

7,316 or 46.21% of the victims were African American although Blacks make up only 13% of the U.S. population (FBI, 2008). Cosby and Poussaint (2007) protest that Black adolescents are six times more likely to die from homicide than White peers and seven times more likely to commit a homicide. Ninety-four percent of victims of Black killers in 2007 were Black. Homicide is the leading cause of death among Blacks, ages 15 to 29 (2007, p. 195). While the homicide rate has declined from the levels of the early 1990s, Cosby, whose son Enis was killed by a robber, contends that the drop is because "so many more black men are in prison" (Cosby & Poussaint, 2007, p. 195). Fields (2008) notes that some homicides are drug and gang related and others a consequence of a "glut of ex-felons re-entering society" (p. A1).

Cosby and Poussaint (2007) lament the conservative pundits who discount homicide as "just part" of the culture of the Black urban poor fueled by wealthy gansta rappers glorifying violence. Many youths "in a twisted way—may feel they gain status among their friends by shooting someone even if they go to jail for years or even for life" (Cosby & Poussaint, 2007, p. 196). Some homicides are part of gang initiation; others are retaliation for previous acts of violence.

McDevitt-Murphy, Neimeyer, Burke, and Williams (2009) document that "the demography of death is not democratic" (p. 3). According to the 2000 Census, African Americans experience homicide at the rate of 22.3 per 100,000, whereas Caucasian homicides are at 2.3 per 100,000. The researchers conclude, "making an understanding of the ways African-Americans experience grief, loss, and trauma is an important public health concern" (p. 3). Thanatologists must be concerned as well.

Implication 2: Underawareness

Grieving multiple homicides is beyond the comprehension of many and feeds the assumptions that it "cannot happen to me" or it "cannot happen in my neighborhood." These long-nurtured assumptions may collapse like dominoes following a homicide. Homicides create a significant multigenerational pool "of survivors who struggle to face life" (McDevitt-Murphy et al., 2009, p. 3).

Rosenblatt and Wallace (2005) point to a troubling barrier to awareness: "European Americans who provide" mental health services "may not have sufficient openness to African-American narratives that speak about racism" (p. 233) and its generational consequences.

Laurie and Neimeyer (2008) note that "distinctions between primary and extended kin and other kin are less pronounced in African-American culture" (citing Sudarkasa, 1997). African Americans grieve for aunts, uncles, cousins, or grandparents who, although not biological kin, provided stability, care, and affirmation. E. Lynn Harris, the African American novelist, talks about those "who have passed through my life and warmed my spirit with kindness, people I love more than words can ever convey" (2003, p. 257). Harris also notes that aunts and uncles may fill the roles of mothers and fathers more than actual parents. Dexter King recalls:

> I never knew a man with so many brothers and sisters as my father—and resulting aunts and uncles for me and my brother and sisters. Not only was there Uncle A.D. and Aunt Naomi, or Aunt Christine and Uncle Isaac, our own blood relatives and his in-laws, there was also Uncle Andy, Uncle Ralph, Uncle Henry, Uncle Bob, Uncle Julius. ... Everybody was related, even if not by blood. (D. S. King, 2003, p. 23)

Implication 3: Different Impact on Family Members

McCarty (2009) reports that members of the King family processed the trio of tragedies differently. Young (1996) supports that by noting that A. D. Williams King, the associate pastor of Ebenezer, immediately after Martin's death:

> didn't seem to be able to accept it at all. He was crying and drinking and screaming as he raged around the room that he was going to get a pistol and "kill all the motherfuckers who killed my brother." Then he would shift abruptly into another state, tearfully admonishing himself, "I've got to be nonviolent. That's what Martin would expect. Martin wouldn't want me to take revenge. Why am I saying that I want to kill someone?" (p. 468)

Three weeks after Martin's assassination, Coretta addressing a peace rally in New York City, acknowledged: "I come to New York today with the strong feeling that my husband ... would have wanted me to be present today." She continued: "Though my heart is heavy with grief from having suffered an irreparable loss, my faith in the redemptive will of God is stronger today than ever before" (Vivian, 1970, p. 101).

To assess grief among the Kings one must consider family dynamics: "Daddy" was Martin Luther King, Sr., the patriarch, and "Big Momma" was Alberta King, the matriarch. Dexter King experienced his grandfather as the dominant personality who set the pace for grief (D. S. King, 2003). Moreover, the Kings were highly visible members of an entrenched African American gentry in Atlanta (Frady, 2002) and knew their grief behaviors were watched closely. They "needed" to set the example.

Implication 4: Keep the Primary Residence an Oasis of Safety for Children

Grieving children are influenced by their environment. Dexter King, the youngest son, described the shattering of the siblings' childhoods:

> We were watching television. That's how I learned. TV told me. Special Bulletin. ... Martin [III] and I were sitting on the floor. ... The Special Bulletin came on, and an unforgettable voice said, "Dr. Martin Luther King, Jr., has been shot in Memphis at 6:01 P.M." Martin and I looked at each other. We said nothing. We both jumped up and ran into our parent's bedroom. (D. S. King, 2003, pp. 47–48)

The boys found their mom, Coretta, talking by telephone with Jesse Jackson, a King aide who had called immediately after the shooting. Dexter heard his mother repeatedly and calmly respond, "I understand." He reflected, "I'll never forget those words, how I couldn't understand why she would keep repeating them. I wanted her to get off the phone and make me understand" (D. S. King, 2003, p. 48).

Coretta softly explained, "Your father—there's been an accident." (Many homicide survivors reject the use of *accident*, even in explaining a death to children.) Assuming her husband was alive, she left to fly to Memphis. However, in a women's restroom at the Atlanta airport, Mayor Ivan Allen broke the news. "Mrs. King, I have been asked to tell you that Dr. King is dead" (D. S. King, 2003, p. 49).

When Coretta returned home Dexter remembers, "We had no time to sit and talk or break down or anything else on our own because people started coming to the house right away" (D. S. King, 2003, p. 49). Dexter wondered why someone had shot his father. An exhausted Coretta responded that an answer could wait until morning. Before she left his bedroom, Dexter asked, "Are you going to sleep here? Where will you be" (D. S. King, 2003, p. 50)? Dexter, like many children touched by trauma, wanted safety and stability. That was challenged by what Dexter termed "this great droning hubbub of guests" his mother felt obligated to host at 234 Sunset; aides filled the house negotiating details for returning Dr. King's body to Atlanta for funeral services. A fictive uncle, Andrew Young, a trusted King aide, reached out to the children. "It was Uncle Andy who actually told us my father was dead. He told us, and said we'd talk more about it later, but that we would have to look after our mother now, because that's what our father would have wanted" (D. S. King, 2003, p. 51).

Strength, according to Dexter, "was the way of our people." The Kings, in time, would get back to "normal" and accept the changes imposed on their daily lives.

> Funeral over, repast done, visitors gone home. For the survivors the river of life goes on, but the comforting course it takes has been unalterably diverted. Extended family leaves. You're there alone. Just your mother, sisters, brother, and conscience. Mother told Martin he was the man of the house now; Martin took it to heart, causing difficulties between him, me, and Yolanda, with his suddenly trying to be the man, with no model. (D. S. King, 2003, p. 61)

Homicide grievers can appreciate postritual changes. Roles changed immediately for Coretta, now a single parent and civil rights activist. As Jackie Kennedy had acted decisively following the assassination to control John Kennedy's legacy (Rubin, 2005), Coretta moved to protect Dr. King's. "The first thing," the widow did, "was germinate the idea for the King Center. She transferred her grieving into work, then immersed herself in that" (D. S. King, 2003, p. 61).

Coretta's decision "to rededicate myself to the completion of his work" (Dosekun, 2006) complicated the mourning for the King children because she began traveling extensively speaking and raising funds. Moreover, her decision threatened the transition within the patriarchal Southern Christian Leadership Conference. Coretta learned to ignore criticism of her efforts (King, 1969).

Dexter acknowledged that it was years before he comprehended what his mother went through transitioning from Mrs. Martin Luther King, Jr., to Coretta Scott King; moreover, the relationship with her in-laws had to be renegotiated. Dexter recalled, "Granddaddy became a surrogate father too. He was conscientious, tried not to usurp Mother. He respected the fact that I had had a father. ... But he was also a disciplinarian" (D. S. King, 2003, p. 64).

Alberta King's murder on June 20, 1974, imploded the Kings' assumptive world. The King family had always assumed Ebenezer Baptist Church was a safe place for them and for members of the congregation. Alberta King had not been active in the movement. As a pastor's wife, mother, grandmother, and church musician, she was the "behind-the-scenes mover and shaker of the family" (D. S. King, 2003, p. 79). This third homicide, according to Christine King Farris, shook the family: "Why [did] these terrible things continue to happen to our family" (Farris, 2009, p. 124)? Asking why is common, but as pastor-father-grandfather, Daddy King explained, "we have to give thanks to God for what is left" (M. L. King, Sr., 1980b, p. 124).

Thankful? For what? Admittedly, Chenault's rampage in the church could have been worse: As Derek King leaped to tackle Chenault, the gun misfired. Dexter wrestled with guilt. "If only we hadn't gone to Carters between Sunday school and Morning Worship. ... If I'd been there, maybe I could have done something." Dexter fantasized that he could have taken the bullet and saved his grandmother's life (D. S. King, 2003, p. 84).

The patriarch conducted a family conference immediately after his wife was pronounced dead. After 4 hours, Daddy King said, "I think—I think that I have to—we have to—forgive this, and forgive this man. Even this." Then he eyed each family member: "Do you all follow me?" Dexter although confused, could not challenge his grandfather. He later reflected on his grandfather's example:

> If he, an elderly person, not as physically strong as he once was, could endure this, have it taken out of him like that and still have faith and move on, then the least I could do was move on too. But to what? To what? (D. S. King, 2003, p. 87)

When reporters eventually asked M. L. King, Sr., if he hated James Earl Ray, his son's assassin, or Marcus Chenault, his wife's assailant, he said, "I don't hate either one. There is no time for that, and no reason either. Nothing a man does takes him lower than when he allows himself to hate someone" (Farris, 2009, p. 198).

These responses may sound unrealistic to some survivors of multiple homicides; others with strong Christian faiths may agree with them. Tensions erupt when one family member—particularly during criminal proceedings—takes a "no hate" stance that others have not embraced yet. One family member wanting revenge or threatening retaliation may compromise the family equilibrium. Borrowing from the King narrative, the clinician might ask:

> How much space does hate toward the murderer(s) take up in your life?
> What are you pretending not to know about the consequences of nurturing this hated?
> How do your emotions impact other family members?
> In what ways is your anger interfering with integrating this grief?

A clinician can borrow narratives to generate therapeutic conversation. As fictive kin is a reality for some grievers, fictive heroes might be a resource for grievers to draw upon. As clinician and client explore how others have faced such tragedies, the clinician might ask:

> How do you think Coretta Scott King would react in your particular situation?
> What counsel might Martin Luther King, Sr., offer you?
> What might Dexter or Bernice King, as survivors of violence, say that would be helpful to you?

Implication 5: Work Toward Sense Making

Currier, Holland, and Neimeyer (2010) contend that sense making—"the formulation of a subjective understanding of the loss in the restoration process" (p. 403)—is the key ingredient in absorbing traumatic death. Admittedly, a particular death in a series of homicides, or a retaliatory homicide, will prove challenging because of the assumption, or the promise, that police would protect family members. Survivors experience heightened death anxiety. Consequently, Fields (2008) reports that funeral directors are seeing an increase in violence, shootings, and killings at funerals in churches and burials.

M. L. King, Sr., had, at Ebenezer, for a period of time, a White associate, Gurion Brewster. As soon as Brewster learned of Martin's assassination he flew to Atlanta and showed up at Daddy King's front door. Daddy King welcomed him: "I've been expecting you. It's bad, Brewster, bad. I don't understand it. Why did they kill him? I am hurt by this, hurt in many ways; hurt too bad and I don't know how I'll ever get over it. I don't think I can" (Brewster, 2007, pp. 227–228).

In the presence of a trusted colleague, Daddy King laid down his armor and gave his grief a voice. Brewster became chauffeur-confidant for several days as King carried out his pastoral responsibilities; in fact, King conducted two funerals. King later confessed to Brewster: "On the day [Martin died] something inside me was killed. After he died, I rarely spoke about my experience with anyone" (Brewster, 2007, p. xi).

Brewster extended an invitation to Daddy King to deliver a lecture at the university where he taught. Faculty and students were taken by King's candor.

> I've lost so much, but I can always imagine that I can lose some more. I could have turned into a man of hate. I could have turned into a man against God. I could have turned away from life because God had taken so much from me. But God has given me even more, so I am grateful. … I am a grateful man. No one can take my gratitude away from me. (Brewster, 2007, p. 230)

M. L. King, Sr.'s, sense making and gratitude was not fully shared by other family members. Christine King Farris, at 1 A.M., 7 hours after her brother died, walked into her parent's home and found her mother cooking. Farris later conjectured, "I suppose she was just trying to keep busy and to keep her mind off what had transpired" (Farris, 2009, p. 131). The grandchildren would look to her for comfort in the days ahead.

Farris described her emotional state during the difficult days following her brother's death. "I felt as if, without bothering to knock, grief had decided to open my door, walked into my house, and stayed" (2009, p. 175). Farris, years after the deaths, offered a perspective that may resonate with other survivors of multiple homicides: "We had all seen and experienced so much in our lives. We agreed that there were times when survival can be painful, to be sure—but it is also extraordinary and wonderful" (2009, p. 208).

The King biographical slices may be particularly beneficial to homicide grievers who define themselves as very religious or spiritual.

Neimeyer (2006) concludes that a survivor must create a way to symbolize and speak about the experience "in a comprehensible account" within the survivor's "self-narrative" (Neimeyer, 2006). Not surprisingly Farris titled her memoir, *Through It All.*

Implication 6: Be Cautious of the "Lead Dog" in Grief

Borrowing an analogy, a grieving family may function like a dogsled team—pulling grief together. Dexter King's words haunt me: "We followed Mother's lead: lick your wounds, keep moving, don't question" (D. S. King, 2003, p. 62). One borrowable lesson from the Kings is to remind the lead griever that she or he sets an example, a pace, particularly in seeking counseling or participating in a support group, that frees others to acknowledge and experience the grief and seek pastoral care or counseling.

Implication 7: Arrange Counseling for Children

Andrew Young, almost a year after Dr. King's assassination, suggested to Coretta that the children should see a counselor, noting that the Kennedys had arranged counseling for their children. Clinicians may be aware of the reluctance of many African Americans to seek counseling for grief. Barrett (1994), Cooper-Patrick et al. (1999), and Laurie and Neimeyer (2008) report that African Americans are skeptical of mental health professionals. Grief is perceived—even following homicide—as a spiritual challenge; grievers turn to a pastor or minister (Laurie & Neimeyer, 2008). For the Kings, spiritual counseling was complicated because Daddy King was their pastor.

Although Young recommended Robert Coles, the Harvard psychiatrist who had treated members of the Kennedy family, Coretta chose Lonnie McDonald, a New York psychiatrist who commuted to Atlanta on weekends to spend time with the children. Dexter was reluctant to be transparent:

> I regarded him warily, decided not to tell him of my dreams, but we continued to know him, not professionally, just to know him as a family friend, over the years. Looking back, I wish I had told him about my dreams. Maybe he could've brought me out of them. But to what? The realities of 1969, the early 70s? More to the reality of how and why my dad died? (D. S. King, 2003, p. 62)

Many African Americans find support in a community of faith, especially one well acquainted with grief. Frady (2002) points out that care was, to some degree, unavailable to Coretta and the extended King family at Ebenezer. The family were grievers-in-residence.

> Through the months that followed it was as if the funeral still went on from Sunday to Sunday around her, the hymning and unceasing elegies still grieving for him, heads dropping and handkerchiefs wiping the eyes in the congregation to which he had confided his spirit's anguishing over the years. As [Coretta] sat in the same pew near the front, her face lifted slightly with its grave, masklike composure as she listened to Daddy King cry out from the pulpit in a shivering voice, "It was the *hate* in this land that took my son away from me." (Frady, 2002, p. 210)

Implication 8: Honoring Why Questions

Neimeyer (1998) theorizes that grievers must restore coherence to life narratives. I would contend that some have to restore coherence in their spiritual narratives. In some instances the "truth, the whole truth, and nothing but the truth" is not available, at least initially—particularly during a homicide investigation. To his credit, as his grandchildren aged, M. L. King, Sr., re-received their question, "Why did God let this happen?" and answered as grandfather and as one of the nation's leading Black ministers. Andrew Young, who sat in one family conference, recalled King "let his grandchildren express their bitterness and cry their tears" (Yang, 1980, p. 12). Young observed that the grandchildren asked "the questions that Job asked" and Daddy King answered "with the faith of the prophets" (Young, 1980, p. 12).

Daddy King was often asked if he thought James Earl Ray had acted alone in shooting Martin. "I have never believed that Ray was alone in his plan. In my heart I can only wonder why there seems to be so much that points to others working with him. Why? That question is always there, of course" (M. L. King, Sr., 1980b, p. 208).

Daddy King, however, carefully chose the environments in which he rehearsed his doubts. Six years after A. D.'s death Daddy King acknowledged, "I had questions then about A.D.'s death, and I still have them now. He was a good swimmer. Why did he drown? I don't know—I don't know that we will ever know what happened" (M. L. King, Sr., 1980b, p. 192). Daddy King eventually revised his conclusion about A. D.'s death, in an article in *Ebony*:

> I realized that he had simply decided, sitting in the living room of his home that night, that he didn't want to be here anymore. His brother's death has been the severest kind of blow. A.D had long considered himself the protector of those around him that he loved. He had been there in Memphis, just steps away, when his brother was shot down. I think this hurt him more than any of us could ever know. (M. L. King, Sr., 1980a, p. 112)

Conclusion

Coretta Scott King was unwilling for King's aides or his critics like Hoover, the young Black firebrands as well as several Southern senators to determine her husband's legacy. Although she was elected to the board of the SCLC, Turk (1997) reports that the widow "did not feel comfortable in the organization's offices or with any of the new leaders" (p. 85). In the March on Washington in August 1963, no women were allowed to march in the front; Coretta reluctantly walked behind her husband. No women were invited to speak to the throng gathered at the Lincoln Memorial (although Mahalia Jackson sang). With Martin's passing, those days were over. To the consternation of the SCLC, she announced that she intended to be an active presence in the primarily male-dominated civil rights movement. Turk (1997) commented, "She had no intention of remaining the silent widow of a great leader" (p. 91).

Conclusion

My general impression, after reading several autobiographies, is that an autobiography is not merely a catalogue of events and experiences in which a person has been involved, but that it also serves as some blueprint on which others may well model their own lives.

Nelson Mandela (2010, p. 409)

Nelson Mandela concluded that one of the few fringe benefits of prison is lots of time to read and to offer hospitality to the ideas and narratives of others. That may also be the only fringe benefit in grief.

Mathematicians insist that the shortest distance between two points is a straight line. Perhaps the shortest distance between a griever and a clinician is a borrowed narrative that might, over time, become something of a blueprint.

Borrowed Narratives Jump-Start Futures

Certainly through borrowed stories, adapting the words of Oprah Winfrey, individuals "can see a world beyond the front porch" of their grief and find the power to imagine a "next" with their initials on it. By hosting the stories of others, grievers may find a seedling of hope. Oprah notes that her dreams began, "When I heard the stories of my rich heritage. When I read about Sojourner Truth and Harriett Tubman and Mary McLeod Bethune and Frederick Douglass. I knew that there was possibility for me" (Kniffel, 2011, p. 40). I believe when grievers are exposed to the narratives of other grievers they too will conclude, "I know there is a possibility for me."

Stories Bridge Yesterday and Tomorrow

Two-year-olds sometimes loudly protest, *"Me* do it!" Unfortunately, that is the attitude of some grievers, stumbling about in the darkness, ignoring "the flashlights" of experience and wisdom available in the narratives of other grievers. Perhaps before they can accept the narratives of others they need to reflect on their own wound.

Three Useful Questions

Alan Jones (1982) formulated three significant questions that I have paraphrased to offer grievers for their reflection

> Do I believe that my life comes to me as a gift and that there is in me a terrific thing?
>
> Am I, in the middle of my grief, daring enough to ask for help, seek guidance from other grievers?
>
> Am I willing to face and respond to my longings, especially when I fear the changes?

Grievers must find and free that "terrific thing" within them in order to find meaning and survive a loss. That pursuit may take some work as Grace Coolidge discovered after the death of her husband, former president Calvin Coolidge, in 1933, when she admitted, "I am just a lost soul. Nobody is going to believe how much I miss being told what to do. My father always told me what to do. Then Calvin told me what I had to do" (B. Harris, 2005, p. 462). As Grace Coolidge—rather than Mrs. Calvin Coolidge—she raised millions as a trustee of the Clarke School for the needs of the hearing impaired over the remaining years of her life. Grace Coolidge harnessed the terrific thing within her.

Second, borrowing from Jones's construct, how do we encourage grievers to be "daring enough to ask for help, seek guidance from other grievers?" One might seek help by seeing a grief counselor or by participating in grief groups. I am amazed as I watch a room of strangers in Grief Gatherings become friends.

Third, Jones asks, "Am I willing to face and respond to my longings, especially when I fear the changes?" Some grievers get stuck because, like a want-to-be trapeze artist, they cannot let go of the familiar bar to reach out to the new bar. My friend Jan Greathouse shared this insight from Chris Cleare: "This is the forked tongue of grief again. It whispers in one ear: return to what you once loved best, and in the other ear it whispers, move on" (2010, p. 233) or as I prefer, move *forward*. Some grievers turn up the volume on the familiar to drown out the invitation to a future. Grace Coolidge had never been to Europe. Finally, in 1935, her friend Florence Adams overcame Coolidge's fears of "being recognized" and they sailed on the adventure of Grace's life. Someone tipped off a Swiss hotel to expect a Mrs. Adams and the widow of a former president. The manager explained to Adams after she checked in that he and his hotel were prepared to respond to any request of "Mrs. Lincoln." Coolidge delighted in the confusion. She discovered little gifts come to those who adventure out of their safe zone.

"Don't Know Much About History"

The excuse "don't know much about history" is alarming. In a recent examination of historical awareness of fourth graders, few could identify why Abraham Lincoln is significant. Buchanan (2011) observes, "Knowing something about the past entails coming to grips with complexities and learning [how] real people wrestled with life-and-death questions and made tragic or wise choices" (p. 7). Grievers today need to know how "real people" like those included in this book have grieved and grown.

Howard Zinn (1980/2003), the legendary teacher of American history, groaned at the imposition of the regimen of facts that today makes up the teaching of history in our educational system—facts that can be easily tested on uniform exams of educational progress. He borrowed the counsel of Dickens's character in *Hard Times,* the pedant Gradgrind, who admonished a younger teacher: "Teach nothing but fact, fact, fact" (Zinn, 1980/2003, p. 684).

The field of thanatology is overpopulated with theories, theories, and theories. Our equivalent of "facts." I sometime suspect that many assume that Moses descended from the mountain with the Ten Commandments under one arm and the five stages of grief under the other. Few can name one historical personality who demonstrates the reality of those stages. In teaching theory, I have worked hard to hang faces and stories on the concepts. I would suggest to clinicians: Stories, stories, stories!

Few remember the theoretical structure I rely on to meet objectives in a presentation, but many will remember a story or the gist of a story about a griever named Coretta, Abraham, Cory, Dwight, Condoleezza, Andrew, Rigoberta, or Leland.

Stories are everywhere waiting to be discovered and recovered just as one would find an old couch or chair, and imagining a future, recover it with new fabric.

In a recent grief group I facilitated, I asked participants why they returned for the second session. One woman, through tears, responded, "I was so touched by the stories last week." And we had been touched by *her* story. Some grievers are willing to go to outrageous lengths to find someone who will not try to "fix" them but will listen to the end of their sentences that make up their story.

I cannot "fix" anyone's grief. I can listen, without interruption, as I did so many years ago in Indiana farmhouses as grandfathers spun stories on Saturday afternoons. And I can suggest a borrowed narrative for a griever's consideration.

The Queen's Guest

In August 1942, during the dark days of World War II, as King George VI walked the dogs one evening, Queen Elizabeth dressed for dinner in her Windsor Palace bedroom. Suddenly, from behind thick drapes, someone grabbed her leg. A man stepped out and, after releasing his grasp, dropped to the floor. The man wanted someone to listen to his lament. The queen, determined to remain calm, quietly summoned a page.

The queen invited the intruder to talk.

In the moments that followed, the Queen of the British Empire and her page patiently listened to a military deserter, who obtained a job with a company doing repairs at the Windsor. He got to the queen's bedroom by pretending that he needed to change a light bulb. All of the man's family had died in the German aerial bombings in England.

That night, a despondent man needed someone who would listen to his lament (Swift, 2004, pp. 187–188) and knowingly or unknowingly, the queen listened all the way to the end of the story without interrupting, without offering clichés or easy answers, and without interjecting, "There. There." Elizabeth and a stranger created a sacred moment.

That night the queen made the floor of her bedroom a safe place for an emotionally wounded subject to tell his story.

I wish I knew the rest of the story. Realistically, some of the best stories do not end, "And they lived happily ever after."

Grievers need safe places to tell their stories and safe persons to receive the stories. And perhaps someone who can offer, in response, a borrowed narrative.

Many grievers express their pain by wrapping it in words and sentences, and, more important, in stories. A passing awareness of the narratives of that long fraternity of grievers stretching back through humankind's history can make a difference.

Never underestimate the power of a borrowed narrative to make a difference in the darkness of grief.

References

The A to Z of Women in World History. (2002). New York: Facts on File.

Abernathy, R. D. (1989). *And the walls came tumbling down.* New York: Harper and Row.

Alford, H. (2009). *How to live: A search for wisdom from old people (while they are still on Earth).* New York: 12 Publishing.

Algeo, M. (2011). *The president is a sick man: Wherein the supposedly virtuous Grover Cleveland survives a secret surgery at sea and vilifies the courageous newspapermen who dared expose the story.* Chicago, IL: Chicago Review Press.

Altevogt, J. D. (1998, December 16). Requiem for a beloved dog. *The Kansas City Star,* p. B7.

American Pet Products Association. (n.d.). *Industry statistics & trends.* Retrieved July 19, 2011, from http://www.americanpetproducts.org/press_industrytrends.asp

American Psychological Association. (2001). *Publication Manual of the American Psychological Association* (5th ed.). Washington, DC: Author.

Andersen, C. (1996). *Jack and Jackie: Portrait of an American marriage.* New York: William Morrow.

Andersen, C. (2000). *The day John died.* New York: William Morrow.

Andersen, C. (2009). *Barack and Michelle: Portrait of an American marriage.* New York: William Morrow.

Angelou, M. (2002). *A song slung up to heaven.* New York: Random House.

Angelou, M. (2011, February 1). *Black history special, Talk of the Nation.* National Public Radio.

Anglican Church of Aotearoa, New Zealand and Polynesia. (1989). *A New Zealand prayer book.* San Francisco, CA: HarperSanFrancisco.

Aquino, Benigno. (1989). In T. Ainslie & D. Embree (Eds.), *Encyclopedia of Asian history* (Vol. 6, pp. 77–78). New York: Charles Scribners.

Arax, M. (2011, February 6). For a Hmong hero, a lavish farewell. *The New York Times*, p. A11.

Arnott, A. (1975). *The secret country of C. S. Lewis*. Grand Rapids, MI: Eerdmans.

Aronson, T. (1993). *The royal family at war*. London: John Murray.

Ashe, A., & McNabe, A. (1995). *Arthur Ashe on tennis: Strokes, strategies, traditions, players, psychology, and wisdom*. New York: Knopf.

Ashe, A., & Rampersad, A. (1993). *Days of grace: A memoir*. New York: Knopf.

Ashenburg, K. (2003). *Mourner's dance: What we do when people die*. New York: North Point Press.

Attenborough, R. (Director). (1999). *Shadowlands*. United States: HBO.

Attig, T. (2000). *The heart of grief: Death and the search for lasting love*. New York: Oxford University Press.

Attig, T. (2001). Relearning the world: Making and finding new meanings. In R. A. Neimeyer (Ed.), *Meaning reconstruction & the experience of loss* (pp. 33–53). Washington, DC: American Psychological Association.

Balaswamy, S., & Richardson, V. E. (2001). The cumulative effects of life event, personal and social resources on subjective well-being of elderly widowers. *International Journal of Aging and Human Development, 53*(4), 311–327.

Banner, L. W. (2009). AHR roundtable: Biography as history. *American Historical Review, 114*(3), 579–586.

Barker, B., & Diehl, D. (2009). *Priceless memories*. New York: Center Street.

Barkin, L. (2011). *The comfort garden: Tales from the trauma unit*. San Francisco, CA: Fresh Pond Press.

Barrett, R. (1994, October). Affirming and reclaiming African-American funeral rites. *The Director, 66*(10), 36–40.

Beasley, M. H. (2010). *Eleanor Roosevelt: Transformative first lady*. Lawrence, KS: The University of Kansas Press.

Bennett, L., Jr. (1968). *A biography of Martin Luther King, Jr*. New York: Johnson Publishing.

Birmingham, S. (1978). *Jacqueline Bouvier Kennedy Onassis*. New York: Grosset & Dunlap.

Black, A. M. (2003). Hickok, Lorena. In J. W. Jeffries, K.L. Segrue, & G.B. Nash (Eds.). *Encyclopedia of American history: The great depression and World War II, 1929 to 1945* (Vol. 3, pp. 431–432). New York: Facts on File.

Black, C. (2003). *Franklin Delano Roosevelt: Champion of freedom*. New York: Public Affairs Press.

Blair, T. (2010). *A journey: My political life*. New York: Knopf.

Bonanno, G. (2009). *The other side of sadness: What the new science of bereavement tells us about life after loss*. New York: Basic Books.

Bosman, J. (2010, August 11). Quick change in strategy for a bookseller. *The New York Times* [Electronic]. Retrieved August 12, 2010, from www.nytimes.com/2010/08/12/ business/media/12bookstore

Boss, P. (2011, June 25). *Plenary session: Ambiguous loss: A unique kind of loss when loved ones disappear.* Symposium conducted at Association for Death Education and Counseling, Miami, FL.

Bowlby, J. (1980). *Attachment and loss: Loss, sadness & depression.* New York: Basic Books.

Bradford, S. (2000). *America's queen: The life of Jacqueline Kennedy Onassis.* New York: Viking Press.

Bradlee, B. (1995). *A good life: Newspapering and other adventures.* New York: Simon & Schuster.

Brady, S. R. (2011). *A box of darkness: The story of a marriage.* New York: St. Martin's Press.

Bram, C. (2009). *Mapping the territory: A memoir.* New York: Allyson.

Branch, T. (1988). *Parting the waters: America in the King years, 1954–1963.* New York: Simon and Schuster.

Branch, T. (2006). *At Canaan's edge: America in the King years, 1965–1968.* New York: Simon and Schuster.

Brands, H. W. (1997). *T.R. [Theodore Roosevelt]: The last romantic.* New York: Basic Books.

Bremer, J. (1998a). Clive Staples Lewis, 1895–1965: A brief biography. In J. D. Schultz & J. G. West, Jr. (Eds.), *The C. S. Lewis readers' encyclopedia* (pp. 9–66). Grand Rapids, MI: Zondervan.

Bremer, J. (1998b). Jamie King Askins Moore, 1872–1951. In J. D. Schultz & J. G. West, Jr. (Eds.), *The C. S. Lewis readers' encyclopedia* (pp. 285–286). Grand Rapids, MI: Zondervan.

Brener, A. (1993). *Mourning & Mitzvah: A guided journal for walking the mourner's path through grief to healing.* Woodstock, VT: Jewish Lights.

Brewster, G. (2007). *No turning back: My summer with Daddy King.* Maryknoll, NY: Orbis Books.

Briggs, D. (2001, July 10). Do all (pets) go to heaven? Theologians speculate. *The Kansas City Star,* p. G2.

Brooks, J. (1999). *Midlife orphan: Facing life's changes now that your parents are gone.* New York: Berkley Books.

Brown, B. (2010, August 5). *Up to Date.* KCUR-FM, Kansas City, MO.

Bryant, N. (2006). *The bystander: John F. Kennedy and the struggle for black equality.* New York: Free Press.

Buchanan, J. (2011, July 12). Don't know much about history. *The Christian Century,* 7.

Buckley, C. (2009). *Losing Mum and Pup: A memoir.* New York: Twelve Press.

Buddemeyer-Porter, Mary. (2005). *Will I see Fido in heaven?* No place of publication: Eden Publishing.

Bullard, S. (1993). *Free at last: A history of the civil rights movement and those who died in the struggle.* New York: Oxford University Press.

Bumiller, E. (2007). *Condoleezza Rice: An American life: A biography.* New York: Random House.

Bureau of Justice Statistics. (2011). Total correctional population. Retrieved November 11, 2011, from http://bjs.ojp.usdoj.gov/index.cfm?ty=tp&tid=11

Burch, B. (1999). *Writing for your portfolio*. Boston, MA: Allyn and Bacon.

Burlingame, M. (2008). *Abraham Lincoln: A life* (2 vols.). Baltimore, MD: The John Hopkins University Press.

Burton, S. (1989). *Impossible dream: The Marcoses, the Aquinos, and the unfinished revolution*. New York: Warner Books.

Burton, S. (1990, July 16). A muddle-through mode. *Time, 36*, 40.

Bush, B. (1994). *Barbara Bush: A memoir*. New York: Charles Scribner's Sons.

Bush, B. (2003). *Reflections: Life after the White House*. New York: Lisa Drew/Scribner.

Bush, G. W. (1999). *A charge to keep*. New York: William Morrow.

Bush, L. (2010). *Laura Bush: Spoken from the heart*. New York: Scribner.

Cain, H. (2011). *This boy's faith: Notes from a Southern Baptist upbringing: A memoir*. New York: Crown.

Caldwell, G. (2010). *Let's take the long way home: A memoir of friendship*. New York: Random House.

Carlson, K. (2010). *Heart broke open: A memoir through loss to self discovery*. New York: HarperStudio.

Carmack, B. J. (2003). *Grieving the death of a pet*. Minneapolis, MN: Augsburg.

Carpenter, F. G. (1887, June 4). Colonel Ellsworth: A tragedy of twenty-six years ago graphically retold. *The Los Angeles Times*.

Carson, C. (Ed.). (1992). *Called to serve Jan 1929–June 1951*. Vol. 1: *The papers of Martin Luther King*. Berkeley, CA: The University of California Press.

Carson, C., & Holloran, P. (Eds.). (1998). *A knock at midnight: Inspiration from the great sermons of Reverend Martin Luther King*. New York: Warner.

Carwardine, R. (2008). Lincoln's religion. In E. Foner (Ed.), *Our Lincoln: New perspectives on Lincoln and his world* (pp. 223–248). New York: W.W. Norton.

CBS News. (2003, November 12). Jackie's letters: Private anguish. Retrieved July 23, 2007 from http://www.cbsnews.com/stories/2003/11/12/eveningnews/printable583327.shtml

Chinese proverbs: Ancient wisdom for the 21st century (5th ed.). (2010). Hong Kong: FormAsia Books Limited.

Chochinov, H. M. (2005). Vicarious grief and response to global disasters. *The Lancet, 366*(9487), 697–698.

Chua-Eoan, H. (1988). *Corazon Aquino*. Philadelphia, PA: Chelsea House.

Cienfuegos, A. J., & Monelli, C. (1983). The testimony of political repression as a therapeutic instrument. *American Journal of Orthopsychiatry, 53*(1), 43–51.

Clark, M. H. (2002). *Kitchen privileges: A memoir*. New York: Simon & Schuster.

Claypool, J. R. (2005). *God the ingenious alchemist: Transforming tragedy into blessing*. Harrisburg, PA: Morehouse.

Cleare, C. (2010). *Little bee*. New York: Simon & Schuster.

Clift, E. (2008). *Two weeks of life: A memoir of love, death, and politics*. New York: Basic Books.

Clinton, C. (2009a). *Mrs. Lincoln.* New York: Harper.

Clinton, C. (2009b, May 14). *Lecture on Mrs. Lincoln.* Presented at Kansas City Public Library, Missouri.

CNN. (2003, November 13). Priest papers revealed Jacqueline Kennedy's grief. Retrieved December 17, 2007, from http://www.cnn.com/2003/ ALLPOLITICS/11/13JACKIE.ap/Index.html

CNN Wire Staff. (2010, June 29). *Benigno Aquino III takes office as president of Philippines.* Retrieved 2011, August 17, 2011, from http:// articles.cnn.com/2010-06-29/world/philippines.aquino_1_corazon-aquino-benigno-aquino-iii-people-power-movement?_s=PM:WORLD

Cobb, W. J. (2010). *The substance of hope: Barack Obama and the paradox of progress.* New York: Walker & Company.

Cohen, D. E., & Battersby, J. D. (2009). *Nelson Mandela: A life in photographs.* New York: Sterling.

Cole, N. (with Ritz, D.). (2010). *Love brought me back: A journey of loss and grace.* New York: Simon and Schuster.

Commire, A. (Ed.). (1999). *Women in world history.* Detroit, MI: Gale.

Como, J. T. (Ed.). (1998). *C. S. Lewis at the breakfast table and other reminiscences.* New York: Macmillan.

Congalton, D. (2000). *Three cats, two dogs: One journey through multiple pet loss.* Troutdale, OR: NewSage Press.

Cook, B. W. (1992). *Eleanor Roosevelt. Volume l: 1884–1933.* New York: Viking.

Coolidge, C. (1929). *The autobiography of Calvin Coolidge.* New York: Cosmopolitan Book Corporation.

Cooper-Patrick, L., Gallo, J. J., Gonzales, J. J., Hong, T. V., Powe, N. R., Nelson, C., & Ford, D. E. (1999). The patient-physician relationship: Race, gender, and partnership in the patient-physician relationship. *JAMA, 282*(6), 583–589.

Cornelius, J. M. (2010, summer). How many "books on Lincoln" are there? *For the People, 12*(2), 6–7.

Corr, C. A. (2003–2004). Pet loss in death related literature for children. *Omega, 48*(4), 399–414.

Corr, C. A., Nabe, C. M., & Corr, D. M. (1997). *Death and dying, life and living* (2nd. ed.). Pacific Grove, CA: Brooks/Cole.

Corr, C. A., Nabe, C. M., & Corr, D. M. (2006). *Death and dying, life and living* (5th ed.). Pacific Grove, CA: Brooks/Cole.

Cosby, B., & Poussaint, A. F. (2007). *Come on, people: On the path from victims to victors.* Nashville, TN: Thomas Nelson.

Coubeil, J. C., & Archambault, A. (Eds.). (2010). *Merriam-Webster visual dictionary.* Springfield, MA: Merriam-Webster.

Cowley, R. (Ed.). (2001). *The collected what if? Eminent historians imagine what might have been.* New York: G. P. Putnam.

Cox, G. (2010). *Death and the American Indian.* Omaha, NE: Grief Illustrated Press.

Crenshaw, D. A. (2007). Life span issues and assessment and intervention. In D. Balk (Ed.), *Handbook of thanatology: The essential body of knowledge for the study of death, dying, and bereavement* (pp. 227–234). Deerfield, IL: Association for Death Education and Counseling.

Crittenden, L. (2007). *The water will hold you: A skeptic learns to pray.* New York: Harmony Books.

Crouse, K. (2011, January 9). Reed pushes grief aside and provides stability. *The New York Times Digest,* 8.

Cruz, D. (2011). "Pointing to the Heart": Transpacific Filipinas and the question of the Cold-War Philippine-U.S. relations. *American Quarterly, 63*(1), 1–32.

Currier, J. M., Holland, J. M., & Neimeyer, R. A. (2010). Sense-making, grief, and the experience of violent loss: Toward a meditational model. *Death Studies, 30*(5), 403–428.

Curry, M., & Denk, P. (2007, January 29). Kentucky Derby winner Barbaro euthanized. *Thoroughbred Times.* Retrieved December 31, 2010, from http://www.thoroughbredtimes.com

Cutler, J. H. (1970). *Cardinal Cushing of Boston.* New York: Hawthorn.

Daily, A., & Daily, A. (2010). *Out of the canyon: A true story of loss and love.* New York: Harmony Books.

Dann, P. (2007). *The goldfish went on vacation. A memoir of loss (and learning to tell the truth about* it). New York: Trumpeter.

Davis, J. H. (1996). *Jacqueline Bouvier: An intimate memoir.* New York: Wiley.

Davis, P. (2004). *The long goodbye.* New York: Knopf.

DeBourgh, G. A. (2008, January). *Interactive instruction: Tips, tools, and techniques to involve learners and promote reasoning skills.* San Francisco, CA: Mosby's Faculty Development Institute.

D'Este, C. (2002). *Eisenhower: A soldier's life.* New York: Henry Holt.

Didion, J. (2007). *The year of magical thinking.* New York: Knopf.

Doka, K. J. (1989). Introduction. In K. J. Doka (Ed.), *Disenfranchised grief: Recognizing hidden sorrow.* Lexington, MA: Lexington Books.

Doka, K. J., & Martin, T. L. (2010). *Grieving beyond gender: Understanding the ways men and women mourn (rev. ed.).* New York: Routledge.

Donohue, K. M. (2005). Pet Loss: Implications for social work practice. *Social Work, 50*(2), 187–190.

Dorsett, L. W. (1992). Research C. S. Lewis. In A. Walker & J. Patrick, (Eds.). *A Christian for all seasons: Essays in honor of C. S. Lewis* (p. 213). New York: Regnery Gateway.

Dorsett, L. W. (2009). *And God came in: The extraordinary story of Joy Davidson: Her life and marriage to C. S. Lewis.* Peabody, MA: Hendrickson.

Dosekun, S. (2006, December). A tribute to Coretta Scott King: 1927–2006. *Feminist Africa 7: Diaspora Voices, 7,* 107–113.

Doty, M. (2007). *Dog years: A memoir.* New York: HarperCollins.

Douglas, J. (2008). *JFK and the unspeakable: Why he died & why it matters.* Maryknoll, NY: Orbis Books.

Downing, D. C. (2005). *C. S. Lewis and the Narnia Chronicles*. San Francisco: Jossey-Bass.

Duiker, W. J. (2000). *Ho Chi Minh: A life*. New York: Hyperion.

Duncan, J. R. (2001). *The magic never ends: An oral history of the life and work of C. S. Lewis*. Nashville, TN: W Publishing.

Dungy, T. (2007). *A quiet strength: The principles, practices and priorities of a winning coach*. Wheaton, IL: Tyndale.

Dupre, J. (2007). *Monuments: America's history in art and memory*. New York: Random House.

Dyson, M. E. (2008). *April 4, 1968: Martin Luther King, Jr.'s death and how it changed America*. New York: Basic Civitas Books.

Eck, D. L. (2001). *A new religious America: How a "Christian country" has become the world's most religiously diverse nation*. San Francisco, CA: HarperSanFrancisco.

Editorial. (1963, August 10). *The New York Times*, p. 44.

Eisenhower, D. (1967). *At ease: Stories I tell my friends*. Garden City, NY: Doubleday.

Eisenhower, J. S. D. (2003). *General Ike: A personal reminiscence*. New York: Free Press.

Eisenhower, S. (1996). *Mrs. Ike: Memories and reflections on the life of Mamie Eisenhower*. New York: Farrar, Straus & Giroux.

The electric Ben Franklin: The quotable Franklin. (n.d.). Retrieved March 30, 2011, from http://www.ushistory.org/franklin/quotable/quote67.htm

Eliot, M. (2008). *Reagan: The Hollywood years*. New York: Harmony.

Embree, A. T. (Ed.). (1989). *The encyclopedia of Asian history*. New York: Scribners.

Epstein, D. M. (2009). *Lincoln's men: The president and his private secretaries*. Washington, DC: Smithsonian Books.

Faber, D. (1980). *The life of Lorena Hickok: E.R.'s friend*. New York: William Morrow.

Faithful Fido. (2006, May 21). *The Christian Century*, 7.

Farrer, A. (1979). In his image. In J. T. Como (Ed.), *C. S. Lewis at breakfast table and other reminiscences* (pp. 242–244). New York: Macmillan.

Farris, C. K. (2009). *Through it all: Reflections on my life, my family, and my faith*. NY: Atria.

Federal Bureau of Investigation. (2008). Expanded homicide data: 2008 Crime. Retrieved March 12, 2008, from http://www.fbi.gov/cius2008/offenses/ecxpanded_information

Felix, A. (2002). *Condi: The Condoleezza Rice story*. New York: Newmarket Press.

Fields, G. (2008, March 16). Deadly business: Violence roils black funeral parlors. *The Wall Street Journal*, p. A1.

Fonda, J. (2005). *My life so far*. New York: Random House.

Foner, E. (Ed.). (2008). *Our Lincoln: New perspectives on Lincoln and his world* (pp. 223–248). New York: W.W. Norton.

Fowler, A. (2006). Supervisor. In H. L. Poe & R. W. Poe (Eds.), *C. S. Lewis remembered* (pp. 98–114). Grand Rapids, MI: Zondervan.

Frady, M. (2002). *Martin Luther King, Jr.* New York: Lipper Viking.

Frank, T. (2011, April). Easy chair: Check it yourself. *Harper's Magazine*, 7–9.

Frayer, L. (2010, June 11). Mandela family death casts pall over world cup. *AOL News*. Retrieved February 18, 2011, from http://www.aolnews.com/2010/06/11/mandela-family-death-dampens-start-of-world-cup/

Frye, J. (2003). *A million little pieces*. New York: Nan A. Talese.

Gaunt, W. (1971). *Turner*. London: Phaidon.

Ghaemi, N. (2011). *A first-rate madness: Uncovering the links between leadership and mental health*. New York: Penguin.

Giglio, J. N. (1991). *The presidency of John F. Kennedy*. Lawrence, KS: The University of Kansas Press.

Giglio, J. N. (2006). Growing up Kennedy: The role of medical ailments in the life of JFK, 1920–1957. *Journal of Family History, 31*, 358–385.

Gilbert, D. (2006). *Stumbling on happiness*. New York: Scribner.

Gilbert, S. M. (2006). *Death's door: Modern dying and the ways we grieve*. New York: Norton.

Gillman, T. J. (2009, January 7). Bush family cat India dies at White House. Retrieved January 4, 2011, from http://www.dallasnews.com/shared content/dws/fea/pets/stories/010608dnmetfirstpet.3e6aae)

Goldman, A. (2003). *Living a year of Kaddish: A memoir*. New York: Schocken.

Goodwin, D. K. (1991). *Lyndon Johnson and the American dream*. New York: St. Martin's Griffin.

Goodwin, D. K. (2005). *Team of rivals: The political genius of Abraham Lincoln*. New York: Simon and Schuster.

Goolrick, R. (2007). *The end of the world as we know it: Scenes from a life*. Chapel Hill, NC: Algonquin Books of Chapel Hill.

Gordon, M. (2007). *Circling my mother: A memoir*. New York: Pantheon.

Gordon-Reed, A. (2011). *Andrew Johnson*. New York: Times/Henry Holt.

Gormley, B. (1998). *C. S. Lewis: Christian and storyteller*. Grand Rapids, MI: Eerdmans.

Gottlieb, A. H., Gottlieb, H., Bowers, B., & Bowers, B. (1998/2006). *1,000 years, 1,000 people: Ranking the men and women who shaped the millennium*. New York: Barnes & Noble.

Gresham, D. H. (1988). *Lenten lands*. New York: Macmillian.

Gresham, D. (2005). *Jack's life: The life story of C. S. Lewis*. Nashville: Abingdon.

Grid. (2010). In A. Stevenson & C. A. Lindberg (Eds.), *New Oxford American dictionary* (3rd ed.). New York: Oxford University Press.

Grogan, J. (2005). *Marley & me: Life and love with the world's worst dog*. New York: William Morrow.

Gusewelle, C. W. (1996, January 18). Farewell to a friend: A partner with heart and style in the hunt. *The Kansas City Star*, pp. C-1, C-8.

Haag, C. (2011). *Come to the edge: A memoir*. New York: Spiegel & Grau.

Haag, J. (1999). Aquino, Corazon. In *Women in world history: A biographical encyclopedia* (pp. 425–432). Detroit, MI: Yorkin/Gale.

Hadas, R. (2011). *Strange relation: A memoir of marriage, dementia, and poetry*. Philadelphia, PA: Paul Dry Books.

Hagman, G. (2001). Beyond decathexis: Toward a new psychoanalytic under-standing and treatment of mourning. In R. A. Neimeyer (Ed.), *Meaning reconstruction & the experience of loss* (pp. 13–32). Washington, DC: American Psychological Association.

Haley, J. (1994, March 16). Wonderful friendship undiminished by inevitable brevity. *The Kansas City Star*, p. C-5.

Haley, J. (1997, November 5). Readers offer comfort and insight after "Juliet" column. *The Kansas City Star*, p. C-9.

Hall, D. (1998). *Without: poems.* Boston, MA: Houghton-Mifflin.

Hall, D. (2008). *Unpacking the boxes: A memoir of a life in poetry.* Boston, MA: Houghton-Mifflin.

Halpern-Lewis, J. G. (1996, May/June). Missing Colleena. *Forum, X,* 1, 18.

Hamilton, N. (2008). *How to do biography: A primer.* Cambridge, MA: Harvard University Press.

Hansberry, L. (1960). *A raisin in the sun: A drama in three acts.* New York: Methuen.

Hansen, D. D. (2003). *The dream: Martin Luther King Jr. and the speech that inspired a nation.* New York: Ecco/Harper Collins.

Harkins, K. (2008, Winter). The fabric of memoir. *Viewpoint, 20*(1), 6–7.

Harlow, S. (2003, December 23). Groups aid people mourning pet deaths. *The Kansas City Star,* p. B4.

Harris, B. (2005). *The First Ladies fact book: The stories of the women of the White House from Martha Washington to Laura Bush.* New York: Black Dog & Leventhal.

Harris, E. L. (2003). *What becomes of the brokehearted: A memoir.* New York: Anchor Books.

Haskins, J. (1988). *Corazon Aquino: Leader of the Philippines.* Hillsdale, NJ: Enslow Publications.

Hayes, R. B. (1885, March 5). Diary. Rutherford B. Hayes Presidential Library, Fremont, Ohio.

Henson, M. S. (1999). Lamar, Maribeau Buonaparte. In J. A. Garraty & M. C. Carnes (Eds.), *American National Biography* (Vol. 13, pp. 70–71). New York: Oxford University Press.

Heymann, C. D. (2009). *Bobby and Jackie: A love story.* New York: Astra.

Helm, K. (2007). *The true story of Mary, wife of Lincoln.* Rutland, VT: Sharp and Company.

Helmsley has last word, and it's "fetch." (2007, August 30). *The Kansas City Star*, p. A1.

Hickok, L. A. (1962). *Reluctant First Lady: The intimate story of Eleanor Roosevelt's early public life.* New York: Dodd, Mead.

Hine, D. C. (Ed.). (1993). *Black women in America: An historical encyclopedia* (2 vols.). New York: Oxford University Press.

Hirschfeld, R. (2008). *Swizzle, stay with me.* Retrieved July 3, 2011, from www.mypetprotection.com

Hirschfeld, R. (2010). *Petriarch: The complete guide to financial and legal planning for a pet's continual care.* New York: AICPA.

Homes, A.M. (2007). *The mistress's daughter.* New York: Viking.

Hospital vigil over the Kennedy baby: Lighted window a compassion nation watched. (1963, August 16). *Life,* Cover.

Hotchner, A. E. (2010). *Paul and me: 53 years of adventure and misadventure with my pal Paul Newman.* New York: Doubleday.

Hoy, W. G. (2010, November). Remembering Pirate. *Grief Connections, 9*(11). Greenville, SC: Thomas McAfee Funeral Homes.

Hsu, A.Y. (2002). *Grieving a suicide: A loved one's search for comfort, answers, & hope.* Downers Grove, IL: InterVarsity Press.

Humphrey, K. (2009). *Counseling strategies for loss and grief.* Alexander, VA: American Counseling Association.

Iggulden, A. (2006, January 10). Exclusive interview with J.K. Rowling: Harry Potter was born the day my mother died. *The Telegraph.* Retrieved April 4, 2011, from http://www.telegraph.co.uk/news/uknews/1507437/ Exclusive-interview-with-J-K-Rowling-Harry-Potter-was-born-the-day-my-mother-died.html

Isay, R. A. (2006). *Commitment and healing.* New York: John Wiley.

Jackson, K. F., & Samuels, G. M. (2011). Multiracial competence in social work: Recommendations for culturally attuned work with multiracial people. *Social Work, 56*(3), 235–245.

Jacobs, A. (2005). *The Narnian: The life and imagination of C.S. Lewis.* San Francisco, CA: HarperSanFrancisco.

Jacqueline Onassis estate. (1996, December 22). *The Kansas City Star,* p. A-27.

Jeffreys, J. S. (2011). *Helping grieving people: When tears are not enough. A handbook for care providers* (2nd ed.). New York: Brunner-Routledge.

Jennings, K. (2006). *Mama's boy, preacher's son.* Boston, MA: Beacon Press.

J. K. Rowling Official Site: Biography. (n.d.). Retrieved April 4, 2011, from www.jkrowling.com/textonly/en/biography.cfm

Jones, A. (1982). *Exploring spiritual direction: An essay on Christian friendship.* New York: Seabury.

Jones, B. F., & Olken, B. A. (2009). Hit or miss? The effect of assassinations on institutions and war. *American Economic Journal: Macroeconomics, 1*(2), 55–87.

Jones, K. (2009, February 20). Socks the cat dies. *Huffington Post.* Retrieved August 18, 2011, from http://www.huffingtonpost.com/2009/02/20/ socks-the-clintons-cat-di_n_168721.html

Kalicak, L. (2002, January 8). Letter to the editor. "Poor Buddy" column. *The Kansas City Star,* p. B6.

Kamen, P. (2007). *Finding Iris Chang: Friendship, ambition and the loss of an extraordinary mind.* New York: Da Capo Press.

Karbell, Z. (2004). Chester Alan Arthur. In *The American president series.* New York: Times Book.

Karbo, K. (2003). *The stuff of life: A daughter's memoir.* New York: Bloomsburg.

Kathrada, A. (2004). *No break for Mandela: Memoirs of Ahmed Kathrada, prisoner no. 468/64.* Lexington, KY: The University of Kentucky Press.

Katz, J. (2011). *Going home: Finding peace when pets die.* New York: Villard.

Kauffman, J. (2002). Safety and the assumptive world: A theory of traumatic loss. In J. Kauffman (Ed.), *Loss of the assumptive world: A theory of traumatic loss* (pp. 205–212). New York: Brunner-Routledge.

Keck, W. (2007, May 14). The time is right for Barker: "Price is Right" host retiring after 50 years in TV game. *USA Today*, 1D, 2D.

Keenan, P. A. (2008). *Why we love them so much: Surviving the loss of an animal friend.* New York: Universe.

Keller, R. S. (2006). Women's spiritual biography and autobiography. In R. S. Skinner & R. R. Reuther (Eds.), *Encyclopedia of women and religion in North America* (pp. 68–79). Bloomington, IN: Indiana University Press.

Kelley, K. (2010). *Oprah: A biography.* New York: Crown Archtype.

Kelly, G. A. (1955). *The psychology of personal constructs.* New York: Routledge.

Kennedy baby dies at Boston Hospital; President at hand. (1963, August 9). *The Kansas City Star,* p. A1.

Kennedy, J. F. (1963). J.F.K. Personal Papers: Death of Patrick, 1963. Boston, MA: John F. Kennedy Presidential Library.

Kennedy, R. F. (1974). *Times to remember.* Garden City, NY: Doubleday.

Kilian, P. (2002). *Barbara Bush: Matriarch of a dynasty.* New York: Thomas Dunne Books/St. Martin's Press.

King, C. S. (1969). *My life with Martin Luther King, Jr.* New York: Holt, Rinehart and Winston.

King, D. S. (with Wiley, R.). (2003). *Growing up King: An intimate biography.* New York: Wiley.

King, M. L., Sr. (1980a, October). How much grief can one man bear? *Ebony,* 110–112, 114–116, 118.

King, M. L., Sr. (with Riley, C.). (1980b). *Daddy King: An autobiography.* New York: William Morrow.

Klass, D., & Walter, T. (2001). Processes of grieving: How bonds are continued. In M. S. Stroebe, R. O. Hansson, W. Stroebe, & H. Schut (Eds.), *Handbook of bereavement research: Consequences, coping, and care* (pp. 431–448). Washington, DC: American Psychological Association.

Klemesrud, J. (1968, October 20). Jacqueline Kennedy: A stranger in Camelot. *The New York Times,* p. 4E.

Kniffel, L. (2011, May/June). Reading for life: Oprah Winfrey. *American Libraries,* pp. 38–41.

Knowles, E. (Ed.). (2009). *Little Oxford dictionary of proverbs.* New York: Oxford University Press.

Kochmann, R. M. (1997). *Presidents: Birthplaces, homes and burial sites.* Bemidji, MN: Arrow Printing.

Komisar, L. (1987). *Corazon Aquino: The story of a revolution.* New York: George Braziller.

Kornblut, A. E. (2009, November 20). Barack Obama's personal story infused tour of Asia. *The China Post.* Retrieved March 7, 2011, from http://www.chinpost.com.tv/print/233499.htm

Kosloff, S., Greenberg, J., Weise, D., & Solomon, S. (2010). The effects of mortality salience on political preferences: The roles of charisma and political orientation. *The Journal of Experimental Social Psychology, 46*(1), 139–145.

Krasnow, I. (2006). *I am my mother's daughter: Making peace with Mom—Before it's too late.* New York: Basic Books.

Krugman, P. (2007, 21 January). Debunking the Reagan myth. *The New York Times.* Retrieved from http://www.nytimes.com

Kuhlman, E. A. (Ed.). (2002). *The A to Z of women in world history.* New York: Facts on File.

Kuhn, W. (2010). *Reading Jackie: Her autobiography in books.* New York: Nan A. Talese/Doubleday.

Kurzman, D. (1998). *Soldier of peace: The life of Yitzhak Rabin, 1922–1995.* New York: HarperCollins.

LaGanga, M. L. (2000, May 28). In race for White House, the "cult of Condi" plays growing role. *The Los Angeles Times,* p. A3.

LaGrand, L. (2006). *Love lives on: Learning from extraordinary encounters of the bereaved.* New York: Berkley Books.

Lash, J. (1971). *Eleanor and Franklin.* New York: W.W. Norton.

Lash, J. P. (1984). *A world of love: Eleanor Roosevelt and her friends.* Garden City, NJ: Doubleday.

Laurie, A., & Neimeyer, R. A. (2008). African Americans in bereavement: Grief as a function of ethnicity. *Omega, 57*(2), 173–193.

Lawrence, G. (2011). *Jackie as editor: The literary life of Jackie Kennedy Onassis.* New York: Thomas Dunne Books.

Leaming, B. (2001). *Mrs. Kennedy: The missing history of the Kennedy years.* New York: Free Press.

Lengle, E. G. (2011). *George Washington: America's founder, in myth and memory.* New York: HarperCollins.

Lepore, J. (2010). *The whites of their eyes: The Tea Party's revolution and the battle over American history.* Princeton, NJ: Princeton University Press.

Levy, H. (2010). *Henry Morgenthau, Jr.: The remarkable life of FDR's treasury secretary.* New York: Skyhorse.

Levy, W. T. (1999). *The extraordinary Mrs. R: A friend remembers Eleanor Roosevelt.* New York: John Wiley & Sons.

Lewis, C. S. (1955). *Surprised by joy: The shape of my early life.* San Diego, CA: Harvest/Harcourt.

Lewis, C. S. (1961). *A grief observed.* New York: Bantam.

Lewis, C. S. (1966). Preface. In D. Sayers, J. R. R. Tolkien, C. S., Lewis, A. O. Barfield, G. Mathew, & W. H. Lewis, *Essays presented to Charles Williams* (pp. vi–xiv). Grand Rapids, MI: William B. Eerdmans.

Lewis, C. S. (1979). *The letters of C.S. Lewis to Arthur Greeves (1914–1963)* (W. R. Hooper, Ed.). New York: Collier Books.

Lewis, W. H. (1982). *Brothers and friends: The diaries of Major Warren Hamilton Lewis.* New York: Harper & Brothers.

Lincoln, A. (1851, January 12). Letter to Johnson, J. D. In *The collected works of Lincoln* (Vol. 2, p. 97). New Brunswick, NJ: Rutgers University Press.

Lindskoog, K. (2001). *Sleuthing C. S. Lewis: More light in the Shadowlands*. Macon, GA: Mercer University Press.

Lopata, H. Z. (1981). Widowhood and husband sanctification. *Journal of Marriage and the Family, 43*, 439–450.

Lord, L. K., Wittum, T. E., Ferketich, A. K., Funk, J. A., & Rajala-Schultz, P. J. (2007). Search and identification methods that owners use to find a lost dog. *The Journal of Veterinary Medical Association, 230*(2), 211–216.

Lowery, J. E. (2011). *Singing the Lord's song in a strange land*. Nashville, TN: Abingdon.

Maharaj, M., & Kothrada, A. (2006). *Mandela: The authorized portrait*. Kansas City, MO: Andrews McMeel.

Malinoswki, S. (Ed.). (1995). *Notable Native Americans*. Detroit, MI: Gale.

Mandela, N. (1994). *Long walk to freedom: The autobiography of Nelson Mandela*. Boston, MA: Little, Brown.

Mandela, N. (2010). *Conversations with myself*. New York: Farrar, Strauss, & Giroux.

Mankiller, W., & Wallis, M. (1993). *Mankiller: A chief and her people*. New York: St. Martin's Press.

Mankiller, Wilma. (1998). In *The Encyclopedia of world biography* (Vol. 10, 2nd ed., pp. 198–199). Detroit, MI: Gale Publishing.

Martin, G. (2009). *Gabriel Garcia Marquez: A life*. New York: Knopf.

Martin, L. (1996, May 28). Owner finds loss of pet still difficult to take. *The Greenville News*, p. 8B.

Martin, S., & Flacco, A. (2009). *Publishing your nonfiction book*. Cincinnati, OH: Writer's Digest.

Malinowski, S. (Ed) (1995). *Notable Native Americans*. Detroit, MI: Gale.

Matlins, S. M. (Ed.). (2000). *The perfect stranger's guide to funerals and grieving practices: A guide to etiquette in other people's religious ceremonies*. Woodstock, VT: Skylight Paths.

Matuz, R. (2004). *The president's fact book: A comprehensive handbook to the achievements, events, people, triumphs, and tragedies of every president from George Washington to George W. Bush*. New York: Black Dog & Leventhal.

Mayo, E. P. (Ed). (1996). *The Smithsonian book of First Ladies: Their lives, thoughts, and issues*. New York: Henry Holt.

McCarty, L. T. (2009). *Coretta Scott King: A biography*. Westport, CT: Greenwood Press.

McCourt, F. (1996). *Angela's ashes: A memoir*. New York: Scribner

McCracken, E. (2008). *An exact replication of a figment of my imagination*. New York: Little, Brown and Company.

McDevitt-Murphy, M. E, Neimeyer, R. A., Burke, L. A., & Williams, J. L. (2009, April). *Assessing the toll of traumatic loss: Psychological symptoms in African Americans bereaved by homicide*. Concurrent session, presented at 31st ADEC Conference, Dallas, Texas.

McElrath, J. (2007). *The everything Martin Luther King Jr. book: The struggle, the tragedy, the dream.* Avon, MA: Adamsmedia.

McElroy, S. C. (2003). Foreword. In B. Carmack, *Grieving the death of a pet* (pp. xiii–xv). Minneapolis, MN: Augsburg.

McKinstry, C. M. (2011). *While the world watched: A Birmingham bombing survivor comes of age during the Civil Rights movement.* Wheaton, IL: Tyndale.

McLaughlin, W. G. (1993). *After the trail of tears: The Cherokees' Struggle for sovereignty, 1839–1880.* Chapel Hill, NC: University of North Carolina Press.

McPherson, J. M. (1999). Lincoln, Abraham. In *American national biography* (Vol. 13, pp. 662–673). New York: Oxford University Press.

Meacham, J. (2008). *American lion: Andrew Jackson in the White House.* New York: Random House.

Menchu. (1998). In *The encyclopedia of world biography* (2nd ed.). Detroit, MI: Gale.

Menchú, R. (1984). *I, Rigoberto Menchú: An Indian woman in Guatemala* (Elisabeth Burgess-Deboy, Ed., & Ann Wright, Trans.). London: Verso.

Mercado, M. A. (Ed.). (1986). *People Power: An eyewitness history: The Philippine Revolution of 1986.* Manila, Philippines: James B. Reuter, SJ, Foundation.

Meredith, M. (2010). *Mandela: A biography.* New York: Public Affairs.

Metaxes, E. (2010). *Bonhoeffer: Pastor, martyr, prophet, spy.* Nashville, TN: Thomas Nelson.

Millan, C. (with Peltier, M. J.). (2008). *A member of the family: Cesar Millan's guide to a lifetime of fulfillment with your dog.* New York: Harmony Books.

Millard, C. (2005). *The River of Doubt: Theodore Roosevelt's darkest journey.* New York: Doubleday.

Miller, E. (2011, April 30). Letter to the editor. *The Wall Street Journal,* p. A14.

Miller, R. L. (2006). *Lincoln and his world: The early years: Birth to Illinois legislature.* Mechanicsburg, PA: Stackpole Press.

Miller, S. [Scott]. (2011). *The president and the assassin: McKinley, terror, and empire at the dawn of the American century.* New York: Random House.

Miller, S. [Sue]. (2003). *The story of my father.* New York: Knopf.

Miller, W. L. (2008). *President Lincoln: The duty of a statesman.* New York: Knopf.

Minzesheimer, B. (2008, February 28). Everybody has a story to tell, so memoirs sell. *USA Today,* p. 1D.

Mitchell, C. (1998). Forward. In J. D. Schultz & J. D. West, Jr. (Eds.), *The C. S. Lewis reader's encyclopedia.* Grand Rapids, MI: Zondervan.

Mitchell, E. (2005, March 19). Learning now to grieve "just a bird." *The San Francisco Chronicle,* p. F2.

Momigliano, A. (1993). *The development of Greek biography.* Cambridge, MA: Harvard University Press.

Moore, H. (2008). *The bishop's daughter: A memoir.* New York: Norton.

Morris, E. (1979). *The Rise of T. R.* [Theodore Roosevelt]. New York: Coward, McGann & Geoghegan.

Morris, S. J. (1980). *Edith Kermit Roosevelt: Portrait of a First Lady.* New York: Coward, McCann, & Geoghegan.

Mrs. Roosevelt in peril. (1933, February 16). *The Kansas City Star,* p. 1.

Mucha, C. M. (2006). *Gently grieving: Taking care of yourself by telling your story.* New York: Paulist Press.

Murphy, S. A., Johnson, L. C., & Weber, N. A. (2002). Coping strategies following a child's violent death. How parents differ in their responses. *OMEGA, 45*(2), 99–118.

National Alliance for Caregiving/American Association of Retired Persons. (2009, November). *Executive summary of caregiving in the United States.* Washington, DC: Author.

Neimeyer, R. A. (1998). *Lessons of loss: A guide to coping.* New York: McGraw-Hill/Primis Custom Publishing.

Neimeyer, R. A. (2000). Searching for the meaning of meaning: Grief therapy and the process of reconstruction. *Death Studies, 24,* 541–558.

Neimeyer, R. A. (2006). Re-storying the loss: Fostering growth in the posttraumatic narrative. In L. Calhoun & R. Tedeschi (Eds.), *Handbook of posttraumatic growth and practice* (pp. 68–80). Mahwah, NJ: Lawrence Erlbaum.

Neimeyer, R. A. (2009). *Constructivist psychotherapy: Distinctive features series.* New York: Routledge.

Neimeyer, R. A. (2010, April 10). *Loss, grief and the reconstruction of meaning.* Plenary session presented at Association for Death Education and Counseling, Kansas City, MO.

Neven, T. (2001, November). In Lenten lands. *Focus on the Family,* 17–19.

Nguyen, D. N. (2008). *Ho Chi Minh thought on diplomacy.* Hanoi, Vietnam: The Gioi Publishers.

Nolan, T. (2010, March 30). Tales from inner space: A cultural conversation with Ray Bradbury. *The Wall Street Journal,* p. D7.

Norenzayan, A., Dar-Nimrod, I., Hansen, I. G., & Proulx, T. (2007). Mortality salience and religion: Divergent effects on the defense of cultural worldviews for the religious and the non-religious. *The European Journal of Social Psychology, 39,* 101–113.

Norrell, R. J. (2009). *Up from history: The life of Booker T. Washington.* Cambridge, MA: Belknap Press of Harvard University.

Norris, M. (2010). *The silence of grace.* New York: Pantheon.

Nuland, S. B. (2003). *Lost in America: My life with my father.* New York: Alfred N. Knopf.

Obama, B. (2004). *Dreams from my father: A story of race and inheritance.* New York: Crown.

The Obituary Record. (1894, August 16). Elliott Roosevelt. *The New York Times.*

O'Neill, P. (1968, November 1). For the beautiful Queen Jacqueline, Goodbye Camelot, hello Scorpios. *Life.*

Oring, E. (2008, spring). Legendry and the rhetoric of truth. *The Journal of American Folklore, 121,* pp. 127–166.

Orr, G. (2002). *The blessing: The memoir.* San Francisco, CA: Council Oak Books.

O'Rourke, M. (2011). *The long goodbye: A memoir.* New York: Riverhead.

Packman, W., Carmack, B., & Romen, R. (in press). Continuing bonds expressions following the death of a pet. *Omega.*

Parker, L. (2005, March 15). When pets die at the vet, grieving owners call lawyers. *USA Today,* pp. 1A–2A.

Parkes, C. M. (1986–1987). Research: Bereavement. *Omega, 18,* 365–377.

Parks, L. R. (1961). *My thirty years backstairs at the White House.* New York: Fleet Publishing.

Paul, D., & Spencer, R. (2001). Handel. *The New Grove dictionary of music and musicians* (Vol. 10, 2nd ed., pp. 747–813). New York: Macmillan Publishing Limited.

Pearson, H. (2002). *When Harlem nearly killed King.* New York: Seven Stories Press.

Perret, G. (2001). *Jack: A life like no other.* New York: Random House.

Peters, S. L. (2009, May 27). Euthanasia veterinarians provide a peaceful death. *USA Today,* p. 5D.

Peterson, R. D., & Krivo, L. J. (1993). Racial segregation and black urban homicide. *Social Forces, 71*(4), 1001–1026.

Picardie, J. (2008, October 17). *We read to know we are not alone.* Retrieved July 20, 2011, from http:oxford-reader.blogspot.com/2008/10/we-read-to-know-we-are-not-alone.html

Pitts, D. (2007). *Jack and Lem: John F. Kennedy and Lem Billings: The untold story of an extraordinary friendship.* New York: Carroll & Graf.

Platt, S. (Ed.). (1989). *Respectfully quoted: A dictionary of quotations requested from the Congressional Research Service.* Washington, DC: The Library of Congress.

Pollitt, R., & Wiltse, V. (1994). *Helen Steiner Rice: Ambassador of sunshine.* Carmel, NY: Guideposts.

Ponton, L. (2002). *Killing monsters: Why children need fantasy, superheroes, and make-believe violence.* New York: Basic Books.

Pope, K. J. (2005). *Beside every great man … is a great woman: African American women of courage, intellect, strength, beauty and perseverance.* Phoenix, AZ: Amber Books.

Pottker, J. (2001). *Janet & Jackie: The story of a mother and her daughter, Jacqueline Kennedy Onassis.* New York: St. Martin's.

Ramirez, J. R. M. (2009, February 26). *Reminiscing with Cory.* Retrieved April 10, 2011, from http://www.philstar.com/Article.aspx?articleid=443566

Raymond, C. (2005, July). Dog years. *The Director,* 6.

Reagan, R. [Ron]. (2011). *My father at 100.* New York: Viking.

Reagan, R. [Ronald]. (1990). *Ronald Reagan: An American life.* New York: Simon and Schuster.

Reagan, R. [Ronald] (with Hubler, R. G.). (1965). *Where's the rest of me?* New York: Duell, Sloan, & Pierce.

Reisner, C. F. (1922). *Roosevelt's religion.* New York: The Abingdon Press.

Remnick, D. (2010). *The bridge: The life and rise of Barack Obama.* New York: Knopf.

Rice, C. (2002, June 16). *Acknowledge that you have an obligation to search for the truth.* Address to the graduating class of Stanford University, Palo Alto, CA.

Rice, C. (2010). *Extraordinary, ordinary people: A memoir of family.* New York: Crown/Archtype.

Rieff, D. (2008). *Swimming in a sea of death: A son's memoir.* New York: Simon & Schuster.

Rodis, R. (2008, January 16). Global networking: How many Filipinos are really in the US? *The Philippine Daily Inquirer.* Retrieved April 23, 2011, from http://Services.inquirer.net/print.php?article_id=20080226-112806

Rohr, R. (2011). *Falling upward: A spirituality for the two halves of life.* San Francisco, CA: Jossey-Bass.

Roosevelt, E. (1937). *This is my story.* New York: Harper & Brothers.

Roosevelt, E. (1945, May 19). Letter to E. Woodward, Ellen Woodward Papers. Jackson, MS: Mississippi State Archives.

Roosevelt, E. (1960). *You learn by living.* Philadelphia, PA: The Westminster Press.

Roosevelt, E. (1992). *The autobiography of Eleanor Roosevelt.* New York: Da Capo Press.

Roosevelt, T. (1913). *An autobiography.* New York: Macmillan.

Roosevelt, T. (1954). *The letters of Theodore Roosevelt: The days of armageddon, 1914–1919,* (Vol. 8) (E. E. Morison, Ed.). Cambridge MA: Harvard University Press.

Rose, P. R. (2011). *Cultural competency for health administration and public health.* Sudbury, MA: Jones and Bartlett.

Rosenblatt, P. C., & Wallace, B. R. (2005). Narratives of grieving African-Americans about racism in the lives of deceased family members. *Death Studies, 29*(3), 217–235.

Ross, C. B., & Baron-Sorenson, J. (2007). *Pet loss and human emotion: A guide to recovery.* New York: Routledge.

Roth, L. (2002, January 8). Letter to the editor: The stir over "Poor Buddy." *The Kansas City Star,* p. B6.

Rowan, R., & Janis, B. (2009). *First dogs: American presidents and their best friends.* Chapel Hill, NC: Algonquin Books.

Rubin, G. (2005). *Forty ways to look at JFK.* New York: Ballantine.

Rush, P. (2003, January 18). Can we hope to be reunited with our beloved pets after death: In heaven there is no worry. *The Kansas City Star,* p. H1.

Rushton, P. (2007). Widower responses to the death of a wife: The impact on family members. *Topics in Advance Practice Nursing eJournal, 7*(2). Retrieved from http://www.medscape.com/viewarticle/506196

Rylant, C. (1995). *Dog heaven.* New York: Blue Sky Press.

Rylant, C. (1997). *Cat heaven.* New York: Blue Sky Press.

Rynearson, E. K. (2011, June 24). *Understanding the impact of violent death.* Concurrent session panel with L.A. Burke, J.R. Jordan, R. A. Neimeyer, presented at Association for Death Education and Counseling, Miami, FL.

Saari, P. (Ed.). *Prominent women of the 20th century.* Detroit, MI: UXL/Gale.

Sadie, S. (2001). Introduction. *The New Grove dictionary of music and musicians* (Vol. 1, 2nd ed., pp. vii–ix). New York: Macmillan.

Schlesinger, A. S., Jr. (1979, September 25). Interview with Arthur Schlesinger by E. Williams. Eleanor Roosevelt Oral Histories (Box 5, p. 8). Franklin Delano Roosevelt Library, Hyde Park, New York.

Schneider, D., & Schneider, C. J. (2001). *First ladies: A biographical dictionary.* New York: Checkmark Books.

Schulte Nordholt, J. W. (1991). *Woodrow Wilson: A life for world peace.* Berkeley, CA: The University of California Press.

Seel, P. (1995). *I, Pierre Seel, deported homosexual: A memoir of Nazi terror* (J. Neugroschel, Trans.). New York: Basic Books.

Sell, S. L. (2010). *Bess Wallace Truman: Harry's White House "Boss."* Lawrence, KS: The University of Kansas Press.

Selwyn, P. A. (1998). *Surviving the fall: The personal journey of an AIDS doctor.* New Haven, CT: Yale University Press.

Silen, J. G. (2006). *My father's keeper: The story of a gay son and his aging parents.* Boston, MA: Beacon Press.

Sills, B., & Linderman, L. (1987). *Beverly: An autobiography.* New York: Bantam.

Silverman, P. R., & Klass, D. (1996). Introduction: What's the problem? In D. Klass, P. R. Silverman, & S. L. Nickman (Eds.), *Continuing bonds: New understandings of grief* (pp. 3–27). Washington, DC: Taylor & Francis.

Silverstone, M. (1999). *Rigoberta Menchu: Defending human rights in Guatemala.* New York: The Feminist Press at the City University of New York.

Simon, S. (2009, August 1). *Simon says: The Philippines loses its sincere revolutionary.* National Public Radio.

Simpson, J., & Speake, J. (Eds.). (1998). *The concise Oxford dictionary of proverbs.* New York: Oxford University Press.

Sitkoff, H. (2008). *King: Pilgrimage to the mountain top.* New York: Hill and Wang.

Skidmore, M. J. (2004). *After the White House: Former presidents as private citizens.* New York: Palgrave Macmillan.

Smith, D. J. (2010). *Young Mandela: The revolutionary years.* New York: Little, Brown.

Smith, G. (2006). *Remembering Garrett: One family's battle with a child's depression.* New York: Carroll & Graf.

Smith, H. I. (1996). *Grieving the death of a friend.* Minneapolis, MN: Augsburg.

Smith, H. I. (2001a). *Friendgrief: An absence called presence.* Amityville, NY: Baywood.

Smith, H. I. (2001b). *A Decembered grief.* Kansas City, MO: Beacon Hill Press.

Smith, H. I. (2002). *When your friend dies.* Minneapolis, MN: Augsburg.

Smith, H. I. (2004a). *Grief Keeping: Learning how long grief lasts.* New York: Crossroad.

Smith, H. I. (2004b). *When a child you love is grieving.* Kansas City, MO: Beacon Hill Press.

Smith, H. I. (2006a). *A long shadowed grief: Suicide and its aftermath.* Boston, MA: Cowley Press.

Smith, H. I. (2006b). Does my grief count? When ex-family grieve. *Illness, Crisis and Loss, 14*(4), 355–372.

Smith, H. I. (2007, April). *Eleanor Roosevelt: The transformative power of grief over a lifetime.* Concurrent session presented at Association for Death Education and Counseling, Indianapolis, IN.

Smith, H. I. (2011, June). *Corazon Aquino as a role model of resilience.* Poster presented at Association for Death Education and Counseling, Miami, FL.

Smith, H. I. (in press). En-training memoir slices. In R. A. Neimeyer (Ed.), *Techniques of grief therapy*. New York: Routledge.

Smith, H. I. & Johnson, J. (2008). *Partnered grief*. Omaha, NE: Centering Corporation.

Smith, J. C. (Ed.) (2002). *Notable Black American women*. Detroit: Gale.

Smith, S. B. (2004). *Grace and power: The private world of the Kennedy White House*. New York: Random House.

Smock, R.W. (2009). *Booker T. Washington: Black leadership in the age of Jim Crow*. Chicago, IL: Ivan Dee.

Sobel, R. (1998). *Coolidge: An American enigma*. Washington, DC: Regnery.

Sonneborn, L. (Ed.). (1998). *The A to Z of Native American Women*. New York: Facts on File.

Spoto, D. (2000). *Jacqueline Bouvier Kennedy Onassis: A life*. New York: St. Martin's Press.

Spring, J. A. (with Spring, M.) (2009). *Life with pop: Lessons on caring for an aging parent*. New York: Avery.

Stanford University. (n.d.). *Jane Stanford: The woman behind Stanford University*. Retrieved August 18, 2011, from http://janestanford.stanford.edu/biography.html

Steffens, B. (2002). *J. K. Rowling*. Detroit, MI: Thomson Gale.

Stepanek, J., and Linder, L. (2009). *Messenger: The legacy of Mattie J. T. Stepanek and heartsongs*. New York: New American Library.

Stewart, W., & Sindayen, N. (1987, January 5). Woman of the year: A Christmas conversation. *Time*, 32–33.

Stimmel, S. (1928). *Personal reminiscences of Abraham Lincoln*. Minneapolis, MN: H. M. Adams.

Stone, J. R. (2006). *The Routledge book of world proverbs*. New York: Routledge.

Strathern, P. (1997). *Socrates in 90 minutes*. Chicago, IL: Ivan Dee.

Strauss, D. (2010). *Half a life*. San Francisco, CA: McSweeney's.

Stylianos, S., & Vachon, M. (1993). The role of social support in bereavement. In M. Stroebe, W. Stroebe, & R. Hansson (Eds.), *The handbook of bereavement: Theory, research and intervention* (pp. 397–410). Cambridge, UK: Cambridge University Press.

Styron, A. (2011). *Reading my father*. New York: Scribner.

The Subject Guide to Books in Print, 2006–2007. (2006). New York: R.R. Bowker.

Sue, S. W., & Sue, D. (2003). *Counseling the culturally diverse: Theory and practice* (4th ed.). New York: Wiley.

Sudarkasa, N. (1997). African American families and family values. In H. P. McAdoo (Ed.), *Black families* (3rd ed., pp. 9–40). Thousand Oaks, CA: Sage.

Swift, W. (2004). *The Roosevelts and the royals: Franklin and Eleanor, the king and queen of England, and the friendship that changed history*. New York: John Wiley.

Talking story. (n.d.). Retrieved January 27, 2011, from http://www.eyeofhawaii.com/Talk_Story/talk_story.htm

Tatad, F. (1886). *People power: An eyewitness history, the Philippine Revolution of 1986*. San Francisco, CA: James B. Reuter, S.J., Foundation.

Taylor, D. (2005). *Tell me a story: The life-shaping power of our stories*. Minneapolis, MN: Bog Walk Press.

Telgen, D., & Kamp, J. (Eds.). (1993). *Notable Hispanic American women*. Detroit, MI: Gale.

Terry, L. (n.d.). Lincoln in Ebony. Retrieved January 27, 2011, from http://www.cbn.com/spirituallife/devotions/terry_by_and_by.aspx

Thomas, A. (2008a). *Thinking about memoir*. New York: AARP/Sterling.

Thomas, A. (2008b). *A three dog life: A memoir*. Orlando, FL: Harvest/Harcourt.

Thomas, M. (1998, February 1). Medicine for the soul. *Florida Magazine, 26*.

Thomas, M. (2004, May 14). Kitty heaven is a balm for the world-weary. *Orlando Sentinel*, B1.

Titcombe, L. (2001, May/June). The need to grieve. *PETS Magazine, 40*.

Tram, D. T. (2007). Last night I dream of peace: *The diary of Dang Thuy Tram*. Translated by A. X. Pham. New York: Harmony Books.

Truman, M. (1986). *Bess W. Truman*. New York: Macmillan.

Trillin, C. (1993). *Remembering Denny*. New York: Farrar, Straus, Giroux.

Trillin, C. (1996). *Messages from my father*. New York: Farrar, Straus, Giroux.

Trillin, C. (2006). *About Alice*. New York: Random House.

Tuffy, D. (2003, January 18). Can we hope to be reunited with our beloved pets after death: Spirit is everywhere, in everything. *The Kansas City Star*, p. H-1.

Turk, R. (1997). *Coretta Scott King: Fighter for justice*. Boston, MA: Braden.

Tutu, D. (2011). *God is not a Christian and other provocations* (J. Allen, Ed.). New York: HarperOne.

Van Lippe-Biesterfeld, I., & van Tijn, J. (2005). *Science, soul and the spirit of nature: Leading thinkers on the restoration of man and creation*. Rochester, VT: Bear & Company.

VandenBos, G. R. (2007). *APA dictionary of psychology*. Washington, DC: The American Psychological Association.

Verbeten, S. (2011, April). Guiding the soul. *The American Funeral Director,* 36–40.

Vivian, O. (1970). *The life of Mrs. Martin Luther King, Jr.* Philadelphia, PA: Fortress.

Vonnegut, M. (2010). *Just like someone without mental illness only more so: A memoir*. New York: Delacorte Press.

Walmsey, L. (1998). *C. S. Lewis on grief*. Nashville, TN: Thomas Nelson.

Walsh, C. (1976). Afterword. In C. S. Lewis, *A grief observed* (pp. 93–151). New York: Bantam.

Walter, T. (1999). *On bereavement: The culture of grief*. Philadelphia, PA: Open University Press.

Ward, L. (2007*). Coffins, kits, and more: Stories of the Civil War embalmer*. Independence, MO: Two Trails Publishing.

Warwick, D. (with Wooley, D. F.). (2010). *My life, as I see it: An autobiography*. New York: Atria.

Wead, D. (2003). *All the presidents' children: Triumph and tragedy in the lives of America's first families.* New York: Altra.

Webb, W. (1999). *Solutioning: Solution-focused interventions for counselors.* Philadelphia, PA: Accelerated Development.

Webster New Oxford American Dictionary. (2010). New York: Oxford University Press.

Weise, D. R., Pyszczyski, T., Cox, C. R., Ardnt, J., Greenberg, J., Solomon, S., & Kosloff, S. (2008). Interpersonal politics: The role of terror management and attachment processes in shaping political preferences. *Psychological Science, 19*(5), 448–455.

Weller, S. (2005). *The Bradbury chronicles.* New York: William Morrow.

Welwood, J. (2002). *Toward a psychology of awakening: Buddhism, psychotherapy, and the path of personal and spiritual transformation.* Boston, MA: Shambhala.

White, R. C., Jr. (2009). *A. Lincoln: A biography.* New York: Random House.

Wickersham, J. (2008). *The suicide index: Putting my father's death in order.* Orlando, FL: Harcourt.

Wilson, A. N. (1990). *C. S. Lewis: A biography.* New York: Fawcett Columbine.

Wilton, A. (2001). Turner, J. M. W., 1775–1851. In *The Dictionary of Art* (Vol. 31, pp. 466–476). New York: Macmillan.

Winfrey, O. (2010, October 3). *Transcript of Oprah interview with J. K. Rowling.* Retrieved April 3, 2011, from www.harrypotterspage.com/2010/1003/transcript-of-oprah-interview-with-j-k-rowling/

Worden, J. W. (2009). *Grief counseling and grief therapy: A handbook for the mental health practitioner* (4th ed.). New York: Springer.

Wythoff, G. (2010, March 11). *"There are eight million stories in the naked city; this has been one of them": Procedurality and The Naked City.* Retrieved from http://mediacommons.futureofthebook.org/imr/2010/03/10/there-are-eight-million-stories-naked-city-has-been-one-them-procedurality-and-naked-city

Yalom, I. D. (2008). *Staring at the sun: Overcoming the terror of death.* San Francisco, CA: Jossey-Bass.

Young, A. (1980). Introduction. In M. L. King, Sr., & Riley, C. (Eds.), *Daddy King: An autobiography* (pp. 9–12). New York: William Morrow.

Young, A. (1996). *An easy burden: The civil rights movement and the transformation of America.* New York: HarperCollins.

Young, T. A., & Bradley, D. H. (2011, March). The power of biography breaks: Talking with Esme Raji Codell. *Book Links, 31*–35.

Zeleny, J. (2008, November 4). Madelyn Dunham, Obama's grandmother, dies at 86. *The New York Times.* Retrieved May 10, 2011, from http://www.nytimes.com/2008/11/04/world/americas/04iht-obama.1.17505156.html

Zinn, H. (2003). *A people's history of the United States: 1492–present.* New York: Harper Perennial/Modern Classics. (Original work published 1980)

Zonnebelt-Smeenge, S. J., & De Vries, R. C. (1998). *Getting to the other side of grief.* Grand Rapids, MI: Baker Books.

Author Index

Name Index

Subject Index

A

"Good steer," A, 33, 101, 143
Abe.com, 31
African American and homicide, 93, 230–232
Afterlife, pets, 159–161
Antecedent losses, 13, 21, 25, 105, 173, 210, 218, 225–227

B

Backstory, 14–15, 46
Bereaving, xii, 17, 42, 105, 109
"Biographical mentor," 207
Bleaching the family narrative, 52
Blessed Mother, The, 195, 197, 201, 207
Bypass, emotional, 17, 100, 107, 148, 175

C

"Camelot martyr," 186

Camouflaging the narrative, 54–55
Caregivers, 79, 97, 99
Celebrity grief, 49, 67, 108, 121, 150
"Cerebral whiplash," 141
Child grievers, 59
"Comprehensive account," 239
Comprehensive grid, 44
Cultural competence, 77

D

Defrosting family narrative, 46
Diversity, 16, 75–76, 77, 82, 89, 93, 94, 142
Dysfunctioning families, 5, 51–52, 142

E

"Event story," 14
Expatriates, 203–204